Second Edition

A Management Guide to PERT/CPM:

with GERT | PDM | DCPM and other Networks

JEROME D. WIEST

Professor of Management
University of Utah

FERDINAND K. LEVY

Professor of Economics
Georgia Institute of Technology

PRENTICE-HALL, INC., Englewood Cliffs, New Jersey   07632

Library of Congress Cataloging in Publication Data

Wiest, Jerome D
  A management guide to PERT/CPM.

  Bibliography: p.
  Includes index.
  1. PERT (Network analysis) 2. Critical path joint
analysis. I. Levy, Ferdinand K.,
author. II. Title.
TS158.2.W53 1977   658.4′032   76-48928
ISBN   0-13-549113-4
ISBN   0-13-549105-3 pbk.

© 1977, 1969 by Prentice-Hall, Inc., Englewood Cliffs, New Jersey   07632

Printed in the United States of America

20 19 18 17 16 15 14 13

Prentice-Hall International, Inc., *London*
Prentice-Hall of Australia Pty. Limited, *Sydney*
Prentice-Hall of Canada, Ltd., *Toronto*
Prentice-Hall of India Private Limited, *New Delhi*
Prentice-Hall of Japan, Inc., *Tokyo*
Prentice-Hall of Southeast Asia Pte. Ltd., *Singapore*
Whitehall Books Limited, *Wellington, New Zealand*

To Yvonne and Mimi

Contents

Preface

The first edition of this book had two purposes. First it was intended to acquaint the student in management-oriented courses with all the fundamental concepts necessary to understand and use PERT/CPM scheduling techniques. Second and equally as important, the book was designed to be a basic guide and reference to those techniques for both potential and actual users in industry. The second edition follows closely the pattern of the first. In addition, applications of these two powerful techniques have been expanded and clarified in exposition. Moreover, the newer network scheduling techniques which PERT/CPM have spawned in the past five or six years, for example, GERT, PDM, etc., have been added to make this edition a more complete reference and study guide.

The emphasis throughout this edition remains on the basic ideas of network scheduling techniques and the variety of management problems to which they are applicable. As in the first edition, more advanced methods using mathematical and computer techniques are fully discussed in appropriate appendices to the chapters. New and expanded exercises, complete with solutions, are included at the end of the book and are designed to make sure that the reader fully understands the fundamentals explained in the body of the book. These exercises are keyed by chapters so that a concept introduced in a specific chapter has a problem that uses it in the exercises.

The literature on network scheduling techniques was voluminous five years ago and has continued to expand at a geometric rate. We have expanded the bibliography at the end of the book which, although not complete, is comprehensive in its coverage of concepts of network scheduling techniques and their myriad of applications. An understanding of the ideas presented in this book should be sufficient background for anyone wanting to pursue reading further in this ever-growing area.

We should like to acknowledge the environment that the Graduate School of Industrial Administration at Carnegie Institute of Technology provided us in the early 1960's so that we were able to collaborate on a series of research papers introducing and developing network scheduling techniques. The first edition of this book was a product of the papers developed at Carnegie and was written at Rice University. The University of Utah and Georgia Institute of Technology have provided partial support for the present edition.

We also want to thank the journals whose work we reproduce here for granting us permission to include material originally presented in them. Finally, we express our deepest appreciation to Ms. Alice Erdman at Prentice-Hall for a competent and thorough editing of the final manuscript and to Mr. Bruce Toth, currently of the Graduate School of Business at Stanford, for his help on the bibliography.

JEROME D. WIEST
Salt Lake City, Utah

FERDINAND K. LEVY
Atlanta, Georgia

1

PERT and CPM
Come of Age

Developed in the late 1950s to aid in the planning and scheduling of large projects, PERT and CPM are today widely used in industry and services throughout the United States and in many other countries around the globe. Their life history to date, although short, has been interesting and rather hectic. In their early years, the tools were heavily promoted, especially by U.S. government agencies, which insisted on their use by contractors on major government projects. There followed a period of critical examination of network techniques, a more rational assessment of their strengths and weaknesses, and a shifting of their use from less appropriate to more suitable applications. Today their use is firmly established among organizations concerned in one way or another with the managing of projects, and surveys indicate that they are among the most commonly used of all quantitative tools of management.

Basic concepts of PERT and CPM, such as activities, events, and predecessors, have become a regular part of the language of project managers and have facilitated communication at every level of management and across organizational lines—between foremen and engineers, managers and technicians. Extensions and modifications of the tools have greatly increased their usefulness and the range of their applications. Although such developments are continuing, PERT and CPM have reached a degree of maturity that justifies the assertion that they have, indeed, come of age.

The historical development of PERT and CPM gives us some idea of their purpose and nature and helps to explain both their similarities and differences. PERT, an acronym for *program evaluation and review technique*, was created as a means to plan and accelerate development of the Polaris ballistic missile. The personnel responsible for the country's defense in the late 1950s were convinced that a nuclear missile launched from beneath the ocean's surface by a mobile submarine would prove to be an effective deterrent against aggression by a potential enemy. Once this concept was adopted, it became necessary to plan the missile's development as quickly as possible. What research had to be done to accomplish this, and how should it be planned? How long would the research take? What stages of development and testing would be necessary for the missile's completion? How fast could the country do this? In summary, when could the United States expect to have an operational Polaris missile? PERT was the planning and scheduling technique developed to answer these questions and to accelerate the realization of the Polaris missile.

Obviously, there were uncertainties in the development program. Answers to some of the above questions were conditional in nature: for instance, "If development of the propulsion system proceeds as planned, *then* we can launch a test missile on such-and-such a date." PERT incorporated this uncertainty into a model which provides a reasonable framework for answering such queries. It has proved to be a useful tool in planning and scheduling large projects, such as the Polaris, which consist of numerous activities whose completion times are uncertain and which, although they must be completed in some order, are independent of one another. Fundamental to PERT is the concept of an "event" or the reaching of a certain stage of completion of a project. Also basic is the expected time required to complete activities leading up to that event.

Closely akin to PERT, but developed independently, is the technique known as the *critical path method*, or CPM, which is basically concerned with obtaining the trade-off between cost and completion date for large projects. CPM emphasizes the relationship between applying more men or other resources to shorten the duration of given jobs in a project and the increased cost of these additional resources. With CPM the amount of time needed to complete various facets of the project is assumed to be known with certainty; moreover, the relation between the amount of resources employed and the time needed to complete the project is also assumed known. Thus CPM is not concerned with uncertain job times as is PERT; rather it deals with time–cost trade-offs. Because of these differences, PERT is used more in research and development projects, and CPM is used more in projects such as construction, where there has been some experience in handling similar endeavors.

Widely diverse kinds of projects lend themselves to analysis by either PERT or CPM, as the following list of applications suggests:

The construction of a building or of a highway

Planning and launching a new product

A turnaround in an oil refinery (or other maintenance projects)

Installing and debugging a computer system

Scheduling ship construction and repairs

The manufacture and assembly of a large generator (or other large job-lot operations)

Missile countdown procedures

End-of-the month closing of accounting records

Each of these projects has several characteristics that are essential for analysis by CPM or PERT:

1. The project consists of a well-defined collection of jobs, or activities, which when completed marks the end of the project.

2. The jobs may be started and stopped independently of each other, within a given sequence. (This requirement eliminates continuous-flow processes, such as oil refining, where "jobs" or operations necessarily follow one after another with essentially no time separation.)

3. The jobs are ordered; that is, they must be performed in technological sequence. (For example, the foundation of a house must be constructed before the walls are erected.)

As the use of PERT and CPM has increased, so have their refinements, extensions, and cost efficiencies. There are few firms employing these techniques that do not have computerized packages to handle them. Moreover, the usefulness of these techniques in scheduling with limited resources and in handling projects where precedence relations are not clearly defined has now been well demonstrated. Like all growing techniques, both the practitioner and theoretician have contributed to their developments. This primer is designed to be an up-to-date guide to the basics and the most recent additions to using PERT and CPM in planning, scheduling, and controlling large projects.

Plan of the Guide

As we shall see, most large projects can be portrayed by a graph, or network, of jobs. Such a network provides the basic tool for analysis. Chapter 2 begins with a discussion of how this network can be drawn for given projects, and we define the basic concepts and terminology associated with networks. Then Chapter 3 introduces the notion of a critical path through a network and develops methods for project scheduling based on the network. Chapters 4 and 5 present the basic PERT and CPM models. In keeping with the spirit of a basic guide, the more difficult material is saved for appendixes or, when it is brief, is placed in footnotes. For example, a linear programming or mathematical formulation of network models is presented in the Appendix to Chapter 5. Chapter 6 discusses the use of PERT and CPM as aids to controlling costs, and Chapter 7 shows how projects may be scheduled when some resources, such as men and equipment, are limited in availability. Chapter 8 describes some more recent modifications and extensions of these techniques, including *precedence networks* and *probabilistic networks*. Finally, in Chapter 9, we reexamine the historical development and applications of network techniques, discuss their strengths and practical limitations, and describe some necessary conditions for their successful use.

Planning, Scheduling, and Control

Fundamentally, PERT and CPM are techniques of project management useful in the basic managerial functions of planning, scheduling, and control. The *planning* phase of any venture involves a listing of tasks or jobs that must be performed to bring about the venture's completion. Gross requirements for material, equipment, and manpower are also determined in this phase, and estimates of costs and durations for the various jobs are made. *Scheduling*, on the other hand, is the laying out of the actual jobs of the project in the time order in which they have to be performed. Manpower and material requirements needed at each stage of production are calculated, along with the expected completion time of each of the jobs. *Control*, generally regarded as "the underlying managerial function," begins with reviewing the difference between the schedule and actual performance once the project has begun. The analysis and correction of this difference forms the basic aspect of control. As stated at the outset, PERT and CPM are useful in all three functions—planning, scheduling, and control; and we shall point this out repeatedly throughout the book. Before we examine the techniques in detail, however, we must introduce the basic terminology associated with them—the task assigned to Chapter 2.

2

Planning and Scheduling Networks

In this chapter we develop the terminology necessary for a thorough understanding of CPM and PERT planning and scheduling. As pointed out previously, the prerequisites for using either of these techniques include separating the project to be scheduled into independent jobs, or activities, and determining an order of precedence for these jobs. That is, we must see which jobs have to be completed before others can be started. The next step is drawing a picture, or graph, which portrays each of these jobs and the predecessor and successor relations among them. The concepts associated with constructing and understanding this graph will be our major concern in this chapter.

Let us begin our discussion with a simplified example of the budgeting process in a large manufacturing firm that we shall call the W-L Company. Suppose that the president of W-L wants his next year's operating budget prepared as soon as possible. To accomplish this *project*, the company's salesmen must provide unit sales estimates for the period to both the sales manager and the production manager. The former must estimate market prices on the forecast and give these to the financial officer. The production manager must make machine schedules of the units to be produced and assign machines for their manufacture. Next, he must give these schedules and machine assignments to the accounting manager, who must then provide costs of production to the financial officer. Then the financial officer, using the information provided by the sales and accounting departments and making the necessary arrangements for internal financing, prepares the final budget and submits it to the president.

If we assume that there are no revisions necessary, W-L's budget is basically finished when it is handed to the president. Let us look more closely at how the budget was composed. Before anything else could be done, sales estimates had to be made. Only then could sales be priced and trial production schedules prepared. Forming the sales estimates, pricing the sales, and making the production schedules are three *jobs*, or *activities*,[1] in the *project* of making W-L's budget. Moreover, since the sales forecast had to be done before the pricing and scheduling, we say that it was an *immediate predecessor* of these activities. Similarly, pricing was an *immediate predecessor* of the financial officer's preparing the budget, as was the accounting group's supplying him with cost estimates; and, more generally, the forecast was a *predecessor* of all the subsequent activities. In a like manner preparing the budget is a *successor* of all other activities, and the *immediate successor* of pricing and of cost estimating.

Table 2-1 shows the project of budgeting at W-L broken down into jobs described in column 3. Note that we have estimated the time needed for each job (column 5) and have assigned identifications to each job (column 1). For example, the job of forecasting sales is denoted by a, estimating costs of production by d, and so on. The second column gives alternative job designations and will be explained below.

TABLE 2-1

Budgeting Project: W-L Company

Job Identifica- tion	Alternate	Job Description	Depart- ment	Time to Perform Job (days)
a	(1, 2)	Forecasting unit sales	Sales	14
b	(2, 4)	Pricing sales	Sales	3
c	(2, 3)	Preparing production schedules	Production	7
d	(3, 4)	Costing the production	Accounting	4
e	(4, 5)	Preparing the budget	Treasurer	10

The project of budgeting can be portrayed in a *project graph*, or network, as shown by Figure 2-1. Jobs are shown as *arrows* leading from one circle on the graph to another. These circles are referred to as *nodes*. Moreover, if one job is an immediate predecessor of another, the *terminal*

---

[1]We shall use the terms "job" and "activity" interchangeably throughout this book.

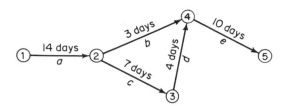

FIGURE 2-1. Project Graph of W-L's Budgetnig Process

node of the predecessor is the *initial node* of its successor. Thus since job *a* is an immediate predecessor of both jobs *b* and *c*, its terminal node, which we have numbered 2 in Figure 2-1, is the initial node for both *b* and *c*.

Reference to Figure 2-1 will also show how we obtained the alternative identification for each job. Job *a* has initial node 1 and terminal node 2, and since a pair of connected nodes on the graph represent a single job or activity, it follows that an activity can also be identified by its node numbers. Thus an alternative name for job *a* is (1, 2), where the number before the comma refers to job *a*'s initial node and the number after the comma corresponds to its terminal node.

Note also that we have indicated the *time* for an activity to be completed adjacent to the arrow corresponding to the activity. In symbols, we denote the time for job *a* to be completed either by $t(a)$ or its alternative $t(1, 2)$. In the example above, $t(a) = 14$ days and $t(c)$ or, equivalently, $t(2, 3) = 7$ days.

What we have basically described is decomposing a *project* into *activities* and then ordering the activities according to which has to be performed first, second, and so on. Then we showed how the activities are named and how they can be portrayed in a *project graph* or *arrow diagram*. In the next section we show how a specific complication in drawing the arrow diagram can arise, and we provide the means to eliminate the complication.

A Complication in Constructing the Arrow Diagram

Suppose that we add another job to the project of budgeting at W-L —a survey of competitive pricing by the sales manager. Let us assume that it takes place simultaneously with the forecasting done by the salesmen. This new activity, which we shall call *a'*, is shown with the others in Table 2-2. It is an immediate predecessor of W-L's pricing of their own sales (as is the forecasting of sales), and it takes 3 days for completion. However, competitive pricing does not affect production decisions, so forecasting remains the lone immediate predecessor of the scheduling activity.

Note that we have eliminated the alternative names for the activities in Table 2-2 and have added a column showing the immediate predecessors

TABLE 2-2

Budgeting Project (Revised): W-L Company

Job Identification	Job Description	Immediate Predecessors	Department	Time to Perform Job (days)
a	Forecasting unit sales	—	Sales	14
a'	Surveying competitive pricing	—	Sales	3
b	Pricing sales	a, a'	Sales	3
c	Preparing production schedules	a	Production	7
d	Costing the production	c	Accounting	4
e	Preparing the budget	b, d	Treasurer	10

of each activity. The complication referred to in this section arises in drawing the arrow diagram of the project. Keep in mind that activities a and a' are both immediate predecessors of activity b, while a alone is the immediate predecessor of activity c. Now an arrow diagram is constructed in such a way that the immediate predecessors of a given job have their terminal nodes identical with the initial node of the given job. If this were done, then a, a', b, and c—the jobs in Table 2-2—would have to be diagrammed as in Figure 2-2.

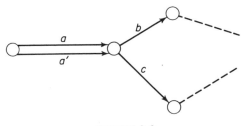

FIGURE 2-2

However, Figure 2-2 also indicates that a' is an immediate predecessor of c (surveying competitors' prices is an immediate predecessor of scheduling production), which is not true. To eliminate this difficulty, we might draw job a twice, as in Figure 2-3. But this is not satisfactory because we should like to employ only one arrow in portraying a single activity. Using more than one arrow for the same activity would not only clutter the graph but would also confuse the graph's user when he was trying to find out where his company stood on a particular project while it was being undertaken.

Finally, if two or more jobs have the same immediate predecessors and the same immediate successors, their initial and terminal nodes will be

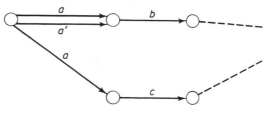

FIGURE 2-3

identical; hence they will have the same alternative job identifications. Since we wish to assign unique names to jobs, we need a device to eliminate this complication in drawing the arrow diagram.

To overcome these difficulties, we introduce the concept of a *dummy job*, or *dummy activity*. A *dummy job* takes zero time to perform and is used solely to illustrate precedence relationship when the use of actual jobs only would lead to the complications outlined above. To illustrate how a dummy job is used, let us return to the budget example. Let f be a dummy activity whose immediate predecessor is job a, and let b have a' and f as immediate predecessors. The arrow diagram of the budget project can then be drawn as in Figure 2-4, with the dummy job indicated by a dashed-line arrow. Notice in Figure 2-4 how the dummy job f is used: a and a' are both immediate predecessors of b. Since a supposedly is an immediate predecessor of dummy activity f, and f is an immediate predecessor of b, then a is no longer an immediate predecessor of b, but is still a predecessor. That is, a still has to be done before b can be started, because it is an immediate predecessor of the dummy f, which must be completed before b can be begun. Also, we are now able to show a as an immediate predecessor of c without showing a' as one, which of course it is not. However, a' is shown as an immediate predecessor of b, and, moreover, all jobs are shown by only one arrow. Thus the addition of dummy jobs eliminates the difficulty encountered when two or more activities have some, but not all, of their immediate predecessors in common. The information on the jobs in Figure 2-4 and their new alternative symbols are shown in Table 2-3.

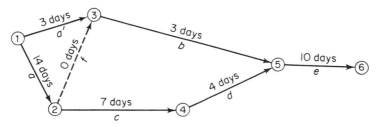

FIGURE 2-4. Arrow Diagram of W-L's Revised Budgeting Project

TABLE 2-3

Budgeting Project (Revised)
with Dummy Jobs for Drawing the Arrow Diagram:
W-L Company

Job Identifi- cation	Alternate	Job Description	Immediate Prede- cessors	Depart- ment	Time to Perform Job (days)
a	(1, 2)	Forecasting unit sales	—	Sales	14
a'	(1, 3)	Surveying competitive pricing	—	Sales	3
f	(2, 3)	Dummy activity	a	—	0
b	(3, 5)	Pricing sales	a', f	Sales	3
c	(2, 4)	Preparing production schedules	a	Production	7
d	(4, 5)	Costing the production	c	Accounting	4
e	(5, 6)	Preparing the budget	b, d	Treasurer	10

A good question to ask at this point is: How do we recognize when the arrow diagram of a project will require dummy jobs? As stated above, there is a need for dummy activities when the project contains groups of two or more jobs which have some, but not all, of their immediate predecessors in common. Jobs that have a single immediate predecessor may be connected directly to the final node of that predecessor; but if a job has more than one predecessor, and one or more of these predecessors is also a predecessor for some other job(s), then dummy jobs are generally required to make the connections.

A simple way to add dummy jobs is to let all the common immediate predecessors of two or more jobs lead into a single node and then let the dummies emanate from this node. We illustrate this with an example of a small project. Suppose that we have the jobs in the project given in Table 2-4 with their immediate predecessors.

TABLE 2-4

Job List—Project I

Job Identification	Immediate Predecessors
a	—
b	—
c	—
d	a, b
e	b, c

Activity *b* is a common immediate predecessor of both *d* and *e*, while *a* is an immediate predecessor of *d* alone, and *c* is one of *e*. We then let *b* lead into two dummy jobs, *f* and *g*, let *f* be an immediate predecessor of *d*, and let *g* be an immediate predecessor of *e*, as shown in Figure 2-5.

By adding jobs to Table 2-4 along with the alternative names for all the jobs, we produce Table 2-5.

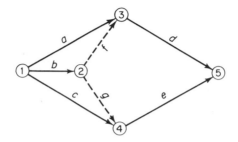

FIGURE 2-5. Arrow Diagram—Project 1

TABLE 2-5

Job List with Dummy Jobs—Project I

Job Identification	Alternate	Immediate Predecessors
a	(1, 3)	—
b	(1, 2)	—
c	(1, 4)	—
f (dummy)	(2, 3)	*b*
g (dummy)	(2, 4)	*b*
d	(3, 5)	*a, f*
e	(4, 5)	*c, g*

A more complicated example of project requiring dummy jobs is given in Table 2-6. Jobs *d*, *e*, and *f* have *a* as a common immediate predecessor, while they have some combination of *b* and *c* as one also. The arrow diagram for that project with the dummies indicated by h_1 to h_5 is shown in Figure 2-6. Notice that job *f* has dummies h_3, h_4, and h_5 for immediate predecessors; these in turn have *a*, *b*, and *c* as immediate predecessors, which really means that *f*'s predecessors are *a*, *b*, and *c*, as indicated in Table 2-6. Similarly, h_1 and h_2 substitute for *a* as immediate predecessors of *d* and *e*, respectively. The complete table of jobs for this project is illustrated in Table 2-7. Note in Table 2-7 that if a job is the sole immediate predecessor of

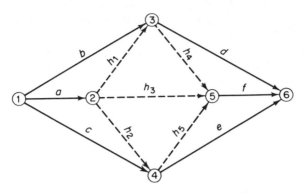

FIGURE 2-6. Arrow Diagram—Project II

TABLE 2-6

Job List—Project II

Job Identification	Immediate Predecessors
a	—
b	—
c	—
d	a, b
e	a, c
f	a, b, c

TABLE 2-7

Job List with Dummy Jobs—Project II

Job Identification	Alternate	Immediate Predecessors
a	(1, 2)	—
b	(1, 3)	—
c	(1, 4)	—
h_1	(2, 3)	a
h_2	(2, 4)	a
h_3	(2, 5)	a
h_4	(3, 5)	b, h_1
h_5	(4, 5)	c, h_2
d	(3, 6)	b, h_1
e	(4, 6)	c, h_2
f	(5, 6)	h_3, h_4, h_5

another activity, the terminal node of the predessor coincides with the initial node of its immediate successor. That is, the two jobs will be directly connected without an intervening dummy job.[2]

The Activity-on-Node Diagram

The addition of dummy jobs to an arrow diagram is a cumbersome procedure, and it adds items to the table of jobs and enlarges the graph. As we shall see in Chapter 3, the calculations necessary to perform critical path or PERT scheduling make use of all jobs, actual and dummy, and hence are lengthened as dummy jobs are added.

A second type of project network has been devised, called the *activity-on-node diagram*, or graph, and it overcomes the foregoing objections to the arrow diagram.[3] The activity-on-node graph, which we shall abbreviate AON, is constructed so that the jobs are denoted by circles, or nodes, and the immediate predecessor relationship between two jobs is shown by an arrow connecting the two nodes. The arrow's point, of course, is at the successor's *node*. Thus, if job *a* is an *immediate predecessor* of job *b*, we portray this relationship on the AON graph as shown in Figure 2-7. These two jobs graphed on an arrow diagram would look as shown in Figure 2-8.

For a more complicated example showing how dummy jobs are not needed in an AON graph, see W-L's revised budgeting project in Table 2-2 worked out in Figure 2-9. Note the ease with which the AON diagram can be drawn. Just draw a circle for each job and then connect each to its immediate successor with a directed arrow. The identifications, or names,

FIGURE 2-7. Two-Activity Example—AON Diagram

FIGURE 2-8. Two-Activity Example—Arrow Diagram

[2]Additional information on when and how to use dummy jobs is contained in the Appendix to this chapter, together with material on *redundant predecessor relationships* and *cycles* in a network—two somewhat technical problems that may be pursued by the interested reader.

[3]This approach to project networking was developed at about the same time as but independently from PERT and CPM by John W. Fondahl in this country and Bernard Roy in France. Fondahl reported his method in "A Non-computer Approach to the Critical Path Method for the Construction Industry," *Technical Report No. 9, Stanford University* (1961; revised 1962), and has since argued strongly for the superiority of "precedence diagrams," as he called them, over arrow diagrams.

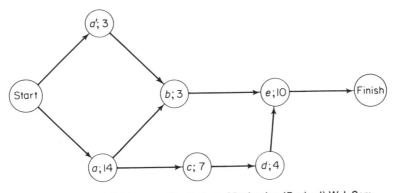

FIGURE 2-9. AON Diagram—The Project of Budgeting (Revised) W-L Company

for a job and the amount of time required to complete a job is usually inserted in the job node. Also, AON graphs usually contain fictitious nodes labeled "start" and "finish" so that there will be a unique beginning and end to the graph of the project. For example, if there were no "start" node in Figure 2-9, it would be difficult to tell whether the project began with job *a* or job *a'*. Figure 2-10 illustrates the use of the AON graph with the data given in Tables 2-4 and 2-6.

An AON diagram seems much simpler to draw than an arrow diagram, and those who have used it report additional advantages: it is simpler to explain, more readily understood by nontechnical users, and easier to revise. Hence a good query is: Why bother with the arrow diagram at all? The truth of the matter is that, even though both are used, the arrow diagram is the more prevalent, primarily because it was used first and became firmly established. The emphasis in the PERT model on "events," which we shall describe in Chapter 4, reinforced the use of arrow diagrams in which *nodes* refer to events. That is, the completion of several activities culminating at a node is referred to as an *event*, or *milestone*. At this point new decisions can be made, schedules reevaluated, and so on. (Event nodes can be introduced in AON diagram if desired, but they are automatically present in arrow diagrams.) Finally, some prefer to use the arrow diagram because it is more suggestive of the work flow associated with activities than are nodes or circle representations.

As we shall see in succeeding chapters, the calculations necessary to do PERT and CPM scheduling make use of the immediate predecessor and successor relationships among jobs in a project. Some people have argued that the arrow-diagramming method is superior for computer-based calculations, because the two-number job identifications used with the arrow diagram automatically supply all necessary precedence relationships. On the other hand, using the AON graph forces us to list each job's immediate

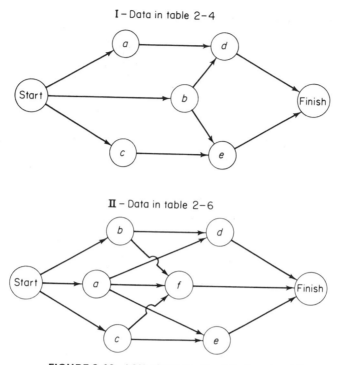

FIGURE 2-10. AON Diagrams—Small Projects I and II

predecessors or successors along with the job (or, alternatively, to list each connecting arrow in two-number form), which generally takes more storage space in a computer. In practice, efficient computer programs have been written for both systems, and differences in running costs between the two are of little practical significance.

Thus, as can be seen, both types of project graphs have their advantages and shortcomings. Because of its better adaptation to PERT procedures and its earlier establishment, the arrow diagram continues to be used more widely than the corresponding activity-on-node graph; but the latter has grown rapidly in popularity, especially in the construction industry. It is even more popular in Europe; according to some reports, its use there exceeds that of arrow diagrams. Not surprisingly, given its ancestry, it has acquired several different acronymns, including PD (for *precedence diagram*) and PN (for *precedence network*). It is the basis for an extension of CPM called the *precedence diagramming method* (PDM), which we will discuss in Chapter 8. Since the term "precedence network" is usually associated with that more complex method, we shall continue to use the title AON to describe simple networks in which jobs are shown as circles and predecessor relationships as arrows. To illustrate and compare AON and arrow diagrams, we turn to a housing construction example.

Example—Building a House[4]

A simple and familiar example should help to clarify the process of drawing a project graph. The project of building a house can be readily analyzed by critical path and PERT techniques. While a contractor might want a more detailed analysis, we shall be satisfied here with the major *jobs*, together with their times and their immediate predecessors shown in Table 2-8. In the table asterisks indicate where dummy jobs may be needed in drawing an arrow diagram.[5] Since the AON diagram can be drawn directly from the table, it is given first as Figure 2-11.

TABLE 2-8

House Construction Project

Job Name	Description	Immediate Predecessors	Time (days)
a	Excavate, pour footers	—	4
b	Pour concrete foundations	a	2
c	Erect frame and roof	b	4
d*	Lay brickwork	c	6
e	Install drains	b	1
f	Pour basement floor	e	2
g	Install rough plumbing	e	3
h*	Install rough wiring	c	2
i*	Install air conditioning	c, f	4
j	Fasten plaster and plaster board	g, h, i	10
k	Lay finished flooring	j	3
l**	Install kitchen equipment	k	1
m**	Install finished plumbing	k	2
n	Finish carpentry	k	3
o	Finish roofing and flashing	d	2
p	Fasten gutters and downspouts	o	1
q	Lay storm drains	b	1
r*	Sand and varnish floors	n, s	2
s	Paint	l, m	3
t*	Finish electrical work	s	1
u	Finish grading	p, q	2
v	Pour walks, and landscape	u	5

[4]This example is derived from a similar one in "The ABC's of the Critical Path Method," by J. D. Wiest, F. K. Levy, and G. L. Thompson, in the *Harvard Business Review* (Sept.-Oct. 1963).

[5]Those jobs with a single asterisk have some, but not all, their immediate predecessors in common. Those with a double asterisk have identical immediate predecessors and successors.

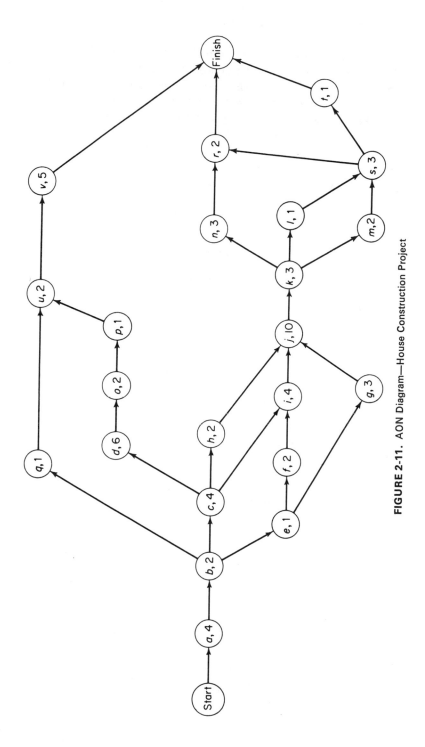

FIGURE 2-11. AON Diagram—House Construction Project

Table 2-9 again lists the jobs in the home construction project but with alternative job names and dummy jobs inserted as necessary to aid in drawing the arrow diagram, which follows in Figure 2-12. Note in the arrow diagram that dummy job D_2 was needed because jobs l and m had k as an identical immediate predecessor, giving them the same initial node, and they also had the same immediate successor s, which gave them both the same terminal node. Thus they would have had identical node numbers; that is, both would have been (10, 12) and would have become indistinguishable had we not inserted the dummy job D_2 as a substitute for k, the immediate predecessor of activity m.

TABLE 2-9

House Construction Project

Job Name	Alternate	Immediate Predecessors	Time (days)
a	(1, 2)	—	4
b	(2, 3)	a	2
c	(3, 4)	b	4
d	(4, 5)	c	6
e	(3, 6)	b	1
f	(6, 7)	e	2
g	(6, 8)	e	3
h	(4, 8)	c	2
D_1 (dummy)	(4, 7)	c	0
i	(7, 8)	D_1, f	4
j	(8, 9)	g, h, i	10
k	(9, 10)	j	3
l	(10, 12)	k	1
D_2 (dummy)	(10, 11)	k	0
m	(11, 12)	D_2	2
n	(10, 13)	k	3
o	(5, 14)	d	2
p	(14, 15)	o	1
q	(3, 15)	b	1
D_3 (dummy)	(13, 16)	s	0
r	(13, 18)	D_3, n	2
s	(12, 16)	l, m	3
t	(16, 18)	s	1
u	(15, 17)	p, q	2
v	(17, 18)	u	5

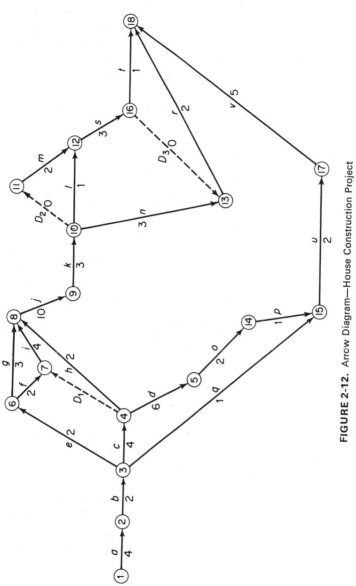

FIGURE 2-12. Arrow Diagram—House Construction Project

19

Network Scheduling—A Summary

This chapter developed the concept of breaking down a *project* into *activities* in order to draw its *graph*, or *network*. This decomposition is necessary for performing the basic calculations necessary to do PERT or critical path scheduling. Before proceeding to show how these calculations are performed, we shall quickly review the terminology and ideas developed in the present chapter.

A *project* is said to consist of a collection of independent *activities*, or *jobs*. If one job has to be completed before another can begin, we say the first job is an *immediate predecessor* of the job following or equivalently, the latter is an *immediate successor* of the former. This predecessor relation among jobs can be shown by a *project graph*, or *network*.

Two types of graphs were illustrated. The *arrow diagram shows* the jobs as *arrows* connecting two *nodes*, or circles, and the immediate predecessor relationship between two jobs is denoted by the predecessor's *terminal (ending) node* being identical with its successor's *initial node*. Reasons for adding *dummy jobs*, that is, jobs requiring zero time for completion, were also given. It was shown that dummy jobs are needed in constructing an arrow diagram if two or more activities in the project have *identical* immediate predecessors and successors, or if two or more jobs have *some, but not all*, of their immediate predecessors in common. A second type of graph, called the *activity-on-node graph*, was illustrated. In the *AON diagram*, jobs are portrayed by nodes and the immediate predecessor relation between two jobs by an arrow from the node representing the predecessor to the node representing the successor.

Appendix: *Dummy Jobs*

When and where to add dummy jobs is a problem which almost always troubles the user's first attempts at drawing project arrow diagrams. It is often simplest to make liberal use of dummies when initially drawing a network and then, after the network is completely drawn, to remove the unnecessary ones. For example, if job *A* is a predecessor to jobs *B*, *C*, and *D*, and in addition one or more of the latter three have other predecessors, not all the same, then *A* can initially be connected by dummies to all three (see Figure 2-13). When the network is completed, unnecessary dummies can be recognized as follows:

1. If a dummy job is the only job emanating from its initial node, it can be removed. (Removing a dummy job does not mean just erasing the dotted arrow, but bringing the final and initial nodes together, with all their connecting jobs, into one node.) Thus dummy job *E* in Figure 2-13 could be eliminated.

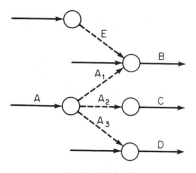

FIGURE 2-13

2. Likewise, if a dummy job is the only job going into its final node, it also can be removed. In Figure 2-13, dummy job A_2 could thus be eliminated.

3. If two (or more) jobs have identical sets of predecessors, some of which also appear in different predecessor sets of other jobs, then the two jobs should emanate from a single node connected to their predecessors by dummy jobs. This usually allows some collapsing of dummy connections. Figure 2-14 is an example. Jobs A and B are the only predecessors for jobs C and D, although they are also among the predecessors for other jobs. C and D can be joined to the same initial node, as shown in Figure 2-15, eliminating two dummy jobs.

FIGURE 2-14

FIGURE 2-15

4. Similarly, if two (or more) jobs have identical sets of successors, the latter having other predecessors as well, then the two can be joined together in their final node and connected by dummy jobs to their successors. For example, the partial network of Figure 2-16(a) can be changed to the simpler network of Figure 2-16(b). Both jobs A and B have as their only successors jobs C and D and can thus be joined to a single final node.

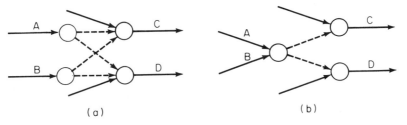

(a)   (b)

FIGURE 2-16

5. Dummy jobs which show predecessor relations already implied by other jobs (dummy or regular) may be removed as redundant. In Figure 2-17, dummy job A_1 is unnecessary. In large networks, such dummies may be difficult to spot visually but may be detected by means of a "redundancy check," as described in the next section.

FIGURE 2-17

Redundant Predecessor Relationships

Since redundancy in predecessor relationships often shows up in a network—and not just in connection with dummy jobs—we ought to say a few words about this problem. When a manager or engineer is trying to write down a list of predecessors for each activity in a network, it is easy to put down more than are necessary—to show as immediate predecessors jobs that are really more distant predecessors (that is, predecessors of predecessors). Actually, as far as the network logic is concerned, this causes no real problem. But it can make drawing the network more difficult, and it usually adds to the number of dummy jobs needed, to the clutter of the network, and to computer time and expense.

Redundancy exists when, among the predecessor set of any job, one of the jobs is a predecessor for some other job in the same set. For example, suppose that job M's predecessor set includes jobs F, G, and H. Suppose further that job H has F and G as predecessors. Then F and G are *redundant* in job M's predecessor set and can safely be eliminated. As long as H precedes M, then F and G will automatically do so also since they precede H. They are not *immediate* predecessors of M but more distant ones. Predecessor lists should contain *immediate predecessors* only.

Often, such redundancy can be spotted easily; but if the trail of predecession is long, redundancy can be well hidden. In the above example, if job F and G were not immediate predecessors of H but were predecessors of job J, which preceded job K, which was a predecessor of H, then the redundancy of F and G in job M's list would not be so obvious.

One method of removing redundancies is to create a table with as many rows and columns as there are jobs in the project. Jobs are then listed in both the rows and the columns in *topological order.*[6] The general procedure is to look at each row and mark the job's immediate predecessors with an $\times$ and its more distant predecessors with a circle. Starting in the row for the first job that has predecessors (beginning jobs will have blank rows, of course), mark an $\times$ in the column corresponding to each immediate predecessor. Then consult the rows of each of these predecessors for *their* predecessors. Whenever the predecessor has a mark in its row—whether an $\times$ or a circle—place a *circle* in the same column position of the original job's row. Do this for each immediate predecessor, and then move on to the next job, first marking its immediate predecessors with $\times$'s and then more distant predecessors with circles. When the table is completed, if any $\times$ is circled, it is a redundant predecessor for the job in its row and can be eliminated from the job's predecessor list.

To illustrate the procedure we use the following small project:

Job	Immediate Predecessors
A	
B	A
C	A
D	B, C
E	B, D
F	C, D
G	B, D, E, F

The jobs are already in topological order, so we create a table with the job names on both rows and columns. The matrix of immediate predecessors (marked with ×'s opposite each job) appears as follows:

		Predecessor						
		A	B	C	D	E	F	G
	A							
	B	×						
	C	×						
Job	D		×	×				
	E		×		×			
	F			×	×			
	G		×		×	×	×	

Now in each row, all immediate predecessors (marked with an ×) are consulted for *their* predecessors (immediate or otherwise), and these are noted in the given row with *circles*. For example, in row D, jobs B and C are shown as predecessors. Both of these have A as a predecessor, so a circle is placed under A in row D. In row E, B appears again, so a circle is placed in the A column. Additionally, D is listed as a predecessor, whose predecessors, in turn, include B and C; so circles are also placed under these columns in row E. Note that this causes the × under B to be circled. If we continue in similar fashion through row G, the table would appear as follows:

		Predecessor						
		A	B	C	D	E	F	G
	A							
	B	×						
	C	×						
Job	D	○	×	×				
	E	○	⊗	○	×			
	F	○	○	⊗	×			
	G	○	⊗	○	⊗	×	×	

We focus our attention on the circled ×'s which signal redundancy. Thus job *B* is a redundant predecessor for job *E* (since predecessor *D* also has *B* as a predecessor); *C* is redundant in *F*'s list; and *B* and *D* are redundant among *G*'s predecessors. All these redundancies could be eliminated without changing the logic of the network. (The × part of the circled ×'s would disappear, but the circles would remain, indicating more distant predecessor relationships.)

The procedure above can easily be performed by hand for small projects, as we have seen, but would be tedious without the help of a computer for large projects. A well-designed computer program for performing project network calculations should have a subroutine that checks for redundancy.

Cycles

Another problem that sometimes occurs in networks is that of *cycles*. A cycle is any path of jobs that leads back into itself. Subroutines that check for redundancy will also turn up any cycles that may exist in a network, which will be indicated if a job shows up as a distant predecessor of itself.[7] Cycles are more serious than simple redundancies, however, as they represent logical errors in the network. They *must* be removed before network calculations can be performed, whereas it is desirable but not absolutely necessary to remove redundancies.

The network calculations of Chapter 3 require that jobs be considered in topological order; calculations must be performed on all of a given job's predecessors before they can be performed on that job. But if a cycle occurs, topological ordering is impossible. For example, if job *A* is followed by *B*, *B* is followed by *C*, and *C* is followed by *A*, then none of these jobs could ever be put in a topologically ordered list since its predecessor would not have been listed. Job *A* cannot be listed until job *C* is listed, which in turn cannot be listed until *B* is. But *B* must follow *A* in the list. Thus none of the three could ever be listed.

One simple way to discover cycles, then, is to attempt to put jobs in topological order. If this can be done successfully, no cycles exist. Otherwise, a circular path of jobs is present and must be removed. While a computer program can check for the existence of cycles, it cannot remove them (except in an arbitrary fashion), because there is no way for the computer to determine which link in the cycle represents a logic error. The person or persons who compiled the project data must recheck for accuracy the stated predecessor relationships of jobs in the cycle.

---

[7]Ordinarily, cycles will be uncovered *before* the redundancy check. They have to be removed before jobs are topologically ordered, as explained above, and such ordering must precede the redundancy subroutine.

3

Finding the Critical Path

Once we reduce a project to a network of activities and events and we estimate activity durations, we are in a position to determine the minimum time required for completion of the whole project. To do so, we must find the *longest path*, or sequence of connected activities, through the network. This is called the *critical path* of the network, and its *length* determines the duration of the project. In this chapter we are primarily concerned with finding and measuring the critical path in a project network. First, however, we must clearly define what we mean by a *path* in a network and by the *length* of a path. We hope to accomplish this with the aid of the following simple example.

Suppose that the W-L Company has two salesmen who meet for dinner one night in San Francisco. They discover that they are both going to Los Angeles the next day and agree to continue their conversation at dinner that night. The first salesman, whom we shall call Mr. Allen, lives in Santa Barbara and plans to go through that city, have lunch with his wife, and then travel on to Los Angeles. Mr. Baker, the other salesman, has an appointment with a customer for lunch in Bakersfield and must go there on the way to Los Angeles. As both have to work in Los Angeles the day after they arrive, they want to meet for dinner as early as possible. Their problem then is to decide the earliest possible time to meet for dinner if they both leave at 8:00 A.M. the next morning.

The driving time from San Francisco is about 8 hours if one goes through Bakersfield on U.S. 99 and about 11 hours if one goes through Santa

Barbara on U.S. 101. This is shown on Figure 3-1. The driving time in hours is shown adjacent to the arrows indicating the direction of travel. (Note the similarity between Figure 3-1 and the arrow diagrams of Chapter 2.) Moreover, if we assume that Allen and Baker will each spend 2 hours for lunch, we can describe their travel to Los Angeles as a project whose final event is their meeting for dinner. The project's activities with their immediate predecessors are given in Table 3-1, and the project's arrow diagram is portrayed in Figure 3-2.

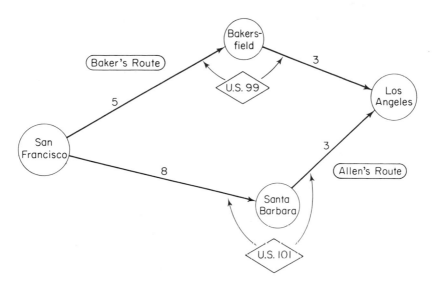

FIGURE 3-1. Routes from San Francisco to Los Angeles

TABLE 3-1

Project of Traveling to Los Angeles

Job Name	Alternate	Job Description	Immediate Predecessors	Time (hours)
a	(1, 2)	Allen drives from San Francisco to Santa Barbara	—	8
b	(2, 3)	Allen lunches with wife	a	2
c	(3, 6)	Allen drives from Santa Barbara to Los Angeles	b	3
d	(1, 4)	Baker drives from San Francisco to Bakersfield	—	5
e	(4, 5)	Baker lunches with customer	d	2
f	(5, 6)	Baker drives from Bakersfield to Los Angeles	e	3

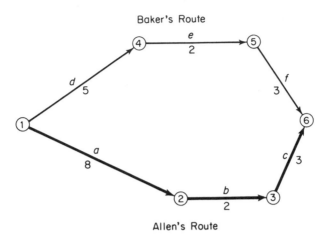

Baker's Route

Allen's Route

FIGURE 3-2. Arrow Diagram of Project of Traveling to Los Angeles

To determine the earliest time that Allen and Baker can meet for dinner, we must find out which one will take longer to reach Los Angeles. From Figure 3-2 it is obvious that Allen will take 13 hours (8 from San Francisco to Santa Barbara, 2 for lunch in Santa Barbara, and 3 from Santa Barbara to Los Angeles), while Baker will need only 10 hours to reach Los Angeles. Thus, if both leave San Francisco at 8 : 00 A.M., the earliest dinner appointment they can make is 9 : 00 P.M. (8 : 00 A.M. + 13 hours).

Notice how we made the calculation. We found Allen's time to reach Los Angeles by beginning at node 1 and seeing how long it took him to reach node 2; then we added this time (8 hours) to the time it took him to reach node 3. Finally, we took this sum and added the time between node 3 and node 6. Similarly, we obtained Baker's time for travel by adding the times between nodes 1 and 4, 4 and 5, and 5 and 6.

On this network there are two ways to start at beginning node 1 and traverse the network to ending node 6. These two ways are called *paths*. A *path* is a set of nodes connected by arrows, which begin at the *initial node* of a network and end at the *terminal node*. In Figure 3-2 there are two paths, 1–2–3–6 and 1–4–5–6, where the numbers refer to the nodes. The *length* of a path in a network is the total time it takes to travel the path. This time is calculated by adding the individual times between connected nodes on the path.

A path is called a *critical path* if it is the longest path in a project network. Thus Allen's path, which we have shown in boldface type, is the only critical path in the project of traveling to Los Angeles. Activities, or jobs, on critical paths are referred to as *critical jobs*, or *critical activities*. These jobs are critical in determining the project's duration: To shorten the time to complete a project, we must shorten the jobs on the longest path in its network—the critical path.

To see this, note that if Mr. Baker decides to eliminate his stopover in Bakersfield, activity (4, 5), thus shortening his travel time to 8 hours, it *still* takes 13 hours before he and Mr. Allen can meet in Los Angeles. On the other hand, if Allen cuts his lunch time in Santa Barbara from 2 hours to 1, then they can meet in 12 rather than 13 hours. Again, Mr. Allen's path and the jobs along it are *critical* in determining the length of the project, that is, when he and Baker can meet in Los Angeles.

As a further exercise in finding paths and their lengths in an arrow diagram, consider the project shown in Figure 3-3. If you list all possible

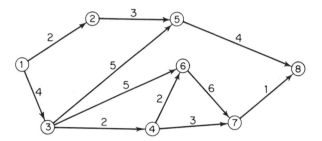

FIGURE 3-3. Example Arrow Diagram

sequences from start to finish, you will discover that there are *five* distinct paths in the network:

    A: 1–2–5–8
    B: 1–3–5–8
    C: 1–3–6–7–8
    D: 1–3–4–6–7–8
    E: 1–3–4–7–8.

From the activity duration given alongside each arrow in Figure 3-3, you should be able to verify that *C* (1–3–6–7–8), is the critical path, with a length of 16.[1]

Thus far we have been using an *arrow diagram* to illustrate the calculation of a project's critical path. The calculation is computed in the same manner for an AON diagram. The only difference is that the activity times we add are given at the *nodes* in this graph rather than along the *arrows* as in the arrow diagram. We will draw an AON diagram, Figure 3-4, using the Allen–Baker trip example of Table 3-1.

The paths in the figure are: (1) start–*a*–*b*–*c*–finish and (2) start–*d*–*e*–

[1] The path lengths are 9(*A*), 13(*B*), 16(*C*), 15(*D*), and 10(*E*).

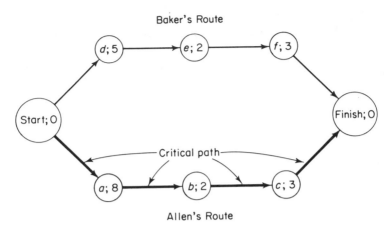

FIGURE 3-4. AON Network of Project of Traveling to Los Angeles

f-finish. The lengths of the paths, computed by adding the time at each node, are $0 + 8 + 2 + 3 + 0 = 13$ hours and $0 + 5 + 2 + 3 + 0 = 10$ hours, respectively. The critical path is (1) since it is longer than (2).

Multiple Critical Paths

We stated earlier that the only way to shorten a project is by reducing the time needed to perform one or more critical activities, that is, jobs on the critical path. However, a project may have more than one critical path. For example, if Baker took 5 hours for his luncheon appointment rather than 2, it would take 13 hours for him to reach Los Angeles; both paths would then be critical. In order for Baker to meet Allen sooner, *both* would have to shorten the time used for their trips. In general, if there are two *independent* critical paths (that is, critical paths with no jobs in common), then at least *two* activities (one on each path) must be shortened to reduce the project length. If the paths share one or more jobs in common, then shortening one of the common jobs will simultaneously shorten both critical paths and hence the project itself. The same considerations hold if there are multiple critical paths. All must be shortened simultaneously if project duration is to be reduced.

As an example in point, consider the project shown in Figure 3-5. Note that all paths are 15 time units long. There are many ways of shortening this project, but to do so at least one—and perhaps as many as five—jobs must be shortened. To cite a few examples, one could reduce project duration by shortening:

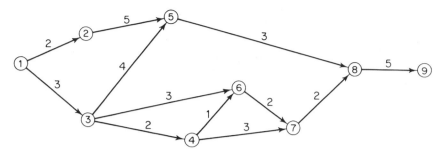

FIGURE 3-5. Arrow Diagram of Project with Multiple Critical Paths

a: job (8, 9)
b: or jobs (1, 2) and (1, 3)
c: or jobs (5, 8), (6, 7), and (4, 7)
d: or jobs (1, 2), (3, 5), (3, 6), and (3, 4)
e: or jobs (2, 5), (3, 5), (3, 6), (4, 6), and (4, 7).[2]

In Chapter 5 we shall discuss how to find the best combination of jobs to shorten, but for now we just observe that alternative ways for reducing project length usually exist.

Job Slack

Going back to our original example where Allen's path is critical, we note that Baker can leave 3 hours later than Allen and still not delay their dinner. Alternatively, Baker could travel more slowly or take longer for lunch in Bakersfield, as long as the total delay did not exceed 3 hours. We say then that Baker has some *slack* in his path, or more generally speaking, that jobs not on the critical path have slack (relative to critical jobs). Such information is extremely useful to project managers because it tells them how much flexibility they have in scheduling various jobs. But before learning how job slack may be calculated, let us first consider an efficient method for finding which jobs are critical.

An Algorithm for Finding the Critical Path

In the previous section we showed how jobs not on the critical path could be delayed or lengthened without changing the time needed to complete the project. In this section we devise a set of procedures that will identify

[2]Such combinations of jobs may be found by taking "cuts" of the network, in which a line is drawn through the network, from above to below, always cutting through arrows oriented counterclockwise to the direction of the cut line. The above examples represent 5 of 15 possible cuts in the network shown.

the critical path and show how the start and finish times of certain activities may be changed without affecting the duration of the project. In general, a set of procedures or collection of rules specifying calculations which lead to a desired result is referred to as an *algorithm*. Hence we shall present an algorithm for finding the critical path of a project and the start and finish times of all the activities within the project.

For purposes of exposition, we shall use the budget example of Chapter 2. Its arrow diagram is reproduced in Figure 3-6. Recall that a job's name is given above the arrow and its duration below. We shall describe shortly what the brackets above and below the arrows denote.

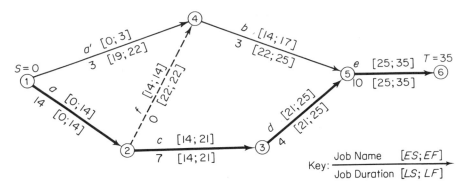

FIGURE 3-6. Arrow Diagram of W-L's Revised Budgeting Project

Early Start and Early Finish Times

We begin with some definitions. The *early start* of a job in a project is the earliest possible time that the job can begin, and we label it *ES( )*, where the job name appears in the parentheses. Thus we denote the early start of job *a* in Figure 3-6 as either $ES(a)$ or $ES(1, 2)$. The *early finish* of a job, denoted by *EF( )*, is its early start time plus the *time* needed to complete the job. For job *a* this would be $EF(a) = ES(a) + t(a)$.

Now, before a job can start, all its immediate predecessors must have been completed. Suppose that the project of budgeting at W-L begins at time 0. Since jobs *a* and *a'* have no predecessors, then $ES(a)$ is 0 and $ES(a')$ is 0 and their corresponding early finish times are $EF(a) = 0 + 14 = 14$ and $EF(a') = 0 + 3 = 3$. In general, we indicate the *start time* of a project by the symbol *S*. For jobs with no predecessors, then $ES = S$. In all examples throughtout this book we will set $S = 0$, but S could just as well be a calendar date.[3]

Once again the early start time of jobs a and a' in our budgeting example is 0, the start time of the project, since both have no predecessors. Now let us look at job c. It cannot start until its immediate predecessor a is completed; hence its earliest start $ES(c)$ is a's earliest finish time, or 14. Job c's early finish time is its early start time plus the time needed to complete it, or $EF(c) = ES(c) + t(c) = 14 + 7 = 21$. Similarly, job f, a dummy activity, can be started only when its immediate predecessor a is completed; thus $ES(f) = 14$. Since f is a dummy job, its duration is zero and hence $EF(f) = 14$.

Early start and early finish times are recorded on Figure 3-6 within the brackets *above* the arrows. The number before the semicolon in the brackets is the early start time, the number following is the early finish time. In symbols, we denote early start and finish times by $[ES, EF]$.

Thus far we have calculated ES and EF for jobs a, a', c, and f. Note that we *cannot* yet calculate these times for job e. Why? Because we do not yet know when its predecessors will be completed. Specifically, we have not calculated early finish times for b and d. Let us do so for job b.

Job b cannot be started until both a' and f are completed. The early finish time of a' is 3 and that of f is 14. Since *both* have to be completed before b begins, b cannot begin until day 14. So we write $ES(b) = 14$. In general, the *early start time* of a job is the largest, or maximum, of the early finish times of *all* its immediate predecessors.

Job d's early start time is 21, the early finish time of c, its only predecessor. It follows that $EF(d) = 21 + 4 = 25$ and $EF(b) = 14 + 3 = 17$. Now we can calculate $ES(e)$ as the maximum of the EF times of b and d, its immediate predecessors. Since 25 is the maximum, then $ES(e) = 25$ and $EF(e) = 35$. Thus the budget can be completed in 35 days. We usually refer to the completion, or finish date, as T, so $T = 35$ in our example.

Obviously, if the earliest completion date of the budget is 35 days after its beginning, the longest path through its network must be 35 days in length. A fast perusal of Figure 3-6 will show this to be correct; the path consisting of jobs a, c, d, and e is 35 days long. This sequence, then, is the project's *critical path*—the longest path in the network.

To briefly summarize our procedure, we start at the beginning of the project network and calculate the early start and then the early finish times for each of the beginning jobs (those with no predecessors). Then we do the

---

[3]Naturally, if calendar dates are used, then the calculations described here have to be "calendarized" to account for changes in months, days not worked, and so on. Thus in the example above, if S is January 20, then $EF(a) = 20 + 14 = 34$ or February 3, assuming that all days are worked.

same for their successors, their successors' successors, and so on until all jobs in the project have been considered. This procedure is called the *forward pass* through the network. Notice that no job can be considered until all its immediate predecessors have been. Thus the jobs are examined in *topological order*. (A list of jobs from a project is in topological order if no job appears in the list until all its predecessors have been listed.)[4] The forward pass, then, yields an *ES* and *EF* for each activity, and the earliest finish date, *T*, for the project.

Late Start and Late Finish Times

As we mentioned before, activities that are not on the critical path can be delayed without delaying the completion date (*T*) of the project. Reasonable questions are: *How much* can they be delayed? *How late* can a particular activity be started and still not lengthen the project's duration? It will be helpful in answering these questions if first we define the *late start* (*LS*) of an activity as the latest time it can begin without pushing the finish date of the project further into the future. Similarly, the *late finish* (*LF*) of an activity is its late start time plus its duration. In symbols for job *a*, $LF(a) = LS(a) + t(a)$, or, in a form that will be more useful, $LS(a) = LF(a) - t(a)$.

To calculate late start and late finish times, we begin at the end of the network and work backward. This time we go through a *backward pass*. In our budget example, that means that we start at node 6. The only job leading into node 6 is job *e*. It must be completed by day 35 so as not to delay the project; therefore, day 35 is its late finish. In general, for jobs with no successors, we set $LF = T$.

Since it takes 10 days to do job *e*, it must begin at day 35 − 10 or day 25, which is its late start. Now there are two jobs, *b* and *d*, which are predecessors of *e*. The *LF* times of both have to be 25, or *e* would be delayed beyond its *LS* and the project not completed by day 35. Then *b*'s late start is 22, since $LS(b) = LF(b) - t(b) = 25 - 3 = 22$. Similarly, *d*'s late start is 21, since the job has a duration of 4 days. Note that we have recorded the late start and late finish times for jobs just below their arrows in Figure 3-6. They are written as [*LS*; *LF*].

Job *c* is the only activity leading into node 3, and its *LF* becomes 21 since that is the *LS* of *c*'s lone successor, job *d*, which emanates from the node. Subtracting *c*'s duration of 7 days, we obtain $LS(c) = 21 - 7 = 14$.

---

[4]Usually, there is not a single topological ordering but several possible ones. Thus in our example job *b* could come before or after *c* in the list, as long as *a*, *a'*. and *f* appear before either of them.

Two jobs lead into node 4, a' and f. Their LF must be 22, the LS of job b emanating from the node. Thus $LS(a') = LF(a') - t(a') = 22 - 3 = 19$, and $LS(f) = 22 - 0 = 22$.

There are two jobs, f and c, which begin at node 2. $LS(f)$ is 22 and $LS(c)$ is 14, so the late finish time of any job leading *into* this node must be the smallest, or the minimum, of the late starts of the jobs beginning at the node. Hence $LF(a)$ is 14, the minimum of 14 and 22. $LS(a)$ then equals $LF(a) - t(a)$ or $14 - 14 = 0$. So a must begin at day 0. We have completed our backward pass, which yielded late start and finish times for all jobs. This information is quite useful, as we shall see below.

Total Slack

Looking a Figure 3-6, we observe that for some of the jobs, *late starts* and *early starts* (or similarly, *last* and *early finishes*) are identical. Thus $ES(a) = LS(a) = 0$ and $EF(d) = LF(d) = 25$. On the other hand, for example, $ES(b)$ is 14 and $LS(b)$ is 22. This means that job b may start any time between day 14 and day 22 and still not delay the completion of the project. We say then that job b has *slack*, and we define the *total slack* (*TS*) of a job, or activity, as the difference between its late start and early start times (or equivalently, as the difference between its late finish and early finish times). For job b, we have

$$TS(b) = LS(b) - ES(b) = 22 - 14 = 8 \text{ days}$$

or

$$TS(b) = LF(b) - EF(b) = 25 - 17 = 8 \text{ days.}$$

Obviously, if a job is on the critical, or longest, path, delaying its start would delay the project finish date. Hence its late and early start times must be identical. A quick glance at Figure 3-6 will show this to be true. It follows that jobs on the critical path have *zero* total slack, for if their $LS = ES$, then the difference between the two must be zero. Another definition of a critical path, therefore, is one whose jobs have zero total slack.

If we delay the start of a noncritical job (one that has *slack*), we shall frequently delay the start of the jobs succeeding it. For example, suppose that we delay job a' until day 18. Then its EF time is $18 + 3 = 21$. If job f is completed by day 14 as before, b still cannot be started until day 21, the completion date of a'. Thus b's ES increases from 14 to 21, and its total slack is reduced from 8 days to 1 day ($22 - 21$). We should be aware that use of the total slack of a job by delaying it will often affect the total slack of succeeding jobs.

Free Slack

However, such is not always the case. For instance, in our budget example notice that the early start time of b is 14. To put it another way, b cannot start until job f is completed on day 14. Job a' is also a *predecessor* of b, but a' takes only 3 days to complete. Thus it can start as late as day 11 and still *not* delay the early start of b. We say then that a' has *free slack* (*FS*), which we define as the amount of time a job can be delayed without affecting the early start time of any other job. For calculation purposes, the *free slack* of job is the difference between its early finish time and the earliest of the early start times of all its immediate successors. Thus

$$FS(a') = ES(b) - EF(a') = 14 - 3 = 11.$$

Free slack, of course, can never exceed total slack;[5] moreover, all jobs that have total slack do not necessarily have free slack. Witness job f, where $TS(f) = 22 - 14 = 8$ days but $FS(f) = ES(b) - EF(f) = 14 - 14 = 0$. The only other job with free slack in our example is b, which has $FS(b) = 8$. In general, a job has free slack if it has more total slack than one of its immediate successors.[6]

Both free slack and total slack have useful managerial interpretations, but total slack is probably the more widely used of the two. Throughout this book, when we refer to slack we will mean to *total* slack, unless we note otherwise. In the next section we shall have more to say about the important concept of slack and about its use.

Use of the AON diagram instead of the arrow diagram does not change any of the above procedures. To calculate the *ES* for a job, one must still examine the *EF* of all predecessors; and the job's *LF* is determined from the *LS* of its successors. *EF*, *LS*, *TS*, and *FS* are calculated as before. The resulting data is recorded by the job *nodes* of the AON diagram, rather than on the arrows.

To summarize the critical path algorithm, jobs in a network are first listed in topological order. Then the following calculations are performed for each job in a *forward pass* through the list (from top to bottom):

$S =$ start time for project (usually $= 0$)
$ES(a) = S$ for all beginning jobs, or
$ES(a) = \max\{EF(\text{all predecessors of } a)\}$
$EF(a) = ES(a) + t(a)$
$T = \max\{EF(\text{all jobs})\} =$ earliest finish time for project.

[5] An exception to this observation is noted in the next section.

[6] Another method of calculating free slack for a job is to determine the difference between its total slack and the *minimum* total slack of all its immediate successors. If a job has no successors, its free slack is taken to be the same as its total slack.

Then in the *backward pass* up through the job list, the following are calculated:

$$LF(a) = T \text{ for all ending jobs, or}$$
$$LF(a) = \min\{LS(\text{all successors of } a)\}$$
$$LS(a) = LF(a) - t(a)$$
$$TS(a) = LS(a) - ES(a) = LF(a) - EF(a)$$
$$FS(a) = \min\{ES \text{ (all of immediate successors of } a)\} - EF(a).$$

Project Due Dates That Differ from Earliest Completion Time

In the backward-pass procedure, we based our calculations on T, the earliest time that the project could be completed as determined by using the forward-pass procedure. Implicitly, we assumed that T represented the *desirable* completion date or target date or due date of the project. Such is not always the case, however. Project planners may wish to establish a target date that permits more slack in the schedule to allow for unforeseen problems or to increase flexibility in allocating resources to jobs. On the other hand, it is also possible that a due date earlier than T may be imposed externally—for example, by the Defense Department on a contractor for a missile project. Pressure would then be on the contractor to find ways of shortening the project duration, or he would face the possible payment of overtime penalties.

These possibilities may easily be incorporated in the critical path algorithm. Instead of setting the late finish times of all ending jobs equal to T, we set them equal to the *desired* project due date, say, D. Backward-pass calculations proceed exactly as before, but some of our previous conclusions would have to be modified.

Note that if the due date D is later than the earliest possible completion time T, then all activities in the project will have slack—including those on the critical path. For example, assume that the W-L Budgeting Project in Figure 3-6 has a target date of 40 days. Since its longest path is 35 days, all jobs on this path have 5 days of slack. Any one of them could be delayed up to 5 days without extending the project finish date beyond the target date of 40. In fact, *every* job in the project has 5 more days of slack than our previous calculations showed.[7] While we can still define the critical path as the longest sequence of jobs in the network, it is no longer true that critical jobs are slackless. But it is true that no job has less slack than critical jobs.

[7]We are talking here about total slack, of course. Free slack is unaffected by a change in target date because free slack is based only on a job's early start and finish times, which are independent of the project target date.

To generalize these observations, if we base calculations in the backward pass on an assumed project due date D, then all jobs will have D minus T more units of slack than they would if the calculations of LS and LF were based on the earliest project completion date T. Thus all critical jobs will have $D - T$ units of slack. If $D = T$, then critical path jobs will be slackless, as before. If D is greater than T, critical path jobs will have positive slack.

What happens, however, if D is less than T: if the due date is earlier than the minimum project completion date? The same analysis holds as above, but since $D - T$ is now negative, some jobs—possibly all of them, but at least the critical path jobs—will have *negative* slack.[8] Critical jobs will have exactly $D - T$ units of slack, the least amount of any jobs. If a project manager sees negative slack figures on project jobs, he knows that one or more of these will have to be expedited or the project probably will not be completed by the due date.

A Digression on Slack

When a job has zero total slack, its scheduled start time is automatically fixed (that is, $ES = LS$), and to delay the calculated start time is to delay the whole project. Jobs with positive total slack, however, allow the scheduler some discretion in setting their start times. This flexibility can be usefully applied to smoothing work schedules. Peak loads that develop in a particular shop—or on a machine, or within an engineering design group, to cite other examples—may be relieved by shifting jobs occurring on peak days to their late starts. Slack allows this kind of juggling without affecting project completion time.[9]

Free slack can also be used effectively at the operating level. For example, if a job has free slack, the foreman may be given some flexibility in deciding when to start the job. Even if he delays the start by an amount equal to or less than the free slack, the delay will not affect the start times or slack of succeeding jobs (which is not true of jobs that have no free slack). For an illustration of these notions, we return to our house-building example.

[8]Since free slack is unaffected by D, then if $D - T$ is negative, it is possible that a job's free slack may exceed its total slack, an exception to the general observation made in an earlier section. We should have said, $TS \geq FS$ (TS is greater than or equal to FS) as long as $D \geq T$.

[9]Chapter 7 presents a full explanation of this idea.

Back to the Contractor

In Figure 3-7 we reproduce the AON diagram of a house-building project, marking the *ES* and *EF* above and the *LS* and *LF* below each job—for example, 0; 4 are above and 3; 7 are below the *a*; 4 circle. We assume that construction begins on day zero and must be completed by day 37. Total slack for each job is not marked. Remember that it is the difference between the numbers representing *LS* and *ES* and those representing *LF* and *EF*. However, jobs that have positive free slack are so marked. There is one critical path, which is shown by heavier lines in the diagram. All critical jobs on this path have total slack of 3 days.

Several observations can immediately be drawn from the diagram:

1. The contractor could postpone starting the house for 3 days and still complete it on schedule, barring unforeseen difficulties (see the difference between early and late times at the finish). This would reduce the total slack of all jobs by 3 days, and hence reduce *TS* for critical jobs to zero.

2. Several jobs have free slack. Thus the contractor could delay the completion of *h* by 2 days, *f* by 1 day, *g* by 4 days, *q* by 12 days, and so on—without affecting succeeding jobs.

3. The series of jobs *d*, *o*, *p*, *u*, and *v* have a comfortable amount of total slack, 11 days. The contractor can use these and other slack jobs as "fill in" jobs for workers who become available when their skills are not needed for currently critical jobs. This is a simple application of workload smoothing: juggling those jobs with slack to reduce peak demands for certain skilled workers or machines.

If the contractor were to effect changes in one or more of the critical jobs, by contrast, the calculations would have to be performed again. This he can easily do, but in large projects with complex sequence relationships, hand calculations are considerably more difficult and liable to error. Computer programs have been developed, however, for calculating *ES*, *LS*, *EF*, *LF*, *TS*, and *FS* for each job in a project, given the set of immediate predecessors and the time required for each job. An example of such programs is given in the Appendix to Chapter 4.

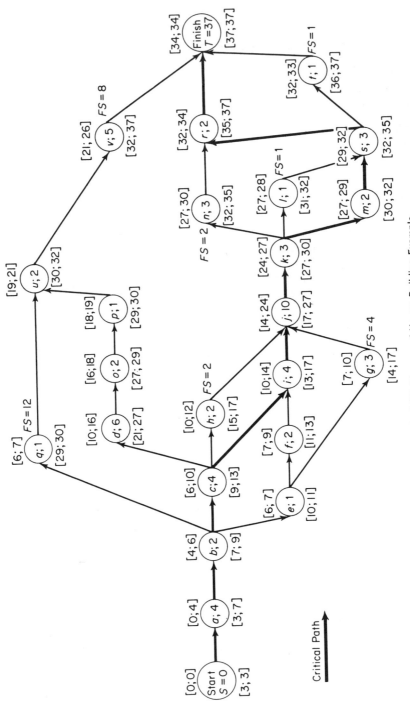

FIGURE 3-7. AON Diagram of House-Building Example

40

4

The PERT Model

Both CPM and PERT, as we have noted, use the project network. It is the basis of both techniques, and the notions of critical paths and activity slack are common to each. How, then, do they differ? Why two models? For historical reasons mainly. The models were developed independently and in somewhat distinct problem settings. As it has turned out in actual applications of the two models, some of their differences have disappeared or at least have become less important. But, traditionally, each has had a special emphasis of its own—each has been concerned with somewhat different aspects of the scheduling problem. Perhaps this is because they were originally applied in different kinds of industries and to somewhat different kinds of problems.

The Problem of Uncertainty

PERT was developed for and has been used most frequently in the aerospace industries—notably in research and development types of programs. These industries are relatively new; their technology is rapidly changing, and their products are nonstandard. CPM, on the other hand, has most frequently been applied to construction projects. For the most part, houses, bridges, and skyscrapers use standard materials whose properties are well known. They employ long-developed and well-seasoned components, and they are based on a more or less stable technology. Changes occur mainly in design—sizes, shapes, and arrangements—rather than in design concepts.

By contrast, while there is some standard hardware in ICBMs and lunar rockets, much of their design and construction requires new developments in materials and technology, and projects are contracted, planned, and scheduled before all technological problems have been solved. All of this is to say that there is a large amount of uncertainty in the development of new weapons systems and spaceships—uncertainty about the times required for developmental research, engineering design, and ultimate construction; about the specific activities; and sometimes about the configuration of the end product itself. There is little past history on which to base network construction and time estimates.

PERT takes some of these uncertainties into specific account. It assumes that the activities and their network relationships have been well defined, but it allows for uncertainties in activity times. For each activity in the project network, not only is an estimate made of the *most probable time* required to complete the activity, but some measure of uncertainty is also noted in this estimate. The person most qualified to know—an engineer, foreman, or worker—is asked to give two other time estimates. One of these is a *pessimistic estimate*—a best guess of the maximum time that would be required to complete the activity if bad luck were encountered at every turn. The estimate does not include possible effects of earthquakes, floods, fires, or other highly unusual catastrophes, but it does reflect the sort of design or construction problems inherent in the situation. The qualified person is also asked to give an *optimistic estimate:* If everything goes right, how long will the activity take at the minimum? In other words, what is the shortest conceivable time for the completion of the activity?

These time estimates are not always easy to prepare, but together they give useful information about the expected uncertainties of an activity. For standard, rather straightforward activities (technologically speaking), the three estimates should not vary much from each other. But the greater the uncertainty of an activity, the wider will be the range of the estimated completion times. And the most probable time is not always the best guess of the time one should *expect* the activity to take. If the most probable time estimate is closer to the optimistic than to the pessimistic time estimate, and if these two extreme values have about the same likelihood of occurrence, then the *average* or *expected time*, over the long run, will be influenced more by the pessimistic time and will be higher than the most probable time. This notion is illustrated below.

Expected Times for Activities

PERT calculates the expected value of an activity duration as a weighted average of the three time estimates. Specifically, it makes the assumption that the optimistic and pessimistic activity times, t_o and t_p, are about equally likely to occur. It also assumes that the most probable activity time, t_m, is four times more likely to occur than either of the other two.[1] So if we apply these weights to the three time estimates, we come up with a formula for the average, or expected, time, t_e, of an activity:

$$t_e = \frac{t_o + 4t_m + t_p}{6}.$$

The *expected time*, as the name implies, is what we would expect the activity duration to be on the average if the activity were repeated a large number of times. In most PERT applications, to be sure, activities do not get repeated a large number of times; they usually occur just once. But t_e is still the best estimate we can make of the time required for a single occurrence of an activity.

To further illustrate these concepts, consider the following example. A design engineer is asked to make three time estimates for the activity "Design stator tube." Based on past experience with similar activities, he decides that the most likely activity time is 8 days. It is possible, he thinks, that the activity might be done in as few as 5 days but if problems arise, it might take as long as 17 days. Implicit in his estimates—and perhaps explicit in his own mind—is a whole range of possible durations; he has assigned to each some likelihood of occurrence. Most probably his likelihood measure was not reduced to quantitative values but thought of only in a relative sense. This might be illustrated by means of a graph showing a distribution of possible durations, each represented by a bar whose height represents some relative measure of likelihood, as in Figure 4-1.

Thus 8 days has the highest likelihood; that is, it is the most likely or most probable time. On either side of 8 days the likelihoods are decreasingly lower. A duration of less than 5 days or more than 17 days is too unlikely to consider.

What we have drawn is very close to what the statistician calls a *probability distribution*—that is, a distribution of probability values for all possible outcomes. All we would have to do is to assign quantitative values, or probabilities, to our likelihood measures. By common agreement among statisticians, probability measures are always between 0 and 1, inclusive. If an

---

[1] For the quantitatively inclined, the weights are based on an approximation of a statistical frequency distribution known as *beta*. The beta distribution was chosen, in turn, as a reasonable approximation of the distribution of activity times for reasons that seemed justifiable to the originators of PERT. The beta distribution is unimodal (has a single peak value), has finite and nonnegative end points, and is not necessarily symmetrical—all of which seem desirable properties for the distribution of activity times. (The normal distribution—more widely used and commonly known—fails to satisfy the last two criteria mentioned.) Note that the choice of a beta distribution was not based on empirical data. Since most activities in development projects occur just once, frequency distributions of such activity times cannot be developed from past data.

FIGURE 4-1. Distribution of Possible Durations for Activity "Design stator tube"

event has a probability of 1, then it is certain to occur, and if its probability is zero, then by definition, it can never occur. Any value between 1 and zero represents a possible occurrence. The closer the value is to 1, the more likely is the event.

In our example since the activity duration may assume any value between 5 and 17 inclusive, and since it must assume one (and only one) of these values, the probability measures assigned to each of these possible outcomes must total 1. This is true of all probability distributions; that is, the sum of all possible, different outcomes must be 1. Sometimes a probability distribution is represented by a curve rather than by a series of bars, indicating that a continuous range of outcomes is possible, not just certain specific values.[2] Since the sum of the probabilities of all outcomes must still be 1, it can be shown that the area under a probability curve is also 1.

Going back to our example again, we can reason that the activity "Design stator tube" would not necessarily take exactly 8 days, 9, 15, or any other integer number of days. It could take on any value between 5 and 17, including fractional values. Thus our probability distribution in this case can best be represented conceptually by a curve, as shown in Figure 4-2.

The three estimates made by the engineer are identified on the curve. If we knew the exact shape of the probability curve, we could accurately calculate the average value of *t*, but since such precise curves are almost never available, we must use an approximation. The average, or *expected*,

[2]For example, if you flip a coin twice, there are just three specific outcomes possible: 0, 1, or 2 heads. Such a process repeated many times gives rise to a *discrete* distribution of outcomes. On the other hand, if the results of a process may take on any value over a range of possible outcomes, then the process yields a *continuous* distribution. Time, weight, distance, pressure, and temperature are all continuous measures.

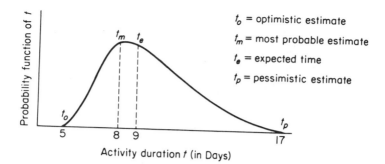

FIGURE 4-2. Continuous Probability Distribution

time as approximated by the PERT formula is

$$t_e = \frac{t_o + 4t_m + t_p}{6} = \frac{5 + 4(8) + 17}{6} = 9 \text{ days.}$$

The fact that the expected time t_e is larger than t_m in this example is a reflection of the extreme position of the pessimistic time t_p. Its influence on this averaging process is to draw the average, or central, point of the distribution to the right of the peak value at t_m.

Variability of Activity Times

Not only is it useful to have a means of calculating the average, or expected, time required for an activity, but we need to know how reliable that estimate is. If the time required for an activity is highly variable—if the range of our estimates is very large—then we will be less confident of the average value we calculate than if the range were narrower. For example, if the three time estimates for the activity "Design stator tube" were 8, 9, and 10 days (for optimistic, most likely, and pessimistic times, respectively), then the average would still be 9 days, and we would be more confident of this figure than in the previous case, where the estimates range from 5 to 17 days. Thus a wide range of estimates represents greater uncertainty and hence less confidence in our ability to correctly anticipate the actual time that the activity will require. What we need, then, is a means of measuring the variability of an activity's time duration. If we know the variability, we can, in turn, measure the reliability of our expected time, as determined from the three time estimates.

One measure of variability of possible activity times is given by the standard deviation of their probability distribution. Standard deviation and variance are commonly used in statistics as measures of variability among the numbers. The *variance* is simply the average squared difference of all numbers from their mean or average value. For example, suppose that three jobs have durations of 3, 4, and 8 months, respectively. Their average duration is 5 months. The squared differences of these durations from 5 are $(3 - 5)^2 = 4$, $(4 - 5)^2 = 1$, and $(8 - 5)^2 = 9$. The average of 4, 1, and 9 is $4\frac{2}{3}$, the *variance* of these job durations. The *standard deviation* is the square root of the variance, or about 2.16 months in this case.

PERT simplifies the calculation of standard deviation (necessarily, as only three out of all possible values of the distribution are given). The standard deviation of t, shown as S_t, is estimated by the formula

$$S_t = \frac{t_p - t_o}{6}.$$

That is, S_t is one-sixth of the difference between the two extreme time estimates.[3] Thus the greater the uncertainty in time estimates, the greater will be the difference in t_o and t_p and the more spread out will be the distribution curve. A high standard deviation, S_t, represents a high degree of uncertainty regarding activity time; there is a greater chance that the actual time required to complete the activity will differ significantly from the expected time, t_e.

In our previous example where the extreme time estimates for the activity "Design stator tube" were given as 5 and 17 days, the standard deviation would, therefore, be estimated as

$$S_t = \frac{t_p - t_o}{6} = \frac{17 - 5}{6} = 2 \text{ days.}$$

Since standard deviation is the square root of the variance of a distribution, then the variance of t is calculated for the above example as

$$V_t = \left(\frac{t_p - t_o}{6}\right)^2 = \left(\frac{17 - 5}{6}\right)^2 = 4.$$

The Expected Length of a Critical Path

The *expected length* of a sequence of independent activities is simply the sum of their separate expected lengths, which gives us a simple means of estimating the expected length of an entire project. We calculate a t_e for every

[3]This formula, too, is an approximation based on the observation that almost all of a unimodal distribution is contained within three standard deviations of the mean. (For a normal distribution this percentage is over 99.7, and no distribution has less than 89 per cent of its area within this range, according to Tchebycheff's inequality.) Hence statisticians frequently estimate the standard deviation of a unimodal distribution as roughly one-sixth of the range of the distribution. This implies—in the case of PERT—that the optimistic and pessimistic estimates are not necessarily the absolute extreme points of the range of possible values but rather the points beyond which there is, at most, only a very small probability of occurrence.

activity in the project network and use these t_e's to identify the critical path in the manner described in Chapter 3. As before, the critical path determines the length of the project; but since we have summed *expected* activity durations along the critical path, we obtain an *expected length of the project,* which we call T_e. (Actually, such a procedure tends to underestimate the actual T_e, as we shall discuss soon, since it ignores the influence of near-critical paths on project length.)

Similarly, the *variance* of a sum of independent activity times is equal to the sum of their individual variances. Since T_e is the sum of t_e's along the critical path, then the variance of T_e equals the sum of all the variances of these activities. We will call this sum V_T; and, similarly, the standard deviation of the project length will be S_T.[4] Either the variance or the standard deviation gives us a measure of the uncertainty surrounding our estimated project time. The higher the S_T, the more likely it is that the actual time required to complete the project will differ from the T_e. As with a single activity, though, the expected value T_e is the best time estimate we can make for the entire project—except in some circumstances that we shall note below.

As a simple example of how these PERT formulas are applied, we shall calculate the project length and variance for the network of activities illustrated in Figure 4.3. Above each activity arrow are numbers representing the three time estimates t_o, t_m, and t_p, in that exact order. We have chosen these numbers for ease of computation rather than to illustrate actual PERT data. Using the PERT formulas for t_e and S_t, we arrive at the following results:

Activity	Expected Time	Standard Deviation	Variance
(1, 2)	6	2	4
(1, 3)	12	3	9
(2, 4)	13	2	4
(3, 4)	5	1	1
(4, 5)	4	1	1
(3, 5)	16	4	16

The longest path of *expected* times, and hence the critical path, consists of activities 1,3 and 3,5, with a length $T_e = 12 + 16 = 28$. The variance of the critical path is then $V_T = 9 + 16 = 25$, which corresponds to a standard deviation $S_T = 5$. You may verify, if you wish, that the next longest path

---

[4]If more than one critical path exists, the one with the largest variance is chosen to determine V_T and S_T. Once again, the effect of other critical or near-critical paths is ignored in calculating the project variance. See page 45.

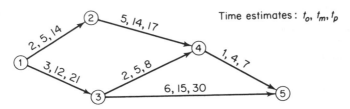

FIGURE 4-3. Example of PERT Calculations

has a length of 23 with a standard deviation of 3 and that its activities all have total slack of 5.

To summarize thus far, PERT differs from CPM in its attempt to recognize uncertainty by using three time estimates. These are reduced to a single time estimate for purposes of calculating a critical path and for obtaining the kinds of network information we described earlier—early and late start times for each job, slack values, and so on. But the standard deviation for each activity and for the entire project gives the manager additional information about variations in job and project times that he can anticipate. He should, therefore, be better able to plan for and cope with such variations.

Probability of Completing a Project by a Given Date

How can S_T or V_T be translated into managerial terms? That is, what does a particular value for S_T tell the manager about the variability of a project's length? We have already indicated a qualitative answer to these questions: A large S_T is associated with a higher variability in the expected project length. But what is a *large* S_T? Can a more quantitative interpretation be given—one that will enable the manager to assess the meaning of a particular S_T for a particular project?

The answer is yes, but an explanation to our answer requires the use of some elementary notions in statistics. The theory underlying these notions is not so simple, but an explanation can be given in a fairly straightforward fashion.

We mentioned earlier that the time required for an activity is uncertain: It may take on any value within a given range. Statisticians refer to such a measure as a random variable. Its value in a particular instance cannot be predicted with certainty, but its average, or expected, value (t_e) can be estimated on the basis of an assumption regarding the nature of its probability distribution and three points on this distribution—stated as the optimistic, most likely, and pessimistic times. As a weighted sum of random variables, t_e is also a random variable.

We calculated the expected project length, T_e, by adding the t_e's along the critical path. Since the t_e's are all random variables, then so is T_e. But the interesting (and fortunate, from a statistical standpoint) result is that T_e does not have the same distribution as the t_e's but follows approximately what is called a *normal distribution*, the familiar bell-shaped curve.[5] A normal distribution is symmetric with a single peak value, and it is described completely by its mean, or average, value and its standard deviation. That is, two normal curves with the same mean and standard deviation are always identical; there is no characteristic in which they can differ. Since we know much about the normal curve, we can infer a good deal of managerial information about a project's length if we know the expected length and standard deviation (T_e and S_T) of its distribution.

For example, 68 per cent of the area under a normal curve is within one standard deviation of the average of the distribution, as illustrated by the shaded region in Figure 4-4. Since the area under a probability curve corresponds directly with probability measures, we can state the following conclusion: A random variable drawn from a normal distribution has a .68 probability of being within one standard deviation of the distribution average. In terms of project duration, the interpretation is analogous: There is a 68 per cent chance that the *actual* project duration will be within one standard deviation, S_T, of the estimated average length of the project, T_e. There is an even greater chance (better than 95 per cent) that the project duration will be within *two* standard deviations of the average, and it is almost certain (99.7 per cent) that the duration will not be more than three standard deviations away. All of this follows from basic statistical notions *if* the random variable "project length" is really normally distributed and *if* the estimated activity times are unbiased[6]—two rather large *if*'s. But even if these assumptions are not completely satisfied, the results of the analysis—if not precise—at least give useful guidelines to the manager. For example, if the above calculations applied to two projects led to estimated probabilities for on-time completions of .20 and .95, respectively, a manager would certainly be more concerned about the former project than the latter and more likely to take corrective action on it, even if he knew that the actual figures might not be precisely correct.

[5]For the technically oriented, this result is inferred from the *Central Limit Theorem*, which implies that the sum of a large number of independent random variables will be approximately normally distributed, regardless of the distribution of the individual random variables.

[6]We use "unbiased" here in the statistical sense. An *unbiased* estimate is one that results from an estimating procedure which, on the average, yields the correct figure. Thus, if an engineer's estimates of activity times tend to be high (or low) on the average, the estimates are biased. If, on the other hand, some are high and some are low but their average is correct, then they are unbiased.

FIGURE 4-4. Normal Probability Distribution

Let us make the procedure above more definite. Suppose that a manager has analyzed the project diagrammed in Figure 4-5 and has calculated the expected activity times and variances as recorded. You may verify that the critical path passes through nodes 1, 2, 4, 5, 8 and has an expected length, or T_e, of 20 months. The variance along this path, by PERT calculations, is the sum of the activity variances, or $V_T = 9$, which is equivalent to a standard deviation, S_T, of 3 months. If we assume that T_e is normally distributed, as illustrated in Figure 4-6, there is a probability of about .68 that the project length will be within one standard deviation of T_e—that is, between 17 and 23 months. This is because 68 per cent of the area under the probability distribution lies between the vertical lines at 17 and 23 months. Similarly, the probability is better than .95 that the project will not exceed the limits 20

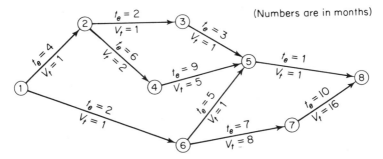

FIGURE 4-5. PERT Network with Expected Activity Times and Variances

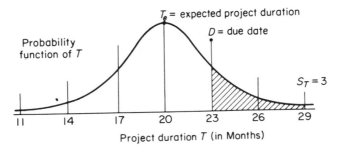

FIGURE 4-6. Distribution of Project Completion Times

$\pm$ 2(3), or 14 months on the low side and 26 months on the high side. One can be virtually certain (over .99 probability) that the project will take no less than 11 and no more than 29 months. Probabilities for any points in between those cited above can be calculated by referring to a standard normal table in almost any statistics book.

The same essential notions may be used to answer the question: What is the probability that the project will be completed by such-and-such a due date? Picture again the distribution of project completion times in Figure 4-6, based on our previous example.

Suppose that the due date, D, is 23 months from the starting point. How likely is it that the project will be finished by then? Such an outcome will occur if the project duration, T, is less than or equal to 23, the probability of which is equal to the area under the curve to the left of 23, as indicated by the unshaded portion of the diagram. Once again, standard normal tables enable us to readily make this calculation. We have only to determine the number of standard deviations D is from T_e, which is equivalent to converting the data for our particular normal distribution to standard normal form.[7] Since T_e and D differ by 3 months, the difference represents one standard deviation (remember that $S_T = 3$). A formula for the calculation may aid the memory:

$$Z = \frac{D - T_e}{S_T}.$$

Here Z is the number of standard deviations by which D exceeds T_e. Note that D might be less than T_e, in which case Z is negative. Now the probability measure originally sought may be obtained by referring to the following table, extracted from a standard normal table:

Z	*Probability of Meeting Due Date*
3.0	.999
2.8	.997
2.6	.995
2.4	.992
2.2	.986
2.0	.977
1.8	.964
1.6	.945
1.4	.919
1.2	.885
1.0	.841

[7]A standard normal distribution has an average value of zero and a standard deviation equal to 1.

.8	.788
.6	.726
.4	.655
.2	.579
0.0	.500
−.2	.421
−.4	.345
−.6	.274
−.8	.212
−1.0	.159
−1.2	.115
−1.4	.081
−1.6	.055
−1.8	.036
−2.0	.023
−2.2	.014
−2.4	.008
−2.6	.005
−2.8	.003
−3.0	.001

In our particular example, since $Z = 1$, then the probability of meeting the due date is about .84. To cite one more example, suppose that the due date is 17 months. How likely is it that the project will be completed by then? As before, calculate Z:

$$Z = \frac{D - T_e}{S_T} = \frac{17 - 20}{3} = -1.0$$

and the associated probability is close to .16. In other words, there is less than one chance in six that the project will be completed on time.

Effects of a Near-Critical Path[8]

We hinted above that T_e, obtained from adding the t_e's of critical path activities, might not always be the best estimate of project length. Here is why. It is possible that, under some combination of activity times and variances, a near-critical path may exist with a higher variance[9] than the "official" critical path. If bad luck is generally experienced with activities

[8] The next four sections may be skipped at first reading if desired.

[9] Actually, it does not have to be higher for the effect described to occur (it can even be lower); but the effect will occur more often in the circumstances described.

along this path and good luck with activities along the critical path, it is quite possible for the former to exceed the latter in length—that is, to become critical itself. Thus, where the possibility of uncertain activity times is admitted, the possibility of alternate critical paths is implied. We may be in error, then, in basing our estimate of T_e on the t_e's of a single critical path. Other paths may become critical and should influence our estimate of T_e. For similar reasons, near-critical paths also influence V_T and S_T, the estimated variance and standard deviation of project length. The user of PERT should be aware that the simple estimating procedures we have shown tend to yield overly optimistic results. Estimates of T_e, V_T, and S_T are lower than they should be, which means that the calculated probabilities for on-time completion of a project are thus higher than they should be.

Other Methods for Calculating Project Length and Variance

To illustrate, we shall again use our sample project of page 50, which is based on Figure 4-5. Recall that the critical path had an expected length, or T_e, of 20 months with an S_T of 3 months. By ordinary PERT methods, we would say that there was a .84 probability of finishing the project in 23 months (which represents one standard deviation above the mean). Actually, this is the probability that activities along the critical path, by themselves, will be completed in 23 months. It is usually assumed that noncritical paths can be ignored because they are shorter and not likely to affect the due date. But examine the sequence of activities along path 1–6–7–8. This path is 19 months long—only 1 less than the critical path. Furthermore, it has a standard deviation of 5 months, 2 *more* than that of the critical path. If we consider this 19-month sequence of activities by itself, the probability of its completion in 23 months is only .79, since

$$Z = \frac{23 - 19}{5} = .8.$$

That is, the expected length of path 1–6–7–8 is 4 months less than the due date of 23 months, while the critical path's expected length is only 3 months shorter than the due date. Comparing just the expected lengths with the due date, we see that path 1–6–7–8 has more slack than the critical path. But because of the greater variability in time estimates of the former path (and hence a larger standard deviation), its chance of completion by the due date is less than that of the critical path. Furthermore, since *all* activities in a network have to be completed before the project is finished, the probability that *both* sequences of activities will be done in 23 months or less is .66, the product of their respective probabilities. (We have made some assumptions here—primarily that the activity durations are independent of each other. Also assumed is that the activities which connect with, but are not a part of, these two sequences do not affect the completion times of the sequences—which is very nearly true in this particular example.)

Thus the normal PERT procedure which bases the estimates of T_e and S_T on a single critical path can grossly overstate the probabilities of completing a project by a given date, especially if there are one or more parallel paths through the network which are nearly critical, and/or which have relatively large variances. The more there are of such paths, the more nearly critical they are, and the larger their variance, the more serious will be the errors. A manager could think his chances of finishing a project on time were very good, when, in fact, they were very poor. On the other hand, if there are many interconnections between such parallel paths, or if the critical path is much longer than any other path, the normal PERT calculations should lead to satisfactory results.[10]

Theoretically, it is possible to arrive at a mathematical expression for the expected length of a project by combining the statistical distributions for jobs in the project network.[11] But the expression becomes exceedingly complex and the calculations enormously tedious for anything but the smallest project and simplest assumed frequency distributions.

Simulation of a Network

A much more easily managed approach is simulation. By use of Monte Carlo sampling technique, activity times are randomly selected for each activity from some appropriate frequency distribution. The project length and critical path data are then calculated in the normal way, based on these times. This procedure is repeated perhaps several thousand times with a computer and a record is kept of the critical path data generated. Finally, an average project length and standard deviation are calculated on the basis of all this simulated data.[12] The resulting estimates should be more reliable than those produced by the normal procedure, since they take into account

[10]For an interesting analysis of errors that may result from the PERT assumptions, see K. R. MacCrimmon and C. A. Ryavec, "An Analytical Study of the PERT Assumptions," *Opns. Res.*, **12**, No. 1 (Jan.-Feb. 1964), 16–37.

[11]See A. Charnes, W. W. Cooper, and G. L. Thompson, "Critical Path Analysis via Chance Constrained and Stochastic Programming," *Opns. Res.*, **12**, No. 3 (May-June 1964), 460–470.

[12]For a more detailed explanation of the methods, see R. M. Van Slyke. "Monte Carlo Methods and the PERT Problem," *Opns. Res.*, **11**, No. 5 (Sept.-Oct. 1963), 839–860.

the effects of near-critical paths which may, in fact, become critical if activities along them take more than their normal times.[13]

Criticality Index

A new and useful measure of criticality can also be obtained from the simulated data. For each activity a record is kept of the proportion of simulation runs in which the activity is critical. For example, if activity a is on a critical path 3,000 times out of 10,000 simulation runs, we would say that a has a criticality index of .30 for the given project. The activity may not have appeared at all on the critical path calculated by normal procedures, but the simulation tells us that the activity has about a 30 per cent chance of being critical, if the data upon which the calculations were made are accurate. Activities with the highest criticality index would be subject to the most managerial scrutiny, since they would have the highest probability of delaying the project. But a moderately high index would also call attention to near-critical activities; there would be less chance of their being ignored than in a case where a single critical path is identified and activities are either critical or not. Additionally, a probability distribution of slack values for each activity could be calculated. Rather than a single slack value, a range of slack values with associated probabilities would be identified with each activity.

Thus the simulation procedure helps to extend the notion of uncertainty to the critical path itself. No single path is identified as critical, but the probability of each activity's being on a critical path is estimated. If the concept of probability is understood by the project manager, the information provided by a simulation calculation should be much more useful than that derived from the conventional PERT calculations.

PERT'S Event Orientation

Some writers have emphasized another difference between PERT and CPM: while CPM is activity-oriented, PERT is often event-oriented. Essentially, this means that in activity-oriented networks, the arrows representing activities or jobs are labeled with some description of the activity; while in event-oriented networks, the events are the objects of interest and are appropriately described. An activity represents a segment of work to be

[13]The extent of PERT's tendency to yield overly optimistic estimates is examined by A. R. Klingel, Jr., in "Bias in PERT Project Completion Time Calculations for a Real Network," *Mgt. Science*, **13**, No. 4 (Dec, 1966), B194–B201.

accomplished over a period of time, but an *event* is a point in time—a milestone representing the beginning or the completion of some activity or group of activities. Thus the activity "Design propulsion system" might appear in a PERT network with an initial node labeled "Begin design of propulsion system" (or perhaps just "Begin systems design" if the design of other components also commences at that point). The final node for the activity might read "Design of propulsion system completed," or "Begin test of propulsion system" if the successor activity involves the work of testing the system. The emphasis on events has its roots in the *milestone method* of management, in which program progress is monitored in terms of success or failure in reaching certain important milestones at scheduled points in time.

Nothing in the network itself is affected by event orientation. The same arrows and nodes with the same interconnections will result from networking a project whether the approach is activity- or event-oriented. In fact, both events and activities can be labeled if desired. The tendency seems to be toward activity labeling, however, as it is the activities with which engineers and managers are most directly concerned. Engineers design *activities*, not *events*. And when projects fall behind schedule, it is the critical *activities* which receive managerial attention. Nevertheless, in some industries, management planning tends to be event-oriented, and a slightly different scheduling algorithm is useful.

Network calculations described in Chapter 3 are activity-oriented: Time calculations center on activities, as illustrated in the network of Figure 4-7. Early and late start times are recorded there for each activity. Finish times can readily be obtained by adding appropriate activity durations.

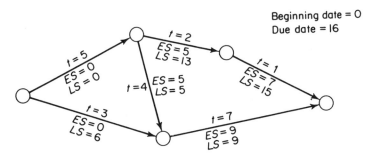

FIGURE 4-7. Activity-Oriented Network Calculations

Event times can be inferred from activity times, or calculated directly. For example, an event's early occurrence time, ET, is the latest early finish (EF) of any activity preceding the event; while its late occurrence time, LT, is the earliest late start (LS) of any following activity.

Event-oriented calculations for the same network would have the results[14] illustrated in Figure 4-8. Since events consume no time, we do not calculate start or finish times, only occurrence times, which may be early or late. Activity times can be derived directly from event times: An activity's early start equals the *ET* of its initial node, and its late finish equals the *LT* of its final node. As before, early finish time is obtained by adding the activity's duration to its early start, and late start equals late finish minus duration. Total slack can be calculated either for an event (*LT* minus *ET*) or for an activity (*LS* minus *ES*). Note that an event's slack is equal to the minimum slack of all paths that pass through the event node.

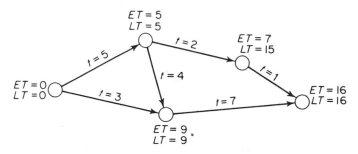

FIGURE 4-8. Event-Oriented Network Calculations

The direct calculation of event times does not require activity times to be computed first. A summary of the method is included in the Appendix to this chapter, and the reader will note its close resemblance to the activity-oriented algorithm. The two methods are equivalent, of course, and lead to the same results; but event-oriented calculations have certain advantages. They are easier to do on a project arrow diagram, and they facilitate computer programming. An example of an event-oriented computer program written in FORTRAN is also given in the Appendix.

The PERT Assumptions

Many thoughtful observers have questioned the assumptions upon which the PERT model is based. Some criticisms are of a technical nature— for example, is the assumption of a beta distribution for activity times appro-

[14]Do not confuse this event-oriented arrow diagram with the AON diagram described in Chapter 2. In the former, activities are still shown as arrows and events as nodes, but network calculations are based on node occurrence times rather than on activity start and finish times.

priate? Or, given that it is appropriate, does the simplified calculation, on pages 45 and 46, of expected activity time and standard deviation lead to error? MacCrimmon and Ryavec,[15] in a searching analysis of the PERT assumptions, concluded that in certain extreme cases the simple formulas could lead to errors as high as 33 per cent in the calculation of activity lengths. If the beta distribution is inappropriate for describing the distribution of activity times (which is not unlikely), then the error could be compounded. Since these errors can be either positive or negative, however, some cancellation of errors is likely to occur when activities are combined in a network.

Another important assumption is that activities are independent—that the time required to complete one activity will have no bearing on the completion times of its successors or of any other activities in the network. Conceptually, this might seem like a reasonable assumption, since activities —by definition—are independent endeavors; but in practice there are often dependencies. If one activity takes longer than expected, especially if it is on the critical path, then management will likely do what it can to expedite successor activities. In this indirect way, the time of one activity can influence the time of another. Availability of resources can also result in dependencies. Two parallel activities which require the same limited resource may take longer than expected if they happen to be scheduled at the same time. (The limited resource problem will be examined in greater detail in Chapter 7.) Technological relationships are another source of dependencies. Such dependencies are supposed to be indicated on the project network by interconnections of activities, but it is not always feasible or desirable to show *all* these relationships, especially if the activities are at a high level of aggregation, encompassing many smaller activities.

Because of these and other sources of dependencies, the estimated project length and variance—especially the latter—may be in error. The first source of dependencies mentioned above (the effect of a job on its successors) would probably *reduce* the actual project variance as compared to the calculated value; the other two causes of dependencies would likely cause *greater* variability in project duration. A manager who is aware of these effects and who is familiar with the characteristics of a particular project might be able to anticipate—at least in some qualitative way—the net effects of these influences on the project duration. But they remain a problem of the PERT assumptions.

Other criticisms of the PERT model have come from *practitioners*— those who have had experience in applying it to "real-world problems." However, we shall save for Chapter 8 our discussion of the difficulties which sometimes arise in applications of the PERT model.

[15]*Op. cit.*

Appendix: *The Event-Oriented Algorithm and a Critical Path Computer Program Written in FORTRAN IV*

The direct calculation of event times closely follows the activity-oriented method of Chapter 3. We let $ET(\ )$ represent the early occurrence time of an event whose number appears in the parentheses; similarly, we let $LT(\ )$ represent the event's late occurrence time. Event i precedes event j if the two are connected by an activity (ij). We represent its duration by $t(ij)$. As before, the algorithm has two sections:

Forward pass

$S =$ start time for the project (usually $= 0$)

$ET(j) = S$ for all beginning events

$ET(j) = \max\limits_{i} \{ET(i) + t(ij)\}$, where the maximization is over all events i that precede event j

$T = \max \{ET(\text{all events})\}$, which is the earliest finish time for the project.

Backward pass

$LT(i) = T$ for all ending events

$LT(i) = \min\limits_{j} \{LT(j) - t(ij)\}$, where the minimization is over all events j that succeed event i.

The relationship between activity and event times is summarized as follows:

$$ES(ij) = ET(i)$$
$$EF(ij) = ET(i) + t(ij)$$
$$LF(ij) = LT(j)$$
$$LS(ij) = LT(j) - t(ij)$$
$$TS(ij) = LT(j) - ET(i) - t(ij)$$
$$FS(ij) = ET(j) - ET(i) - t(ij), \text{ or equivalently,}$$
$$= TS(ij) - LT(j) + ET(j).$$

The following critical path computer program was written to illustrate the preceding notions. It is primarily an event-oriented program, but it also calculates and makes use of activity times. No attempt was made to include the more elaborate features of network programming or to allocate memory space efficiently. It is assumed that the data deck of project activities is in topological order (a subroutine could accomplish this if it is not) and that project data are punched in the following manner:

Card 1
    Field 1 (5 columns) Project Starting Date S
    Field 2 (5 columns) Project Due Date   D
    Field 3 (5 columns) Number of Activities
                in Project   N
Cards 2 through N + 1 (one card for each activity)
    Field 1 (5 columns) Activity Initial Node
                Number   I(n)
    Field 2 (5 columns) Activity Final Node
                Number   J(n)
    Field 3 (5 columns) Activity Duration   T(n)

Subscripted variables may be dimensioned according to the capacity of the computer and the size of the project expected. (A 32K machine should permit dimensions of about 2,500 words per subscripted variable, allowing project of up to 2,500 activities to be handled.) If activity durations are all whole numbers (as assumed in the program below), then all variables should be specified as integers. Otherwise, all but I and J should be declared real variables.

Variable names follow the mnemonic designations of the text (ES, LF, TS, and so on). I(n) and J(n) represent the *i* and *j* node numbers, respectively, of activity *n*, while T(n) is its duration time. All subscripts refer to activity numbers (ordered from 1 to N as they appear in the data deck) except for variables ET(k) and LT(k), for which the subscripts represent node numbers.

No output statements are included in the program. The interested reader may supply these, with output format as desired. The READ statements may have to be modified, depending on the particular compiler used.

```
      DIMENSION I(2500), J(2500), LS(2500), LF(2500)
      INTEGER T(2500), ES(2500), EF(2500), TS(2500), FS(2500), ET(2000),
     XLT(2000), S, D, TMIN
C     READ PROJECT START DATE, DUE DATE, AND NUMBER
      XOF ACTIVITIES
      READ 1, S, D, N
1     FORMAT (3I5)
C     READ ACTIVITY DATA—I NODE, J NODE, AND DURATION
      DO 2 K = 1, N
2     READ 3, I(K), J(K), T(K)
3     FORMAT (3I5)
C     INITIALIZE NODE OCCURRENCE TIMES
      DO 4 K = 1, 2000
      ET(K) = S
```

```
4   LT(K) = D
C   INITIALIZE TMIN, THE MINIMUM PROJECT DURATION
    TMIN = 0
C   FORWARD PASS—CALCULATE ES, EF FOR EACH ACTIVITY,
    XET FOR EACH NODE
    DO 5 K = 1, N
    INODE = I(K)
    JNODE = J(K)
    ES(K) = ET(INODE)
    EF(K) = ES(K) + T(K)
    IF (EF(K) − ET(JNODE)) 6, 6, 7
7   ET(JNODE) = EF(K)
6   IF (EF(K) − TMIN) 5, 5, 8
8   TMIN = EF(K)
5   CONTINUE
C   BACKWARD  PASS—CALCULATE  LF,  LS,  TS  FOR  EACH
    XACTIVITY, LT FOR EACH NODE
    DO 9 K = 1, N
    L = N + 1 − K
    INODE = I(L)
    JNODE = J(L)
    LF(L) = LT(JNODE)
    LS(L) = LF(L) − T(L)
    IF (LS(L) − LT(INODE)) 10, 11, 11
10  LT(INODE) = LS(L)
11  TS(L) = LS(L) − ES(L)
9   CONTINUE
C   CALCULATE   FREE   SLACK = ACTIVITY   TOTAL   SLACK
    XMINUS J NODE TOTAL SLACK
    DO 12 K = 1, N
    JNODE = J(K)
12  FS(K) = TS(K) − LT(JNODE) + ET(JNODE)
C   PRINT OUT RESULTS
    END
```

The preceding program bases the backward-pass calculations on D, the due date. A minor change in the program could be effected if it were desired to base such calculations on TMIN, the minimum project length. Use of the PERT three time estimates could also be incorporated with little difficulty.

5

The CPM Model

The critical path method was originally developed to solve scheduling problems in an industrial setting. For this reason, probably, it was less concerned with the uncertainty problems that PERT attempted to cope with and more concerned with costs of project scheduling and how to minimize them. Thus, unlike PERT, CPM does not make use of probabilistic job times; it is a "deterministic" rather than a "probabilistic" model. It does, however, allow for variations in job times, not as a result of random factors (bad luck or good luck) but as the planned and expected outcome of resource assignments.

Most jobs, CPM argues, can be reduced in duration if extra resources (men, machines, money, and so on) are assigned to them. The cost for getting the job done may increase, but if other advantages outweigh this added cost, the job should be expedited, or *crashed*. On the other hand, if there is no reason to shorten a particular job—if it has a generous amount of slack—the job should be done at its *normal* or most efficient pace, with a lesser assignment of resources. Thus there is no need to crash all jobs to get a project done faster; only the critical jobs need be expedited. Which jobs to expedite and by how much are the problems CPM attempts to solve.

Schedule-Related Project Costs

The cost of a project is not due solely to the direct costs associated with individual activities, or jobs, in the project. Normally, there are indirect expenses as well—overhead items such as managerial services, indirect supplies, equipment rentals, allocation of fixed expenses, and so forth. Many of these are directly affected by the length of the project: The longer the time required for its completion, the higher will be these expenses. In addition, if the project management is under contract to a government agency or some other customer to complete the program by a given due date, often the contract will specify penalties for delay beyond this date. It was reported that Lockheed's contract for the C-5A contained a $12,000 per day late penalty clause, and that General Dynamics was rewarded $800,000 for flying the F-111 10 days ahead of schedule.[1]

Hence project schedules can influence two kinds of costs—direct costs associated with individual activities (which increase if the activities are expedited) and indirect costs associated with the project (which decrease if the project is shortened). Figure 5-1 illustrates these notions.

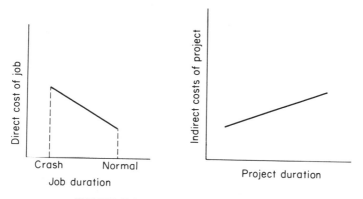

FIGURE 5-1. Costs Associated with a Project

As originally developed, the CPM model made the simplifying assumption that the time–cost trade-off for an individual activity is linear; that is, the relationship can be represented by a straight line on a graph plotting job duration versus cost. The steeper the slope of this line, the higher the cost of expediting the activity. A horizontal line, then, indicates that crashing the job would result in no decreased efficiency and, therefore, no added cost. One would normally expect the line to slope down to the right, indicating that costs go up as duration is reduced. If a job cannot be shortened regardless of the extra resources applied to it, the line would be vertical. All three possibilities would likely be represented on a job's time–cost trade-off graph, such as Figure 5-2. Over a certain range, some decrease in time can be obtained by the application of extra resources (represented by the portion of the figure between "crash" and "normal"). There is probably a minimum duration, however, which cannot be further reduced no matter what the

[1]*Aviation Week*, Feb. 21, 1966.

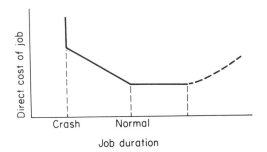

FIGURE 5-2. Time-Cost Trade-off Relationship for a Typical Job

expenditure of resources (vertical portion of line). Similarly, slowing the job will decrease costs only up to a certain point; beyond this point no additional savings are obtained (horizontal portion of line). In fact, costs may take an upward turn if the job is excessively stretched out.

In reality, a curved line may better represent actual costs than a straight line or a piecewise linear line, as in Figure 5-2. Modifications of the original CPM model have made it possible to solve problems with other than linear cost–time relationships, but our discussion here will be confined to the simplest case.[2]

The Lowest-Cost Schedule

From an intuitive viewpoint, it seems likely that there is some optimum project length—a happy medium between one with excessive direct costs for shortening jobs and one with excessive indirect costs for lengthening the project. The CPM model verifies this notion mathematically, and it specifies a method for finding this *optimum point*—the point representing the least-cost schedule. The mathematics of the method are quite sophisticated,[3] but the general procedure can be easily explained.

To begin with, a preliminary schedule is generated in which all jobs are assigned at their early start times and with normal resources. This is the maximum length schedule; it can be reduced only by expediting one or more of the jobs at added cost. If this added cost is less than the savings in indirect costs which result from shortening the project, then a less expensive schedule can be found. Improvements are made in stepwise fashion. New schedules

[2]See the Appendix at the end of this chapter for an analysis of other possible cases.

[3]An outline of a linear programming formulation of CPM is contained in this chapter's Appendix. For an original source, see J. Kelley, "Critical-Path Planning and Scheduling: Mathematical Basis," *Opns. Res.*, **9**, No. 3 (May-June 1961), 296–320.

continue to be generated as long as jobs can be crashed with a net reduction in total costs. The central problem, then, is to determine which jobs to expedite and how far to carry the schedule-shortening procedure.

At each step of the process, only jobs along the critical path are considered for crashing. (We noted earlier that critical jobs are the only ones that affect project length; it can be reduced only by shortening one or more critical jobs.) The cost–time slope of each critical job is examined, and the job with the least slope is determined. This is the job that can be shortened with the least expense of added resources. If the cost of shortening the job one period is less than the resultant savings from shortening the schedule one period, then the job is expedited—up to the point where no further shortening of the schedule is possible (either because the job duration cannot be reduced further or because some other job has become critical along a parallel path). Then the remaining critical jobs are examined, and the one with the flattest cost–time line is selected. If there are parallel critical paths, then one job in each of them must be chosen for crashing. The process is repeated until no further shortening of critical jobs is possible or until the costs of such shortening would exceed the savings that result from reducing the project length.

Step-by-Step Example

A simple example should help to clarify these basic notions. Suppose that we have a project consisting of four activities, connected as in the graph of Figure 5-3. Directly beneath each arrow (activity) is a pair of numbers. The first represents the normal time for the activity—the number of days required to complete the activity at its most efficient pace. The second number represents the minimum time—the crash duration, which results from the application of additional resources. We assume that in-between points are possible, too. Noted in parentheses below the duration times is the cost per

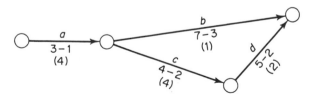

Key: <u>Activity name</u>
         Normal time — Crash time in days
         (Cost of crashing, $/day)

FIGURE 5-3. Example Network

day of crashing—that is, the dollars of additional expense required to reduce the activity's duration by 1 day. For example, activity *a* normally requires 3 days. For $4 added to its base cost, its duration can be reduced to 2 days, and for another $4 it can be reduced to 1 day, the minimum possible time to complete the activity. Since every activity must be performed to complete the project, the *base cost* of every activity must be paid. These costs may be regarded as fixed, or "sunk," costs of the project. For decision-making purposes, the relevant activity costs are those associated with crashing—that is, the incremental expenses for reducing activity completion times.

Figure 5-4 shows the cost–time trade-off lines for each of the activities in our example. The slopes of these lines indicate the relative costs of crashing the activities: The steeper the slope, the more expensive it is to

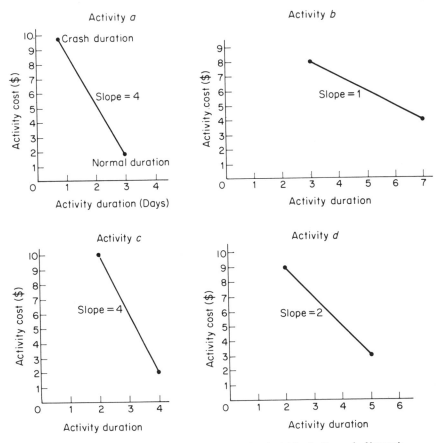

FIGURE 5-4. Cost-Time Trade-off Lines for Activities in Example Network

expedite an activity's completion. For example, activity c has a slope of 4;[4] it requires \$4 to shorten c by 1 day. By contrast, activity b has a flatter cost–time line, with a slope of 1. Thus each day's reduction in activity duration costs just \$1.

Suppose that time-related overhead expenses for this simple project are \$4.50 per day. What is the least-cost schedule for completing the project? How much should each of the activities be accelerated, if at all?

To find the optimum schedule, we start with all activities at normal pace. The critical path then is a–c–d, and it is 12 days long, as shown in the schedule graph[5] of Figure 5-5. If we ignore the base costs of the activities, the cost of this schedule is \$54:

$$
\begin{aligned}
\text{total cost} &= \text{cost of crashing} + \text{cost of overhead} \\
&= 0 \qquad\qquad\quad + (12\ \text{days})\ (\$4.50/\text{day}) \\
&= \$54.
\end{aligned}
$$

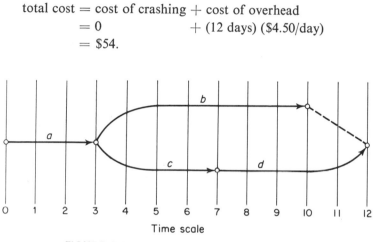

FIGURE 5-5. Schedule Graph for Example Network

To shorten the schedule would require crashing one or more activities on the critical path. Since d has the flattest slope of all critical jobs (see Figure 5-4), it can be shortened least expensively. We note also that b has 2 days of slack, represented by the dashed line. This means that d can be shortened 2 days before b becomes critical. With this change in d, the schedule graph appears as in Figure 5-6. The schedule is now 10 days long and its cost is \$49:

[4]Mathematically, the slope of the cost–time line measures the increase in cost per unit *increase* in time. Thus all the lines shown in Figure 5-4 have negative slope. To simplify our exposition, however, we will ignore the minus signs and speak of the absolute values of the slopes.

[5]A *schedule graph* is a network drawn on a time scale, in which the horizontal length of arrows represents their duration and their placement on the scale reflects their scheduled start and stop times. Dashed lines indicate precedence relations and the existence of slack.

$$\text{total cost} = \text{cost of crashing } d + \text{of cost overhead}$$
$$= (2 \text{ days}) (\$2/\text{day}) + (10 \text{ days}) (\$4.50/\text{day})$$
$$= \$49.$$

Although the cost of crashing increases $4, the overhead costs decrease $9, for a net improvement of $5.

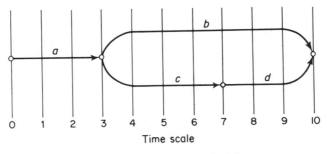

FIGURE 5-6. Ten-Day Schedule

Now we have two critical paths, *a–b* and *a–c–d*, and the schedule can be shortened only by reducing the length of both of them. Since *a* is common to both, a reduction in *a*'s length would accomplish our purpose. Or we could shorten the schedule by crashing one activity on each of the critical paths segments that are parallel to each other. There are two possibilities here: crashing *b* and *c*, or *b* and *d*. When two or more activities must be shortened jointly, their respective cost–time slopes must be added to obtain the cost of crashing. Thus our choices are as follows:

Crash Activity	Total Cost of Crashing ($/Day)
a	4
b and *c*	1 + 4 = 5
b and *d*	1 + 2 = 3

Obviously, the last alternative is the most attractive, but note that *d* can be shortened only 1 more day before it reaches its minimum length of 2 days. (Remember that the second number for each activity in Figure 5-3 gives the minimum time required for the job.) Crashing *b* and *d* 1 day each results in the 9-day schedule of Figure 5-7. Schedule costs are now $47.50:

$$\text{total cost} = \text{cost of crashing } b \text{ and } d + \text{cost of overhead}$$
$$= [(1 \text{ day})(\$1/\text{day}) + (3 \text{ days})(\$2/\text{day})]$$
$$+ (9 \text{ days})(\$4.50/\text{day})$$
$$= \$47.50.$$

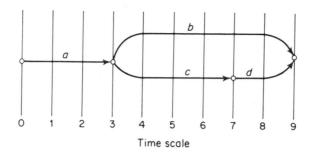

FIGURE 5-7. Nine-Day Schedule

Of the remaining alternatives for reduction in project length, crashing a ($4/day) is less expensive than crashing b and c ($5/day). Activity a can be shortened from 3 days to 1 day, and the schedule resulting from this change appears in Figure 5-8. This seven-day schedule is costed as follows:

$$
\begin{aligned}
\text{total cost} &= \text{cost of crashing } a, b, \text{ and } d + \text{cost of overhead} \\
&= [(2 \text{ days})(\$4/\text{day}) + (1 \text{ day})(\$1/\text{day}) \\
&\quad + (3 \text{ days})(\$2/\text{day})] + (7 \text{ days})(\$4.50/\text{day}) \\
&= \$46.50.
\end{aligned}
$$

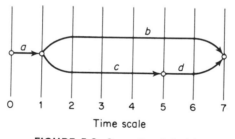

FIGURE 5-8. Seven-Day Schedule

Now there is only one alternative for further reduction in schedule length: shortening b and c. Activity b has already been shortened by 1 day, but it can be reduced another 3 days. However, c can be shortened only 2 days. Even though the cost of crashing b and c exceeds the saving in overhead, we perform this last change, which leads to the schedule graph in Figure 5-9.

This is the minimum length schedule. Even if b were further shortened, the project would still be 5 days long. The cost of the schedule above is

$$
\begin{aligned}
\text{Total cost} ={}& \text{cost of crashing } a, b, c, \text{ and } d \\
&+ \text{cost of overhead} \\
={}& [(2 \text{ days})(\$4/\text{day}) + (3 \text{ days})(\$1/\text{day}) \\
&+ (2 \text{ days})(\$4/\text{day}) + (3 \text{ days})(\$2/\text{day})] \\
&+ (5 \text{ days})(\$4.50/\text{day}) \\
={}& \$47.50,
\end{aligned}
$$

which, as anticipated, exceeds the cost of the previous schedule.

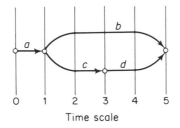

Time scale

FIGURE 5-9. Five-Day Schedule

If we combine all our results in a graph showing how project length affects total schedule costs, we obtain the curve in Figure 5-10. With this information a manager can readily select the most appropriate schedule. Ordinarily, it will be at the low point on the curve, but frequently there are other factors, qualitative in nature, which the manager must also weigh. For example, perhaps the 9-day schedule entails fewer risks and greater safety for employees than the least-cost 7-day schedule. The difference in cost is slight and the increased safety may well be worth it in the manager's judgment. In any event, the project time–cost curve gives the manager explicit and useful information concerning the economic effects of project scheduling

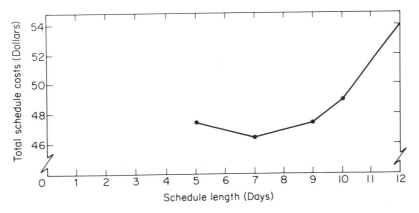

FIGURE 5-10. Project Cost-Time Curve

which, when combined with other relevant data and factors, should enable him to make better decisions.

What About "Stretching" Jobs?

Thus far we have implicity assumed that a job is either done at what we have called its normal pace or else it is speeded up. But what about changing the pace in the other direction? Would it ever make sense for a manager to slow down a job, to stretch out its duration by a lesser application of resources? The answer is: "It all depends." If slowing down a job will result in decreased efficiency and higher costs, there is ordinarily little point to doing it. In most situations that we can think of, a project's utility is inversely related to its length. That is, a short overall project duration is preferred to a long one. This is usually true because it is desired to complete the project as early as possible and hence enjoy its benefits as soon as possible. If for some reason the project is to be completed by a fixed due date, the start date should be delayed as long as is prudently feasible. The latter follows from considerations of the time value of money and from the desire to minimize overhead costs that are related to the time duration of the project. The shorter the time that money is invested in a project before that money begins to reap benefits, the less costly is the financing of the project.

Thus it generally makes little sense to stretch out jobs if the effect is to increase both direct job costs and project overhead and financing costs. (There may be other factors involved, however, such as a limitation on resources that requires some jobs to be stretched out—a problem to be examined in Chapter 7. Also it may be desirable in certain circumstances to stretch a project beyond its optimal duration in order to maintain more stable employment levels, especially for companies engaged in multiproject activities where projects do not always dovetail precisely with each other.)

Is it possible, however, for direct activity costs to be reduced, at least up to some point, by a reduction in pace? If so, then how do we determine the optimum cost schedule by CPM? According to most literature on CPM, this problem would not arise, because the normal job time is defined to be the most efficient time also. An extended cost–time trade-off curve would then appear as in Figure 5-11(a). But it is conceivable that normal time might be defined on some basis other than cost. The normal driving time between two cities might be 1 hour if a normal highway speed of 65 miles per hour is maintained, but a stretched-out travel time of 90 minutes would probably increase the mileage per gallon of gasoline and hence reduce costs. Thus if by normal we mean "what is ordinarily done, the usual or customary procedure," it is conceivable that the cost–time relationship might look as shown in Figure 5-11(b).

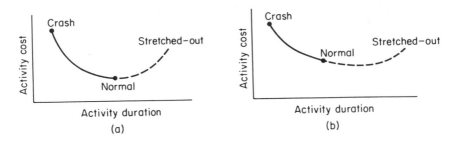

FIGURE 5-11. Two Activity Cost-Time Trade-off Curves

The CPM procedure described above may still be used, however, if we substitute the term "lowest-cost time" or "most-efficient time" for "normal time." This is really what the originators of CPM had in mind, but the meaning of terms differs from person to person, and it is advisable to clarify the point. Regardless of the terminology used, CPM ignores the portion of the cost–time curve (if it exists) to the right of the lowest point, a rule that can be logically defended in the absence of unusual circumstances such as those suggested above.

The Problem of Large Projects

The technique we have just illustrated may be described as an exhaustive search procedure because in the technique we looked at every possible alternative action at each step of the solution. For simple projects not much larger than the one above, the optimum schedule may easily be found by such a manual search technique or by ones similar to it. As projects become larger, however, and as the number of jobs and paths through the network increases, the procedure becomes more and more difficult to follow because of the rapidly expanding number of alternatives to be evaluated at each step. Consider, for example, the 24-job project illustrated in Figure 5-12.

FIGURE 5-12. Twenty-Four-Job Project

There are 20 paths through the network. Can you identify them all? If all activities were critical (as might result from shortening the schedule), every path would have to be made shorter in order to reduce the project length. Somewhere between two and six jobs, depending upon those chosen, would have to be crashed in order for all paths to be shortened, and there are several *hundred* alternative ways of doing this. Clearly, it would require a great input of time and patience just to enumerate these alternatives by hand, and that is just one step in the repetitive procedure necessary to move to an optimum solution. Obviously, a project with several hundred or thousand activities (the typical size for real-life problems) would present an impossible task for a mere human who follows such a method. For most practical-sized problems, then, hand solutions are not feasible. More mathematically sophisticated techniques must be used, combined with the computational power of modern electronic computers.

Solution by Computers

In his original article referred to on page 64, Kelley described a linear programming procedure for finding optimal solutions for networks of jobs with linear cost–time trade-off curves. Other researchers have generalized his methods to handle nonlinear cost–time curves, and more efficient solution procedures based on network flow theory have been devised.[6] The Appendix to this chapter describes some of the linear programming formulations developed for cost optimization of critical path networks.

For the manager with a computer who wishes to apply CPM, more than 60 critical path computer programs are in existence, according to one survey.[7] Several of these programs have cost optimization features outlined in this chapter. One reportedly can solve networks with over 2,000 jobs and 1,000 nodes.

So far we have assumed that resources required for completing a job—whether at normal or at crash pace—are always available. The network calculations of both CPM and PERT are based upon this assumption. In

[6]See E. B. Berman, "Resource Allocation in a PERT Network under Continuous Activity Time–Cost Functions," *Mgt. Science*, **10**, No. 4 (July 1964), 734–745; D. Fulkerson, "A Network Flow Computation for Project Cost Curves," *Mgt. Science*, **7**, No. 2 (Jan. 1961), 167–178; W. L. Meyer and L. R. Shaffer, *Extensions of the Critical Path Method Through the Application of Integer Programming*, Department of Civil Engineering, University of Illinois, July 1963. Kelley, it should be noted, described a network flow algorithm in his 1961 article (*op. cit.*), along with a nonlinear extension of the method.

[7]See J. J. Moder and C. R. Phillips, *Project Management with CPM and PERT*, 2nd ed. (New York: Reinhold Publishing Corp., 1970).

Chapter 7 we shall examine problems that occur with network analysis when resources are limited.

Appendix: *Linear Programming Formulations of Network Problems*

Event-oriented network calculations are directly translatable into a linear programming formulation of the critical path algorithm. Let variable x_i represent the early occurrence time of node i, $i = 1, \ldots, m$, where $m =$ the number of nodes in the network. The objective is to minimize the difference between x_1 and x_m, where 1 is the first node and m is the last node in the network. (It is assumed that there is only one initial and one final node.) The constraints assure that the time difference between any two connected nodes, x_i and x_j, is at least as great as the duration, t_{ij}, of the connecting activity. Thus the general formulation is:

minimize $\quad x_m - x_1$

subject to $\quad x_j - x_i \geq t_{ij}$, all activities ij

$\qquad\qquad x_i \quad$ unconstrained in sign, $i = 1, \ldots, m$.

The usual solution procedure (simplex algorithm) will lead to a solution in which $x_1 = 0$, unless some other value is specified initially. Actually, any other x_i, including x_m, may be arbitrarily assigned an initial value without affecting the value of the minimizing function, since the latter measures only the difference between x_m and x_1 and the two vary directly with each other.

In the simplex solution, each independent variable x_i represents either the early or late occurrence time of its respective node (for nodes on a critical path the two times coincide). If it is desirable for *all* node variables to assume *early* occurrence values, then the following function will assure it:

minimize $\quad x_m - x_1 + \sum_{i=2}^{m-1} x_i$

or, since x_1 is always $\leq x_m$,

minimize $\quad \sum_{i=1}^{m} x_i.$

Similarly, if late occurrence times are desired, the function

minimize $\quad mx_m - \sum_{i=1}^{m-1} x_i$

may be used. The m multiplier for x_m assures that the absolute value of the summation term in the function will never exceed the first term (since every $x_i \leq x_m$), which is necessary for a bounded solution. The effect is to push all x_i ($i < m$) to their upper bound without increasing x_m beyond its minimum value. It is assumed in all of the above, of course, that one x_i is constrained to a particular value, for example, $x_i = 0$.

As an illustration of a basic linear programming formulation of critical path calculations, consider the simple project illustrated in Figure 5-13. Since there are six activities, there will be six constraints, and the linear programming problem becomes:

minimize $\quad x_5 - x_1$
subject to $\quad x_2 - x_1 \geq 2$
$\quad\quad\quad\quad x_3 - x_1 \geq 1$
$\quad\quad\quad\quad x_3 - x_2 \geq 3$
$\quad\quad\quad\quad x_4 - x_2 \geq 2$
$\quad\quad\quad\quad x_5 - x_3 \geq 4$
$\quad\quad\quad\quad x_5 - x_4 \geq 3.$

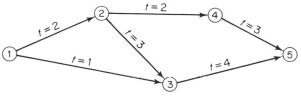

FIGURE 5-13.

We can solve by the simplex method, or if we assign $x_1 = 0$, the solution may easily by obtained by inspection. Each x_i is simply assigned the smallest value permitted by the constraints, with the following results:

$x_1 = 0$
$x_2 = 2$
$x_3 = 5$
$x_4 = 4$
$x_5 = 9.$

Actually, there are alternative solutions to the problem that will yield the same value of the function. Any node with slack may be increased by adding to it some portion of its slack, without changing the value of the function. Nodal slack values may be obtained from node early and late occurrence times; the latter are calculated by assigning each x_i the *largest* value permitted by the constraints (but still maintaining the same x_m), or they may be inferred from activity slack values.

Activity slack is obtained directly from the simplex solution of the linear programming formulation. For example, the problem above has a final simplex tableau as follows[8]:

Basis Variables	Structural Variables					Slack Variables						Right-hand Side
	x_1	x_2	x_3	x_4	x_5	S_{12}	S_{13}	S_{23}	S_{24}	S_{35}	S_{45}	
x_2	-1	1				-1						2
x_3	-1		1			-1		-1				5
S_{13}						-1	1	-1				4
x_4	-1			1		-1			-1			4
S_{45}								-1	1	-1	1	2
x_5	-1				1	-1		-1		-1		9
Indicator Row $z_j - c_j$	1	0	0	0	0	1	0	1	0	1	0	

Since each constraint is associated with an activity, slack variables necessary to convert inequality constraints to equalities are also activity-associated. S_{12}, for example, is the slack variable for the activity connecting nodes 1 and 2. Fortuitously, the terminology of linear programming, or L.P., and CPM coincide: The slack variable (L.P.) takes on a value equal to the slack time (CPM) of an activity. From the tableau above, for example, $S_{13} = 4$, meaning that activity (1, 3) has 4 units of slack. Similarly, activity (4, 5) has slack of 2 units. Notice that slack variable S_{24} does not appear in the basis, indicating that $S_{24} = 0$ and that activity (2, 4) has no slack. By conventional CPM methodology, both (2, 4) and (4, 5) would have 2 units of total slack. At first blush, then, the analogy between conventional CPM calculations and the L.P. model does not seem complete. Slack in the L.P. model is relative to fixed values of node occurrence times (fixed by the solution procedure), and thus slack in a sequence of activities is all assigned to one of them only, depending upon nodal time assignments. If all such times are *early* occurrence times, the slack will show up in the last activity of a sequence that leads into a path with less slack. In this case the slack is analogous to what we have called "free slack"—but in the formulation above, there is nothing to guarantee that all nodal times will be ET's. Notice in the indicator row of the final simplex tableau that there is a zero in the S_{24} column. Since S_{24} is nonbasic, this indicates that an alternative optimum solution exists. If S_{24} is brought into the solution, S_{45} goes out and the only other change is in x_4, which

---

[8] Artificial variables necessary to obtain an initial feasible solution have been omitted from the tableau. The tableau shown is not unique, as alternative solutions are available.

changes to 6. In effect, the alternative solution results in the assignment of node 4 at its late occurrence time, and a shift of slack from activity (4, 5) to activity (2, 4). If the alternative function described on page 74 were used, however, one could be assured that all nodes would be assigned at their ET's and the slack variables would represent activity free slack.

The dual of our original formulation has an interesting interpretation, also. The duality theorem of linear programming states that if a problem of the form (in matrix notation):

minimize $\underset{(1 \times n)\,(n \times 1)}{cx}$

subject to $\underset{(m \times n)\,(n \times 1)}{Ax} \geq \underset{(m \times 1)}{b}$

$\underset{(n \times 1)}{x} \geq \underset{(n \times 1)}{0}$

has a solution x^* which minimizes cx, then there is an analogous problem:

maximize $\underset{(1 \times m)\,(m \times 1)}{wb}$

subiect to $\underset{(1 \times m)\,(m \times n)}{wA} \leq \underset{(1 \times n)}{c}$

$\underset{(1 \times m)}{w} \geq \underset{(1 \times m)}{0}$

which also has an optimum solution w^*, such that $cx^* = w^*b$. One problem is called the *dual* of the other, and it is arbitrary which is designated the *primal* and which the dual.

Note that if a primal has n variables and m constraints, then the dual has m variables and n constraints—just the reverse. There is a dual variable corresponding to each of the primal constraints, and vice versa. It can be shown that if a primal constraint is stated as an equality (without slack variables), the corresponding dual variable is unconstrained in sign. The opposite proposition also holds.

In the *solution* to a problem, if an inequality constraint in the primal is satisfied as an equality, then the corresponding dual variable must be non-negative. But if the inequality constraint is satisfied as an inequality (that is, its slack variable is greater than zero), then the corresponding dual variable must be zero. Once again, the opposite, in an if–then sense, also holds; and for all propositions above, *primal* and *dual* may be interchanged.

The dual to our network problem follows directly from the duality theorem and the propositions above. Its general formulation is:

maximize $\underset{\text{all } ij}{\sum} t_{ij} w_{ij}$

subject to $-\sum w_{1j} = -1$ all $1j$

$\sum w_{ik} - \sum w_{kj} = 0$ all $k \neq 1, m$

$\sum w_{im} = 1$ all im

$w_{ij} \geq 0$ all ij.

As applied to the example network on page 75, the dual becomes:

maximize $\quad 2w_{12} + \quad w_{13} + 3w_{23} + 2w_{24} + 4w_{35} + 3w_{45}$

subject to

$$
\begin{aligned}
-w_{12} - w_{13} & = -1 \\
w_{12} \qquad\qquad -w_{23} - w_{24} & = 0 \\
w_{13} + w_{23} \qquad\qquad -w_{35} & = 0 \\
w_{24} \qquad\qquad -w_{45} & = 0 \\
w_{35} + w_{45} & = 1 \\
w_{12}, \quad w_{13}, \quad w_{23}, \quad w_{24}, \quad w_{35}, \quad w_{45} & \geq 0.
\end{aligned}
$$

So stated, the problem may be given a *network flow* interpretation. The project network becomes a flow network. A hypothetical unit of flow (water, electricity, and so on) enters the initial node, travels through the network, and leaves the terminal node. Each w_{ij} represents flow through branch ij. If we follow the convention that flow into a node is positive and flow out of it is negative, we can write a balancing equation for each node: *flow in = flow out*, or *flow in — flow out = 0*. The only known flows are those into the initial node and out of the final node, so we place these unit constants on the right of the equal sign and all unknowns on the left, as above. Thus there are as many equations as there are nodes. Each constraining equation above represents a flow balance on a particular node. For example, the second contraint says that flow into node 2 (w_{12}) minus the flow out of node 2 (w_{23} and w_{24}) equals zero.

The duration of an activity ij may be viewed as the cost (in time, money, or energy) of pumping a unit of flow from i to j in the network. Thus the problem of finding the critical or longest path in a project network is equivalent to finding the highest cost route through the flow network. The function will be maximized when all flow is along that path which carries the highest costs (longest times). Because of the way the problem is structured —particularly the unit flow imposed on the network—all w_{ij}'s will be integer-valued and either 0 or 1. Thus in the optimum solution the critical path is identified by activities having $w_{ij} = 1$. The function will then have a value equal to the length of the critical path. This will be the same as the optimal solution of the primal problem, which measures the difference between the initial and final node occurrence times. In the problem above w_{12}, w_{23}, and w_{35} are all 1; the remaining w_{ij}'s are all zero, and the function has a value of 9.

A more complete development of the L.P. formulation of critical path scheduling is given by Charnes and Cooper in an article in which they first proposed the model.[9] As they state, linear programming is less efficient

[9] A. Charnes and W. W. Cooper, "A Network Interpretation and a Directed Subdual Algorithm for Critical Path Scheduling," *J. Indust. Eng.*, **13**, No. 4 (July-Aug. 1962), 213–219. The above adaptation of their material follows an opposite convention in signs so that even occurrence times are positive. Also, we have reversed the order of presentation and hence the designation of dual and primal.

than the conventional CPM algorithm for obtaining a network schedule and critical path data, but it offers some advantages in that it provides access to the extensively developed L.P. literature. In particular, the features of duality and sensitivity analyses are available, with their useful managerial interpretations.

Cost Optimization—L.P. Models

The L.P. model above is time-oriented only; it does not consider the cost–time trade-off possibilities that were discussed earlier in this chapter. Further elaboration of the model is required to incorporate cost optimization in the solution procedure.

If we admit the possibility of expediting activities at some extra cost, then the activity time t_{ij} is no longer constant but becomes a variable in the L.P. model. The simplest cost–time relationship that we can assume is a linear one as illustrated in Figure 5-14.

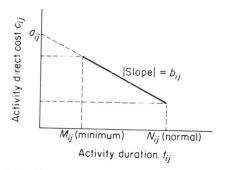

FIGURE 5-14. Linear Cost-Time Relationship: $c_{ij} = a_{ij} - b_{ij}t_{ij}$

If, for convenience, we designate the absolute value of the slope by b_{ij}, then the equation for the line may be expressed as

$$c_{ij} = a_{ij} - b_{ij}t_{ij},$$

where a_{ij} is the intercept of the projected line on the vertical axis, and t_{ij} is limited to values in the interval:

$$M_{ij} \leq t_{ij} \leq N_{ij}.$$

M_{ij} is the minimum duration achieved by crashing activity ij, and N_{ij} is its normal duration. Total costs for all activities would then be a function of the t_{ij}'s, as follows:

$$\text{total direct costs} = \sum_{\text{all } ij} (a_{ij} - b_{ij}t_{ij}).$$

Instead of minimizing project length, as before, the objective is to minimize project direct costs given a project length T. Since the a_{ij} are constant, direct costs can be minimized if we:

maximize $\quad \sum_{\text{all } ij} b_{ij}t_{ij}$

subject to $\quad \begin{aligned} x_j + t_{ij} - x_j &\leq 0 & \text{all } ij \\ t_{ij} &\leq N_{ij} & \text{all } ij \\ t_{ij} &\geq M_{ij} & \text{all } ij \\ x_m - x_1 &\leq T. \end{aligned}$

The first constraint, as in the earlier L.P. model, states that the difference in occurrence times of two connected nodes must be at least as great as the duration of the connecting activity. The next two constraints restrict each activity time t_{ij} to the interval between normal and crash times. Finally, the last constraint puts an upper limit on the project length. Note that T, an input parameter specifying this length, must be feasible. That is, it cannot be less than the length of the critical path with all activities at their minimum, or crash, times.

As a parameter, T may be varied to determine the effect of project length on direct activity costs. A plot of points thus obtained may be combined with indirect, or overhead, expenses corresponding to various project lengths to obtain the U-shaped total cost curve described earlier. Alternatively, x_m could be incorporated in the objective function with a coefficient C representing time-related costs in dollars per time unit. The function would then become:

maximize $\quad \sum_{\text{all } ij} b_{ij}t_{ij} - Cx_m,$

and the last constraint above would be omitted unless it was desired that the schedule length not exceed T. If the constraint is omitted, then one x_i must be fixed, for example, $x_1 = 0$.

Note that, while the simple L.P. model on page 74 contained m variables and n constraints (where m = number of nodes and n = number of activities), the cost-optimization L.P. model contains $(m + n)$ variables and $3n$ constraints. Even a 100-job project—small by most standards—would result in a large L.P. problem and require a considerable amount of computer time to solve. More efficient methods of solving the problem utilizing network flow theory are available.[10] Our purpose here, however, is to show as clearly as possible how CPM cost-optimization problems may be analyzed and formulated.

---

[10] See D. Fulkerson, "A Network Flow Computation for Project Cost Curves," *Mgt. Science*, **7**. No. 2 (Jan. 1961), 167–178, and J. Kelley, "Critical-Path Planning and Scheduling: Mathematical Basis," *Opns. Res.*, **9**, No. 3 (May-June 1961), 296–320.

Nonlinear Cost–Time Trade-off Curves

Suppose that the cost–time relationship for an activity is not linear but curved, as shown in Figure 5-15. The curve implies that successive decreases in activity duration are increasingly expensive as that duration is reduced. This is intuitively plausible: For many activities the first 10 per cent reduction comes relatively easily, but the second 10 per cent is more difficult and therefore more expensive to achieve. Further cuts are even more costly.

FIGURE 5-15. Continuous, Nonincreasing, Convex Cost-Time Curve

The curve that we have shown is continuous, convex, and nonincreasing. A relatively simple way to incorporate such a relationship in the L.P. model is to approximate the curve with linear sections. Any number of sections may be used, depending upon how close an approximation to the curve is desired, but for illustrative purposes, suppose we approximate the above curve with two linear sections, as in Figure 5-16.

In effect we have replaced the original activity with two surrogate activities in sequence, the first having normal and crash times of P and M, respectively, with a cost–time slope of b_1. The second has normal and crash times of $N - P$ and 0, respectively, and a slope of b_2. Since $b_2 < b_1$, the CPM algorithm will always select activity 2 for crashing before activity 1.

FIGURE 5-16. Piecewise Linear Approximation to Convex Cost-Time Curve

If both activites are scheduled at normal pace, their total time will be $P + (N - P) = N$ with a cost of c_1, the same as the original activity. If only activity 2 is crashed, the total duration will be $P + O = P$ with a cost of c_2. If both activities are crashed, the total time will be $M + O = M$ and the cost will be $(c_3 - c_2) + c_2 = c_3$, corresponding once again to the original activity.

The L.P. model will be essentially the same as before (page 80), except for the portions of it pertaining to activity ij:

maximize $\cdots b_1 t_{1ij} + b_2 t_{2ij} \cdots$

.
.
.

subject to

$$x_i + t_{1ij} + t_{2ij} - x_j \leq 0$$
$$M \leq t_{1ij} \leq P$$
$$0 \leq t_{2ij} \leq N - P$$

(Note that b_1, b_2, M, P, and N, while not so subscripted here, still pertain to a particular activity ij.)

If the piecewise-linear approximation to an activity's cost–time curve contains k segments, then the activity is replaced by k surrogate activities in sequence, and the solution procedure is entirely analogous to the above, as long as the cost–time curve is continuous, convex, and nonincreasing.

Nonconvex and Discontinuous Cost–Time Trade-off Curves

Integer programming must be resorted to if an activity's cost–time trade-off relationship is like any of those depicted in Figure 5-17. Curve (a) is continuous, nonincreasing, and—unlike the previous case analyzed—concave. The same method we used on the convex curve (Figure 5-16) could be applied to it, as illustrated in Figure 5-18; but since $b_1 < b_2$, the conventional solution procedure would pick surrogate activity 1 for crashing before surrogate activity 2. In physical terms this is not meaningful. At normal pace

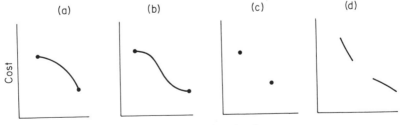

FIGURE 5-17. Other Possible Cost-Time Trade-off Relationships

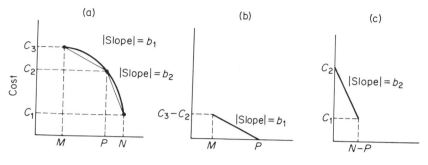

FIGURE 5-18. Piecewise Linear Approximation to Concave Cost-Time Curves

the activity 1 requires N time units. The initial expediting is accomplished at the approximate rate of b_2 dollars per time unit of reduction. Only after the time is reduced to P units can the lower rate of b_1 be realized. Activity 2's duration, t_{2ij}, must therefore be reduced to zero before any decrease in activity 1 is attempted.

One approach for assuring that line segments approximating a curve are brought into the solution in their proper order involves the use of an integer-valued variable, δ. To the constraints on page 82 are added the additional inequalities

$$\delta P \leq t_{1ij}$$
$$\delta(N - P) \geq t_{2ij}$$
$$\delta = \text{a nonnegative integer.}$$

Taken together, these constraints restrict δ to the values of 0 and 1, which can more readily be seen if we solve the first two constraints in terms of δ. Combined they result in

$$t_{2ij}/N - P \leq \delta \leq t_{1ij}/P.$$

If the activity is scheduled at its normal rate, then $t_{2ij} = N - P$ and $t_{1ij} = P$, and consequently $\delta = 1$. If the duration is reduced, then t_{2ij} approaches zero, but as long as $t_{2ij} > 0$, then δ must remain equal to 1 and t_{1ij} equal to P. Only when $t_{2ij} = 0$ can $\delta = 0$ and t_{1ij} take on any value less than P. Thus segment 2 is brought into the solution procedure before segment 1, in accordance with the physical realities of the problem.

The method may readily be extended to more than two segments and to relationships that are neither convex nor concave, as Figure 5-17(b). Suppose that an activity's cost–time curve may be approximated by r linear segments, as in Figure 5-19. In the general model, which has now become a *mixed-integer* programming model, *each* activity *ij* contributes the following terms:

maximize $\sum_{k=1}^{r} b_k t_k$

subject to $d_o + \sum_{k=1}^{r} t_k + x_i - x_j \le 0$

$$0 \le t_k \le d_k - d_{k-1} \qquad\qquad k = 1, \ldots, r$$

$$\frac{t_{k+1}}{d_{k+1} - d_k} \le \delta_k \le \frac{t_k}{d_k - d_{k-1}} \qquad k = 1, \ldots, r-1$$

$$\delta_k \ge 0 \text{ and integer} \qquad k = 1, \ldots, r-1$$

$$x_i, x_j \ge 0$$

.

.

.

The *ij* subscripts were omitted for simplicity of expression. In the complete formulation, all the above terms would be repeated for each activity, and the following variables and constants would contain the subscript *ij*: *b, d, t, r,* and *δ*.

FIGURE 5-19. Piecewise Linear Approximation to General Cost-Time Curve

Activities are frequently encountered which can be expedited only by changing the method of operation, resulting in a discontinuous cost–time trade-off curve. As a simple example, the activity "Mail package from Los Angeles to New York" may require 3 days and \$10 if sent first class by rail, or one day and \$16 if airmailed by jetliner. This would give rise to a relationship such as in Figure 5-17(c). Even more frequently, resources can be increased only in discrete amounts; the result is a discontinuous curve, perhaps with multiple discrete points. Grading a roadbed for highway construction, for example, might be done with one, two, three, or four bulldozers; each possibility results in a distinct point on the cost–time trade-off curve. Where resources are not smoothly divisible, the assumption of a continuous trade-off curve may yield erroneous results.

Suppose that a discontinuous curve for activity ij consists of r discrete points with activity durations $d_1, d_2, \ldots, d_r$ and corresponding costs $c_1, c_2, \ldots, c_r$. Define a variable α_k, $k = 1, \ldots, r$, such that $\alpha_k = 1$ when the duration is d_k, and zero otherwise. Then an integer program may be formulated as follows (we show only the terms involving ij):

minimize $\qquad \cdots + \displaystyle\sum_{k=1}^{r} \alpha_k c_k + \cdots$

subject to

$$x_i + \sum_{k=1}^{r} \alpha_k d_k - x_j \leq 0$$

$$\sum_{k=1}^{r} \alpha_k = 1$$

$$\alpha_k = \text{nonnegative integers}$$

This formulation for discrete cost–time relationships, combined with the formulation for continuous curves on page 84, may be applied to more complicated trade-off functions such as that illustrated in Figure 5-17(d). Meyer and Shaffer develop in detail the procedures required.[11] The difficulty of such formulations, as mentioned above, is in their solution. Even a small project leads to a sizable L.P. model, especially if discontinuities are involved and the model must be augmented to assure integer solutions of certain variables. Meyer and Shaffer stated that a project with no more than 50 activities could be solved using computers and programs available in 1963, the time of their study.[12] Although larger and faster computers are available today, the L.P. approach is still limited to relatively small networks. Much more efficient network flow techniques may be used, however, if the cost–time trade-off curves are continuous, convex, and nonincreasing. Networks with thousands of activities may be solved even on moderate-sized computers. The interested reader is referred to Fulkerson or Kelley[13] or to Moder and Phillips[14] for a concise exposition.

[11]See W. L. Meyer and L. R. Shaffer, *Extensions of the Critical Path Method Through the Application of Integer Programming*, Department of Civil Engineering, University of Illinois, July 1963.

[12]IBM 7090, using SHARE Library Code IP92 integer programming program. The main limitation was computer memory capacity.

[13]D. Fulkerson, "A Network Flow Computation for Project Cost Curves," *Mgt. Science*, **7**, No. 2 (Jan. 1961), 167–178; J. Kelley, "Critical-Path Planning and Scheduling: Mathematical Basis," *Opns. Res.*, **9**, No. 3 (May-June 1961), 296–320.

[14]J. J. Moder and C. R. Phillips, *Project Management with CPM and PERT*, 2nd ed. (New York: Reinhold Publishing Corp., 1970).

6

PERT/Cost: A Network
Cost Accounting System

In their original developments, both PERT and CPM were essentially time-oriented. As planning tools they enabled managers to estimate the *time* required to complete a proposed project. As scheduling techniques they provided a means of establishing *time* schedules for project activities. And as control devices they allowed managers to check scheduled *times* against actual *times* for activity durations or event occurrences. While it is true that CPM included a cost–time trade-off feature, costs were to be considered only as a means of finding activity times. No provision was described in early CPM literature for compiling activity costs which resulted from the optimizing process in order to obtain total project costs, either for predictive or control purposes. Thus the output of the original CPM model was a list of optimal activity *times* (durations), generally with associated early and late start schedules, rather than a list of activity costs or a project cost summary.

Users (and critics) of CPM and PERT early commented on the need for an extension of these network techniques into the area of cost control. They argued that managers are concerned with activity costs as well as with elapsed activity times. Cost control is usually as important as time or schedule control—and frequently even more so. The incorporation of cost features in PERT and CPM seemed like a logical and desirable extension of these models, but several years elapsed after their introduction before network cost control systems were developed and made generally available.

A few individual users devised procedures of their own during the early years of network analysis, but the major impetus to cost-control systems came with the publication in 1962 of a U.S. government manual, *DOD and*

NASA Guide, PERT Cost Systems Design. Within a year the Department of Defense and the National Aeronautics and Space Administration required the user of PERT/Cost procedures on many military research and development contracts. Firms that bid in competition for such contracts—especially those involving large projects—had to demonstrate their capability and intention of using PERT/Cost as a management control technique. Progress reports and auditing procedures were to be tied to such a system.

While the government's sponsorship and endorsement of PERT/Cost undoubtedly accelerated its use and acceptance, such endorsement also had some negative effects. Many firms doing business with the government resented the strong pressure to install a completely new cost accounting system. Not only was it costly and difficult to do so, but they felt it was an unnecessary duplication of their existing systems. Perhaps some of the initial resistance to the PERT/Cost system was due to the government's somewhat forceful method of introducing it. Not only did the coercion cause resentment, but also there was an implied criticism of existing cost accounting systems which firms had developed over a period of years. And (although few firms would admit it publicly) there was the possibility that the PERT/Cost system would supply more information to the government about the firm's costs than the firms would like to give. Whatever the reasons, it is interesting to note that PERT/Cost or CPM/Cost systems were voluntarily adopted by nondefense organizations with fewer complaints and a good deal more enthusiasm than was exhibited by those firms who were forced into adopting them.[1] Over the years, however, managers from both defense and nondefense industries who have used PERT/Cost accounting procedures have recognized the usefulness of information supplied to them by the system.

Basic Concepts of Network Cost Systems

The basic concept of the PERT and CPM cost systems[2] is simple but importantly different from that of most cost accounting systems. In essence it is this: Costs are to be measured and controlled primarily on a project basis rather than according to the functional organization of a firm. That is, individual activities or groups of activities form the micro cost centers for accounting (and therefore management control) purposes, rather than organizational

---

[1] As further verification of the old saw, "You can lead a horse to water, but you can't make him drink," several firms doing business with the government set up PERT/Cost systems *in addition* to their regular cost accounting systems, using the former only to supply required documents and reports to the government and the latter for their own accounting and control purposes.

[2] The term "PERT/Cost" has acquired a somewhat generic status as a description of network cost accounting systems. We will use the term hereafter for convenience and economy of expression.

units (divisions, departments, sections, and so forth). The rationale of the system is the entirely logical notion that responsibility for expenditures should coincide with responsibility for managing that which gives rise to the expenditures. Under a PERT or CPM management system, project managers and submanagers ordinarily are chosen for supervising individual activities or groups of activities. Since they are responsible for seeing that activities are completed on schedule, it is argued, they should also be responsible for controllable costs associated with the activities.

Cost overruns under a PERT/Cost system are more easily detected and corrective action more readily taken. For example, under a departmental cost system, if expenditures were higher than expected in the engineering department, this might be due to any of a number of projects or activities upon which the engineering department was currently working. But if costs were measured and reported on an activity basis, an overrun could be immediately pinpointed to the particular activity responsible, and corrective measures could be initiated. This, basically, is the argument for a project-oriented cost accounting system.

These concepts are easier to describe, however, than to implement. In the first place, not all companies engaged in project work organize on a project basis; some feel that a functional organization is still superior. Others have attempted to combine features of both. Hughes Aircraft Company, for example, developed a "staff overlay" system in which project managers were assigned authority over certain segments of the line organization totally committed to their projects. Even with a project-oriented organization there are questions of how to organize certain functions, such as the legal department, on a project basis—or whether to attempt it at all. Many interests and conflicting views will be present in any firm. Even if organizational problems are resolved in a satisfactory manner, there will still be problems of cost allocations which are not easily solved—such as how to allocate overhead costs to various activities. Some of these problems will be discussed later in this chapter.

We should mention here, however, that a project-oriented cost accounting system does not necessarily replace existing systems based on organizational structure. A firm will probably plan budgets and report expenditures both on a project and on an organizational basis. If costs are identified with the proper degree of detail, cost summaries can readily be generated on either basis. Project-oriented cost control, however, generally requires an increased amount of detail in cost accounting records. Depending on how well the system is designed, it can either assist the manager with better information or deluge him with far too much of it. At least it has the potential, if used properly, of providing him with the kinds of cost information that should enable him to do a better job of planning and control than is possible under conventional cost systems.

Cost Accounting by Work Packages

As noted above, the basic idea of the PERT/Cost system is to measure and control costs in terms of the same entities of the project as are used for planning and scheduling purposes—that is, the activities. Actually, if a project has been broken down into activities small enough to be used for purposes of detailed planning and scheduling, many such activities would be too small to be used conveniently for cost-control purposes. If so, several related activities may be grouped together into larger "work packages." These represent particular units of work for which responsibility can be clearly defined and which are still small enough to be manageable for planning and control purposes. The *DOD and NASA Guide* describes the organization of work packages in the following manner[3]:

> *End Item Subdivisions* The development of the work breakdown structure begins at the highest level of the program with the identification of project end items (hardware, services, equipment, or facilities). The major end items are then divided into their component parts (for example, systems, subsystems, components), and the component parts are further divided and subdivided into more detailed units.... The subdivision of the work breakdown structure continues to successively lower levels, reducing the dollar value and complexity of the units at each level, until it reaches the level where the end item subdivisions finally become manageable units for planning and control purposes. The end item subdivisions appearing at this last level in the work breakdown structure are then divided into major work packages (for example, engineering, manufacturing, testing). At this point, also, responsibility for the work packages will be assigned to corresponding operating units in the contractor's organization.
>
> The configuration and content of the work breakdown structure and the specific work packages to be identified will vary from project to project and will depend on several considerations: the size and complexity of the project, the structure of the organizations concerned, and the manager's judgment concerning the way he wishes to assign responsibility for the work. These considerations will also determine the number of end item subdivisions that will be created on the work breakdown structure before the major work packages are identified and responsibility is assigned to operating units in a contractor's organization.

[3]Pages 27 and 29.

Further Functional or Organizational Subdivisions An organization unit will usually identify smaller work packages within the major work packages assigned to it. This division of work may take the form of more detailed functional (for example, engineering) identification, such as systems engineering, electrical engineering, mechanical engineering, or it may take the form of a more detailed end item identification with engineering, such as instrumentation engineering, power cable engineering, missile section assembly engineering, and so forth. . . . The form chosen for more detailed identification will depend, again, on the structure of the performing organization and the manager's judgment as to the way he wishes to assign responsibility for the work. The *number* of these smaller subdivisions will naturally depend on the dollar value of the major work packages and the amount of detail needed by the manager to plan and control his work. Normally, the *lowest level* work packages will represent a value of no more than $100,000 in cost and no more than 3 months in elapsed time.

The work packages formed at the lowest level of breakdown, then, constitute the basic units in the PERT cost system by which actual costs are (1) collected and (2) compared with estimates for purposes of cost control.

The specific figures of $100,000 and 3 months' duration are intended as guides rather than strict limits. The nature of a particular work package may logically lead to exceeding these figures in some instances. It should be remembered, also, that the *DOD and NASA Guide* was written primarily for the aerospace industry. Other industries or organizations might find different and more suitable methods of breaking down a project network for activity accounting. A construction contractor, for example, might select work packages on the basis of subcontracted jobs or upon the basis of the skills involved. In some cases a work package may be identical to a single activity on the project network, or it may embrace several activities in a subnetwork. The principle stated in the last paragraph quoted above is a generally useful guide to the selection of work packages for activity accounting.

Forecast of Project Costs

For planning and budgeting purposes, it is useful for a manager to know what the time pattern of expenditures will be for a project. If costs are estimated for each activity or work package,[4] then a projection of costs can

---

[4] For convenience, we will continue to use the term "activity" for either activity or work package.

easily be made, based upon an early start or a late start schedule or any other feasible schedule, for that matter. To do this, the assumption is usually made that expenditures for an activity are incurred at a constant rate over the duration of the activity. If this assumption is not valid for certain activities, they should be divided into a sequence of two or more subactivities, each of which has a relatively constant expenditure rate. Then the cost per period of an activity may be approximated by dividing its total cost by its duration in periods. A project cost schedule is then prepared by adding all activity costs, period by period, according to the activity time schedule.

As a simple example, consider again the project network in Figure 4-5, with activity costs added as shown in Figure 6-1. From the data shown on the network, Table 6-1 may be compiled following the methods discussed in

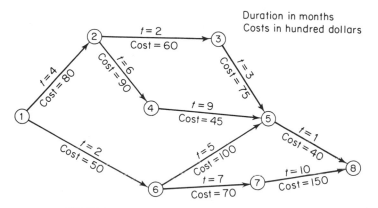

FIGURE 6-1. Project Network with Activity Costs

TABLE 6-1

Activity Costs for Project Network

Activity	Duration (months)	Early Start Time	Late Start Time	Total Cost ($100's)	Cost per Month ($100's)
(1, 2)	4	0	0	80	20
(2, 3)	2	4	14	60	30
(2, 4)	6	4	4	90	15
(3, 5)	3	6	16	75	25
(4, 5)	9	10	10	45	5
(1, 6)	2	0	1	50	25
(6, 5)	5	2	14	100	20
(6, 7)	7	2	3	70	10
(5, 8)	1	19	19	40	40
(7, 8)	10	9	10	150	15

FIGURE 6-2. Early and Late Start Schedule Graphs

Chapter 3. The only new data are the cost figures. A start time of 0 and a due date of 20 months are assumed.

Now a month-by-month summary of cost requirements is calculated for both early and late start schedules. In the first month, for example, activities (1, 2) and (1, 6) are active in the early start schedule, for a total cost of $20 + 25 = 45$ hundred dollars. In the fifth month, to illustrate further, activities (2, 3), (2, 4), (6, 5), and (6, 7) all occur, with joint costs of 75 hundred dollars.

A schedule graph, in which the network is plotted on a time scale and in which the horizontal length and placement of activity arrows indicate activity duration and schedule, facilitates cost calculation. Figure 6-2 shows schedule graphs of the project for both early and late activity start times. Monthly costs and cumulative costs are noted below each graph.

When plotted as in Figure 6-3, the cumulative cost figures illustrate more graphically the budget implications of the early and late start schedules. The area between the two curves represents a range of budgets which are feasible from a technological viewpoint. For budgetary or other reasons, it may be preferable to follow a relatively straight line of cumulative costs from start to finish. As long as this lies in the feasible region, it may be approxi-

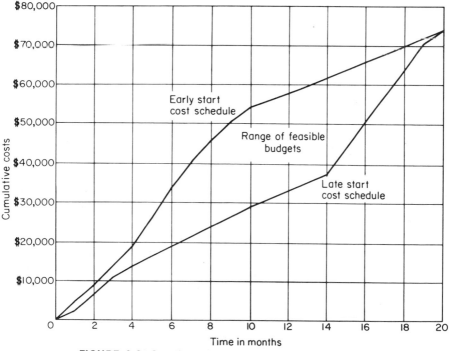

FIGURE 6-3. Cumulative Costs for Early and Late Starts

mately achieved by juggling the scheduled starts of activities between their early and late start times.

Budget restrictions frequently limit the amount of expenditure in any one period, or certain critical resources—men, materials, machinery, and so on—may be available only in limited amounts. If budgetary or other resource constraints are such that even the late-start cost schedule cannot be met, the finish date must be delayed and the activities must be scheduled according to methods such as those to be discussed in Chapter 7. Once a schedule has been found which is feasible in terms of both technology and resource availabilities, however, a cost schedule may be calculated and plotted as above. A computer may be used to advantage for large projects, of course.

Analysis and Control of Project Costs

Basic to most cost-control systems is a procedure for comparing actual costs with budgeted costs. The PERT/Cost system not only permits such a comparison but, because of its integration with project scheduling procedures, also provides a means of comparing work scheduled with work accomplished. The resulting cost and schedule information allows project managers at both top and intermediate organizational levels to detect problem areas and pinpoint their sources much more readily than would be possible with conventional cost accounting procedures. When followed by appropriate managerial action, such information can lead to effective control of project costs and performance.

The first step in control procedure is the measurement and recording of costs which are incurred as the project progresses. Costs should be coded according to network activities and also organizational function to permit summaries and reports to be made on either basis. If possible (and it usually is), the cost data should be collected in such a way as to be useful for payroll and other accounting purposes.

At the same time that costs are reported, an estimate should be made of the percentage of work accomplished. Thus an activity may have incurred, say, 60 per cent of its budgeted costs but be only 40 per cent completed. If the assumption of a linear relationship between costs and time is valid, such an activity would appear to be heading for an overrun in costs. If such an assumption is in error for certain activities, they should be broken into separate activities for which the assumption is more reasonable, as noted above, or else estimates should be made of the cost and time remaining for these partially completed nonlinear activities.

Ordinarily, it would be assumed that if 60 per cent of budgeted costs had been spent, the remaining expenses would amount to no more than 40 per cent of budgeted costs, and similarly for time spent and time remaining.

Of course, it is not unusual for revisions of original cost and time estimates to be made, as additional information and experience is gained during the course of the project, or as unanticipated problems are encountered. Such revisions can be incorporated in updated budgets and time schedules for purposes of managerial control.

Graphic Displays of Cost and Time Data

With the above cost and time data collected from period to period as the project progresses, some very useful graphic reports may be produced that help managers to answer such questions as:

> Is the project on schedule? When is the expected completion time?
> How far over budget are present costs?
> What are the sources of delay and cost overruns? Is a particular activity in trouble or is some department problem affecting several activities?

Answers to most of these questions may be drawn directly from the graphic display; others may require some investigation, the necessity and direction of which are suggested by the display.

For example, assume that the initial planning phase of a project has led to the total cost budget and time schedule illustrated by solid line A in Figure 6-4. This is essentially a plot of cumulative costs corresponding to a particular schedule of activity start times, as discussed above. Note that the project is scheduled to begin in January, 1970, and to end by the first of April, 1971, with a total cost of $6 million. Assume, further, that the project has been under way for some time and that the current date is marked by the vertical line labeled "Today."

Actual costs expended on the project are plotted as dashed line B, indicating that expenditures have exceeded the budgeted rate of line A. Of and by itself this fact is not particularly helpful. It may be that the project is proceeding ahead of schedule and that the higher costs are merely a reflection of this. On the other hand, if the project is just on schedule or—worse yet— behind schedule in terms of work accomplished, then a definite overrun of costs has occurred. We need to know, then, what work has been completed, in terms of dollars budgeted for this work. Dotted line C displays this information. It represents the value of work completed, measured on the basis of the original cost estimates.

The fact that curve C is below curve B indicates that there is an overrun in costs.[5] The amount of overrun at any point in time is represented

---

[5]Similarly, an underrun would result in curve C being above curve B.

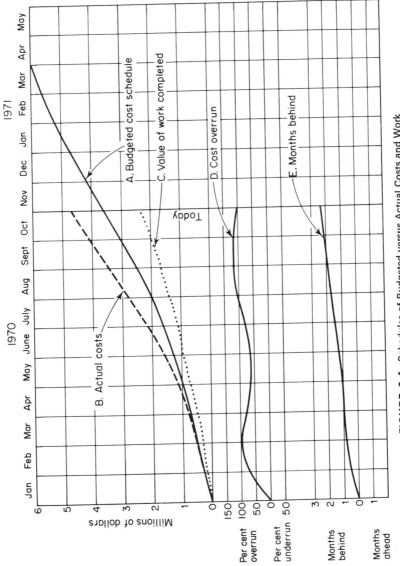

FIGURE 6-4. Schedules of Budgeted versus Actual Costs and Work

by the vertical distance between the two curves. Thus at the present time, actual costs ($4.7 million) exceed the value of work completed ($2.4 million) by $2.3 million, an overrun of some 95 percent. Curve D in the smaller graph in the lower left part of Figure 6-4 is a running calculation of the per cent overrun (or underrun, if it occurs), obtained by the formula

$$\% \text{ overrun (underrun)} = \frac{\text{(actual cost)} - \text{(value of work completed)}}{\text{value of work completed}}.$$

(A negative result indicates an underrun.)

In our particular example, curve C also falls beneath curve A, indicating that the project is behind schedule. The amount of this delay at a particular time point is the *horizontal* distance between curve C at that time point and curve A. For example, at the "present time" (November 1), work valued at $2.4 million has been completed. That same amount of work was originally scheduled to have been completed about the third week in August. Thus we are about $2\frac{1}{4}$ months behind schedule. Curve E at the bottom of Figure 6-4 is a running tally of the number of months behind. It indicates that the project progressively has fallen further and further behind schedule and that initial delays are not being erased by an accelerated pace on subsequent work but are being further compounded.

A manager facing a situation such as the one in our hypothetical example would obviously have serious problems to worry about. After only 10 months, the project is already more than 2 months behind schedule, and costs are almost double what they should be for the work accomplished. With the project due date rapidly approaching, the manager's immediate concern will probably be how soon the project can be completed and at what cost. Projection of the curves into future months should help to answer these questions for him. Figure 6-5 illustrates such projections. Curve F is an extension of curve B and shows the estimated costs necessary to complete the project. These estimates could be drawn directly from the budgeted costs for the activities not yet completed, or they may be modified according to additional information or experience received since the first estimates were made.

Curve G extends curve C to a new completion date and represents a cost budget based on a revised time schedule of activities yet to be performed. The schedule may be based on the original time estimates, or these, too, may be modified as necessary. As with curve A, costs are based on those originally budgeted, so a comparison may be continued between budgeted and anticipated actual costs. The vertical distance between F and G is a projection of cost overruns. Expressed as a per cent of budget cost, it appears as curve H, an extension of curve D. Similarly, the horizontal distance between curves G and A represents an estimate of how far the project will continue to be behind or ahead of schedule. This difference is plotted as curve I, Projected Months Behind, an extension of curve E.

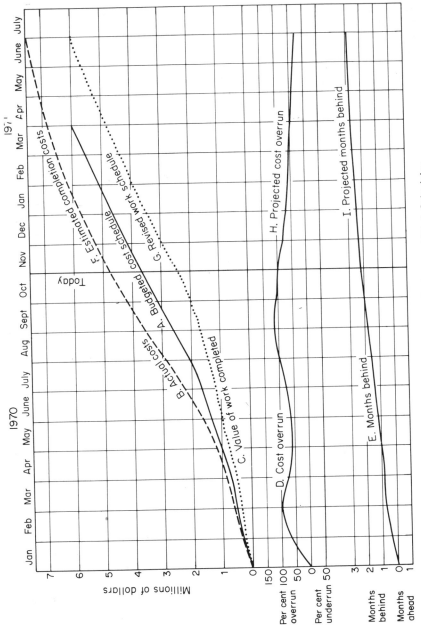

FIGURE 6-5. Projections of Cost Budgets and Work Schedules

The obvious problems in our case example would prompt the manager to examine more detailed reports to determine the source or sources of delay and overruns. Before doing so, however, it would be well for him to check the reasonableness of the summary report, particularly with regard to the curves projected into the future. For example, is it likely that the new estimated completion date will be met? The project is presently $2\frac{1}{4}$ months behind schedule, and the projected completion date is 3 months later than the original due date. Can the delay be reduced by expediting some activities? Is this necessary, or even desirable?

In addition, the manager should ask if project actual costs are reasonable. Curve F shows an estimated overrun at completion of $1.5 million but the current overrun is considerably more than that—2\frac{1}{4}$ million. While estimated additional costs to completion are shown as 2\frac{3}{4}$ million on curve F, the value of work yet remaining is 3\frac{1}{2}$ million (see curve G). Is it likely that the remaining activities can be completed for $$\frac{3}{4}$ million less than their original budgeted costs, as curve F implies—especially when costs to date are almost 100 per cent overrun? On the face of it, the estimated completion costs of curve F appear overly optimistic. Most managers would be quite skeptical of such estimates. A graphic summary such as that in Figure 6-5 would enable a manger to readily detect both wayward performance trends and questionable projections into the future, and to initiate whatever action he deems appropriate.

Cost Curve for Activities and Departments

Project summary curves can clearly signal the existence of cost or schedule problems, but not their source. Less highly aggregated data are needed to detect the specific areas contributing to delays or overruns. Similar cost curves based on major subdivisions of the project and, when appropriate, on departments within the organization can provide this information. Suppose, for example, that our project is the development of a new space vehicle, that the major end items of the project are structure, propulsion system, guidance and control, and payload, and that the responsible organizational departments are research, engineering, manufacturing, and testing. Suppose, further, that "Months Behind" and "Per Cent Overrun" charts for all of these end items and departments appear as in Figure 6-6.

On the basis of these curves, a manager would observe that guidance and control is the end item and engineering the department most responsible for project overrun and schedule delay. To pinpoint the problem, guidance and control should be broken into smaller subdivisions, down to the level of work packages if necessary. Then it will become apparent whether the problem is general, affecting several subsystems, or whether one or two activities

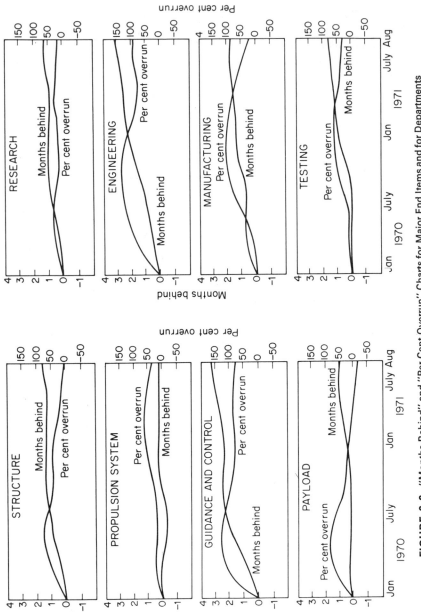

FIGURE 6-6. "Months Behind" and "Per Cent Overrun" Charts for Major End Items and for Departments

100

are the source of most of the problems. If the problem is general to the whole system or to much of it, the manager might suspect a common source of the problem, perhaps traceable to the department responsible. In this case, since engineering shows an overrun in budgeted costs, it should be subjected to further scrutiny. Cost curves similar to the above drawn up for subdivisions of engineering should reveal whether the problem is local or general within the department.

While the specific causes of overruns and delays may not be apparent from the cost curves, their sources may still be determined. The manager will know when to ask questions and of whom. As cost and schedule information is displayed in graphic form, it may be quickly understood and interpreted— much more easily than if it were simply tabulated. Then, without sifting through reams of data, the manager can readily spot problem areas that deserve closer scrutiny and probing.

Possible Accounting Problems with PERT/Cost

The managerial benefits from the PERT/Cost system derive largely from the increased detail with which costs are categorized and reported. As noted above, costs are not only identified by department but also by end item. Although this detail permits closer control of project performance and costs, it is also the cause of some accounting problems. Not the least of these is the additonal work naturally required to obtain the greater amount of detail—a major clerical task for large projects. More specific accounting problems include the following:

1. *Indirect Costs:* Some project costs are not easily identifiable with end items or specific work packages. Conventionally, such items are considered to be a form of overhead and allocated according to a variety of sometimes arbitrary rules. In some industries—particularly aerospace—cost reimbursable contracts have created incentives for firms to include as many support-type functions as possible on a direct cost basis that may be charged to the customer. Such overhead-type functions are often handled either by preparing for each such function a single work package which spans the duration of the project or a series of short duration packages. Effort would then have to be made to prepare budgets and record actual costs for these indirect cost items. Another approach is to allocate such costs as reasonably as possible to work packages, but the likely effect would be some lessening in the degree of control of these indirect costs.

2. *Overhead Control:* PERT/Cost literature suggests reporting overhead as a single line item. Since the overhead is a sizable expense in most firms, and since overruns may result from indirect as well as direct

costs, it seems desirable to provide some means of exerting better control over overhead. One approach is to divide it into separate categories such as indirect labor, indirect materials, and so on, which can be more closely scrutinized. With careful consideration, part of what is ordinarily grouped in overhead might logically be assigned to work packages. For example, supervisory and management overhead can be associated to a large degree with specific work packages. Remaining indirect charges may be handled as in 1 above.

3. *Material Costs:* Frequently, the material requirements for various subsystems within a project are compiled at the same time so that purchase orders may be placed for the total amount of each raw material. The intent is to secure the best possible prices through quantity discounts and to assure the availability of required materials. Provisions for estimated scrappage and other losses are included in the order. Because of the long lead time between engineering's release of material requirements and their eventual use in fabrication, actual costs of materials are often incurred long before work packages in which they are used are scheduled to begin. Since the object of PERT/Cost is to account for costs on the basis of work packages, special provisions must be set up not only to allocate material costs to work packages and to measure costs of excess usage but also to identify material variances soon enough to permit corrective action to be taken. It may be that one set of records is required to provide cash flow data, and another set for control purposes within the PERT/Cost accounting system.

These and other difficulties in the implementation of PERT/Cost have been identified by analysts.[6] One major problem, of course, is natural resistance to change: It is always difficult to make major revisions in well-established procedures, especially those as complex and far-reaching as are most cost accounting systems. Nevertheless, the logical appeal of PERT/Cost, with its emphasis on more careful relating of costs and end items and its ability to predict overruns and delays, has led many managers to apply it or to modify their existing system so as to obtain comparable results.[7] Considerable improvements in project cost control have been widely reported by many who have made such efforts.

---

[6]For a more extensive discussion of these problems, see Larry S. Hill, "Some Cost Accounting Problems in PERT/Cost," *J. Indust. Eng.*, **17**, No. 2 (Feb. 1966), and Eric Jenett, "Experience with and Evaluation of Critical Path Methods," *Chem. Eng.* (Feb. 10, 1969).

[7]For an interesting example of how PERT/Cost has been modified, see Arnold R. Saitow's "CSPC: Reporting Project Progress to the Top," *Harvard Business Review* (January-February, 1969).

7

Network Scheduling
with Limited Resources

Until now we have assumed that the only constraints in scheduling an activity—that is, in assigning to it start and finish dates—have been technological in nature. An activity can be started, we have implied, as soon as all of its technological predecessors have been completed. If all activities were scheduled as soon as technologically possible, we would have an early start schedule, either of the PERT or CPM variety. Similarly, by considering successor activities, we could create a late start schedule, and if this differs from the early start schedule, there are any number of other schedules that we could create by shifting slack jobs back and forth within the limits of their respective slacks. All these schedules may be generated from only two sets of data: (1) activity precedence relations, as exhibited by a network diagram, and (2) activity durations (either expected values based on PERT calculations or optimal durations resulting from CPM procedures).

Implicit in such scheduling procedures is the assumption that the resources required to perform activities are available in unlimited supply, or at least that sufficient resources are available for each activity to be scheduled sometime between its earliest and latest start dates. It is true that, in some instances, estimates for individual activity times are influenced by a consideration of available resources. But such estimates are usually made independently of other activity estimates, and the possible competing claims for the same resources are not explicitly considered. While the assumption of unlimited resources may be justified in some cases, most project managers are faced with the problem of relatively fixed manpower availabilities, a certain number of machines or other pieces of equipment, and—considering money as a resource—a limited budget. Jobs that occur on parallel paths through the network may compete for the same resources, and even though precedence constraints would not prevent their being scheduled simultaneously, a limited supply of resources might force them to be scheduled sequentially.

Consider the small project in Figure 7-1, for example, plotted as a schedule graph with a horizontal time scale. The horizontal length of each activity arrow represents its duration and the number above the arrow represents its manpower resource requirement (we will call it the crew size). Since all the crew sizes are different in this example, we can identify each job by its crew size without confusion. Jobs 4, 6, and 8—all without predecessors—can be scheduled to begin at time 0 by conventional CP calculations, while jobs 2, 3, and 7 can all start at time 2, the second day. Jobs 5 and 1 would follow on the next day. The result is an early start schedule.

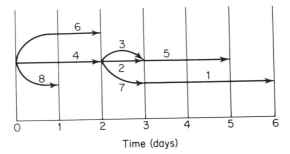

Time (days)

FIGURE 7-1. Schedule Graph, Unlimited Resources

Suppose, however, that there are only 10 men available on any one day. Obviously, jobs 4, 6, and 8 cannot all be active at the same time. This applies to jobs 2, 3, and 7 also. To begin the project, either we could schedule job 8 and postpone 6 and 4 until 8 was finished, or vice versa. With respect to jobs 2, 3, and 7, any two of them may be scheduled at the same time, but not all three. A little juggling around with the jobs can lead to the schedule in Figure 7-2, which is about as good as we can do. Resource requirements do not exceed 10 men on any of the scheduled days, but the completion time has increased from 6 to 7 days. Although there are other feasible schedules, which may be found from a different juggling of jobs, none of them are shorter than that in Figure 7-2. In this case, as frequently happens, the resource limits have resulted in a delayed completion date.

We may observe several things from this exercise. First, limited resources result in *practical* problems for the user of critical path scheduling. They impose a whole new set of constraints on the scheduler: Job start times are constrained not only by precedence relationships but also by resource

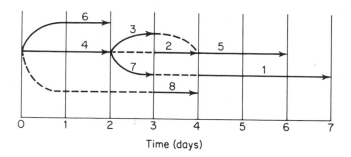

Time (days)

FIGURE 7-2. Schedule Graph, Resource Limit of 10 Men

availabilities. How does one decide which subset of jobs to schedule on a given day when the whole set of jobs that could start, as far as technological constraints are concerned, would require more than the available resources? This is the first problem that we shall look at in this chapter.

Second, limited resources lead to *conceptual* problems in critical path analysis. The usual notions of slack and criticality lose their normal meanings. Notice in Figure 7-2, for instance, that there is no longer a critical path as previously defined—that is, an unbroken sequence of critical jobs from start to finish. Later on in the chapter we shall discuss ways of extending critical path notions to limited resources situations. For now we turn to the practical problems of limited resource scheduling that face the project manager.

The Complexity of Project Scheduling with Limited Resources

Problems of resource scheduling vary in kind and in severity, depending upon the nature of the project and its organizational setting. In some cases there may be just one key resource—perhaps a large crane or a test facility—that is the bottleneck in scheduling a project. Activities must be scheduled so that no two of them requiring the same facility occur at the same time. Or perhaps there is a relatively small number of resources, whose limited availability must be jointly considered in scheduling. At the other extreme are projects requiring many resources, most of which are available in fixed, limited amounts. The problem of scheduling activities so that none of the resource availabilities are exceeded and none of the precedence relations are violated is an exceedingly difficult task for projects of even modest size. This is especially true if one tries, simultaneously, to minimize project duration or meet some other reasonable scheduling criteria.

Scheduling projects with limited resources is a type of problem that mathematicians refer to as a large combinatorial problem. That is, there are a very large number of combinations of activity start times—each combination representing a different schedule—too large to enumerate even with a big computer. One can apply integer programming to the problem. (In the Appendix to this chapter, we have formulated an I. P. model of the problem.) But even this powerful mathematical tool, aided by the largest and fastest computers, can solve only small projects—those well under 100 activities. Unfortunately, analytical techniques are computationally impractical for most real-life problems of this kind. We need to turn to other approaches.

Heuristic Programs

In recent years a good deal of work has been done in the development of heuristic programs for solving large combinatorial problems. By way of definition, a *heuristic* is a guide or method of reducing search in a problem-solving situation, an aid to the discovery of a solution. The phrase "rule of thumb" is often used synonymously with "heuristic."

We all use heuristics in solving the countless problems, large and small, that confront us each day. Drawing on our knowledge and experience, we devise simple rules of thumb that free us from the task of solving the same or similar problems over and over again. If the problem is how to drive to work in the least time, you might use the rule, "When the freeway is crowded, take the surface street to work." This simple heuristic avoids more complicated problem-solving procedures, such as measuring traffic flows, obtaining highway bulletins, gathering statistical data, and so on. We solve many problems of this kind in the same way. Lacking the time or inclination to pursue more thorough problem-solving procedures, we employ simple (if not infallible) rules of thumb.

Business managers, likewise, employ heuristics frequently in their operations. The classic management rule, "Handle only the exceptional problems and let subordinates decide routine matters," is an example in point. While heuristics may not lead to the best solution in each case, experience over a period of time has proved their general usefulness in finding good solutions to recurring problems with a minimum of effort.

In some cases a simple rule of thumb is insufficient. It must be elaborated or combined with other rules to take into account additional factors or exceptional circumstances. A collection of such rules for solving a particular problem is called a *heuristic program*. If sufficiently complex, such a program may require a computer for its solution. Most of the interesting developments in heuristic programming described in recent literature take the form of computer programs. A number of different heuristic programs for scheduling projects with limited resources have been developed in the past few years. Some of these have been outlined in published documents; others, for proprietary reasons, have not.

Heuristic programs for resource scheduling usually take one of two forms:

1. *Resource Leveling Programs* These attempt to reduce peak resource requirements and smooth out period-to-period assignments, within a constraint on project duration.
2. *Resource Allocation Programs* These allocate available resources to project activities in an attempt to find the shortest project schedule consistent with fixed resource limits.

We shall discuss these two approaches in greater detail and give examples of programs based on each of them.

Heuristic Methods for Resource Leveling of Project Schedules

In some project situations resources can be acquired or released in practically any desired amounts if one is willing to pay the expenses involved in changing resource levels, such as the costs of hiring, training, unemployment insurance, and so on. It is usually prudent, however, to maintain relatively stable employment levels and to utilize resources at a more constant rate. In such situations resource leveling programs are most appropriate.

For simple projects, or if just one or two key resources are involved, rather informal methods requiring no computer are often quite satisfactory. We suggested earlier that activity slack was a measure of flexibility in the assignment of activity start times. The scheduler may use activity slack as a means of smoothing peak resource requirements. He starts out by calculating an early start schedule for the project and then plotting a resource loading chart for the schedule. In Figure 7-3, for example, the project's early start schedule graph (a) gives rise to the resource loading chart shown in (b). (As before, the number above each arrow represents its resource requirement in the number of men, and since each activity has a different requirement, this number can be used to identify the activity as well.)

The peak requirement of 24 men occurs on the third day, when jobs 7, 8, and 9 are all active in the early start schedule. Both 8 and 9 have slack (2 and 7 days, respectively), so these jobs could be delayed up to the amount of their slack without delaying the project completion date. Job 7 is on the critical path, so it seems reasonable to examine the possibilities of moving the other jobs. Since job 9 has the most slack, we are inclined to investigate it first.

A look at Figure 7-3 suggests that job 9 could be easily postponed beyond the peak period of day 3 and in fact could be used to help fill up the

(a) Early start schedule graph

(b) Manpower loading chart

FIGURE 7-3.

(a) Schedule graph

(b) Manpower loading chart

FIGURE 7-4.

low point on the loading chart, days 8 through 11. Such a move would yield the graphs of Figure 7-4. Here the manpower loading chart has been smoothed considerably, but even further improvement is possible. Days 3 and 4 are peak days now, and of the two jobs active on those days, only job 8 has slack.

If we delay job 8 by the full amount of its slack, we obtain the results of Figure 7-5. The peak period now occurs on days 1 and 2, spanned by jobs 3, 4, and 6. Job 6 is critical, but both 3 and 4 have two days of slack.

The best results are obtained by delaying job 3, as shown in Figure 7-6. At this point, if not sooner, it becomes obvious that we have concocted an example that gives us very nice results: the ideal, completely flat manpower loading chart. For the duration of this project, we would have no need to incur costs for changing resource levels. Real-life projects, of course, could rarely be smoothed with such notable success, but the approach taken in this imaginary project could be used and has been, by many project schedulers.

(a) Schedule graph

(b) Manpower loading chart

FIGURE 7-5.

(a) Schedule graph

(b) Manpower loading chart

FIGURE 7-6.

For larger and more complex projects, hand-smoothing by juggling slack jobs can be very difficult and time consuming. Just drawing and redrawing the charts can be a tedious task as the number of jobs increases. If there were several resources to level, not only would there be more loading charts to keep track of but also the technological interrelations of jobs would make simultaneous smoothing of all resources a tricky proposition. One might find that delaying a slack job would reduce a peak requirement for resource A but result in new peak requirements for resources B and C, as a result of the the shifts in jobs that succeed the initial one. The ramifications of a single move in a project with many interconnecting activities are difficult to antici-pate and tedious to trace out by hand methods.

A computer can be used to good advantage at this point, however. Several heuristic-type computer programs have been written; their object is to smooth resource requirements by shifting slack jobs beyond periods of peak requirements.[1] Some of these essentially replicate what a human sched-

[1]See, for example, A. R. Burgess and J. B. Killebrew, "Variation in Activity Level on a Cyclical Arrow Diagram," *J. Indust. Eng.*, **13** (March-April 1962); L. De Witte, "Manpower Leveling of PERT Networks," *Data Processing for Science/Engineering*, **2**, No. 2 (1964), 29; R. C. Wilson, "Assembly Line Balancing and Resource Scheduling," University of Michigan Summer Conference, Production and Inventory Control, 1964.

uler would do if he had enough time; others make use of unusual devices or procedures designed especially for the computer. All of them, of course, depend for their success on the tremendous speed and capabilities of electronic computers.

Example of a resource leveling program

One example of such a program and the heuristics upon which it is based is the MS² (for multiship, multishop) workload smoothing program, desigend orginally to smooth manpower requirements in naval shipyards.[2] Each ship needing repairs represents a separate project, whose numerous jobs to be completed can be represented in network form. Since several ships may be worked on at one time and each requires men drawn from several shops or skill groups, the problem is essentially one of multiple project scheduling with limited resources (hence the name "multiship, multishop"). Obviously, such types of problems are not limited to shipyards; they frequently arise in industrial and other settings.

As is true in many project operations, manpower requirements for any one shop in a shipyard may vary greatly from day to day, depending on the arrival of jobs and how big they are. Since shop crew sizes generally must be sufficient to meet maximum manpower requirements, a schedule which reduces peak loads by increasing usage during slack periods would allow smaller shop sizes and hence reduce labor expense. The MS² program attempts to do this by scheduling all jobs at their earliest start times and then shifting some of them that occur during peak periods to later slack periods.

First, an early start schedule, along with total slack values for all jobs, is calculated by regular network procedures. A manpower loading chart is then generated, showing day-by-day manpower requirements in each of the shops for the early start schedule. The program then sets "trigger levels," or resource limits, one unit (man) below the peak requirements in each of the shops, and it attempts to reschedule the jobs so that peak requirements do not exceed the trigger levels. Jobs are then reloaded, or rescheduled, one at a time, until the trigger level is exceeded in some shop. All jobs active on the peak day in that shop are examined, and those which lack sufficient slack to be shifted beyond the peak period are discarded from consideration. Of those which remain, one is chosen at random and rescheduled to start at some point beyond the peak day.[3]

[2]F. K. Levy, G. L. Thompson, and J. D. Wiest, "Multi-ship, Multi-shop, Workload Smoothing Program," *Naval Res. Logistics Quart.* **9**, No. 1 (March 1962).

[3]There are two elements of randomness here—in the selection of a job from the eligibility list and in the determination of the number of days beyond the peak period that the job is shifted. The probability of an eligible job being chosen is inversely proportional to its manpower requirement, and there is a higher probability of a job being moved a minimum distance beyond the peak rather than a maximum distance, as limited by the job's total slack.

Such a move, of course, may affect the early start dates and total slack of jobs following the one moved. These are recalculated and the loading is continued until all jobs are loaded or until the trigger level is again exceeded and another job is shifted. If the trigger levels of each shop are met, then all of them are reduced one unit again, and the process of loading and shifting is repeated.

Should it be impossible for the peaks to be reduced below the trigger levels in one or more shops, then the previous feasible set of trigger levels is called back and the trigger levels are examined on a shop-by-shop basis, starting with the shop with the highest average hourly pay. The trigger level of that shop is lowered, one unit at a time, until no further reduction is possible. Then the next most expensive shop is examined and the trigger levels reduced to the lowest feasible point. This operation is repeated until no trigger levels can be reduced further and a final schedule is reached.

The trigger level can be looked upon as a ceiling pressing down on the manpower requirements. Peaks are reduced by pushing them to the right, as shown in Figure 7-7(a) and (b). The ideal schedule would result in a rectangle, as in (c), but because of fixed sequencing of jobs, variations in crew sizes on different jobs, and the interactions of trigger levels in various shops, the ideal is improbable. It is possible, as we noted earlier, that reducing a peak on one day by shifting a job to the right may result in a second—and perhaps worse—peak later, in the same shop or in a different one.

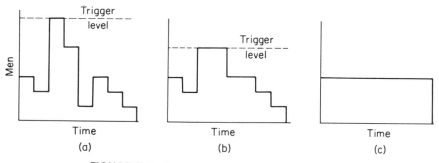

FIGURE 7-7. Smoothing Peak Resource Requirements

Because of the random elements in the program, schedules produced by repeated applications of the program will likely differ from each other. From a set of such schedules generated and evaluated by the computer, the best schedule can be readily chosen—that is, the schedule requiring the least resources.

It is of interest to note the differences between the heuristics of this type of computer program and those followed in the example represented by Figures 7-3 through 7-6. In the hand solution, we made use of the human's ability to take a comprehensive look at a manpower loading chart and to detect particular jobs and peak days that could be shifted to "fill up some hole" elsewhere in the schedule. It is quite difficult to program a computer, however, to do the same thing. What a human grasps at a glance, and the cognitive processes he goes through in picturing a shift in jobs, are not easily reduced to a step-by-step program of heuristic rules. Thus, in the computer scheduling model, we resort to more crude trial-and-error search and to random actions, hoping that the speed of the computer and its ability to rapidly generate many schedules will make up for its lack of human capabilities. Of course, as projects grow larger, the human's advantage dwindles with his ability to perceive the project schedule as a whole. The amount of information to process becomes too great, and the computer's relative value increases. What is humanly possible and desirable for small projects becomes impracticable for large ones.

Heuristic Methods for Resource Allocation in Project Scheduling

For many project managers the resource scheduling problem is not only one of smoothing requirements but also one of allocating resources that are available only in fixed or relatively fixed amounts. The manager may have a limited staff of skilled design engineers or other difficult-to-replace, skilled personnel, or there may be a fixed number of certain machines or pieces of equipment, or perhaps some construction material can be obtained only at a limited rate. Frequently, too, there are budget restrictions. Even if resources could readily be purchased in unlimited quantities, the funds to do so may be limited to certain monthly allowances. As a result, activities can be scheduled only as necessary resources become available, even if the effect is to delay the project completion date.

A modification of the MS^2 program just described conceivably could generate a schedule to satisfy fixed resource limits. You would have to remove the constraint of a fixed due date and push down on the trigger levels until peak requirements were all under the resource limits. If the limits are rather confining, it is likely that many jobs will be squeezed to the right on the schedule chart, delaying the project due date. You cannot have constraints both on resource limits and on the project due date.

Although such an extension of resource leveling techniques is possible, it is not very practical. If the resource limits are tight, there will be considerable scheduling and rescheduling of jobs. As the trigger levels are lowered, jobs on peak days will be squeezed to the right, causing all successor jobs to be rescheduled also. Rather than schedule all jobs at early start and then reschedule them repeatedly until resource restrictions are met, it seems more reasonable to generate a feasible schedule to begin with and minimize the subsequent adjustments. This can be done by scheduling jobs each day only up to the limit of resources and then postponing any remaining jobs until resources are sufficient for scheduling them.

Most resource allocation programs are of this type. Resources are allocated on a period-by-period basis to some subset of the available jobs—those whose predecessors have been completed. The essential heuristics of such programs are those that determine *which* jobs shall be scheduled and *which* shall be postponed in any period. The most obvious approach is to use job slack as a basis of priority, scheduling first the jobs that are most critical. In one form or another, this heuristic appears in most of the existing resource allocation programs, in combination with various other rules or modifying heuristics.

A simple heuristic program

As an illustration of the resource allocation approach to project scheduling, consider the simple program shown in flow-diagram form in Figure 7-8.[4] The program is based essentially on three rules (heuristics):

1. Allocate resources serially in time. That is, start on the first day and schedule all jobs possible, then do the same for the second day, and so on.
2. When several jobs compete for the same resources, give preference to the jobs with the least slack.
3. Reschedule noncritical jobs, if possible, to free resources for scheduling critical or nonslack jobs.

To illustrate how these heuristics operate in the program, let us apply them to a small project consisting of 10 jobs, each of which requires a certain amount of time and a given number of men (crew). For simplicity, let us assume that all the men are interchangeable. In practical situations, however, the various jobs may require men of different skills as well as other resources such as machines, materials, money, and so forth.

Figure 7-9 shows the schedule graph for this small project. All jobs have been started as early as their predecessors will allow. The number above each arrow identifies the job and its crew size. Job 4, for example, requires 4 men on each of days 2, 3, and 4. Thus we can calculate daily manpower requirements for the schedule by summarizing vertically the crew sizes of all jobs active on a given day. In the schedule graph in Figure 7-9, manpower requirements start at 7 on day 1, climb to 13 on days 2 and 3, and so on.

---

[4]The illustration in this section is adapted from J. D. Wiest's "Heuristic Programs for Decision Making," *Harvard Business Review* (Sept.-Oct. 1966). Used by permission of Harvard Business Review.

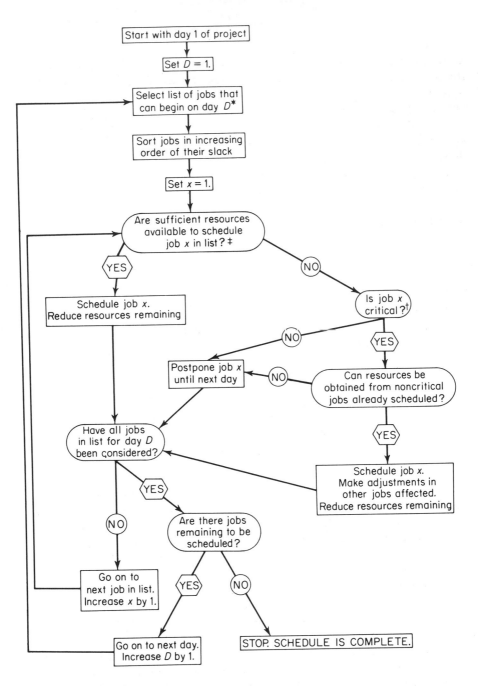

Start with day 1 of project

Set $D = 1$.

Select list of jobs that can begin on day D^*

Sort jobs in increasing order of their slack

Set $x = 1$.

Are sufficient resources available to schedule job x in list? ‡

YES

Schedule job x. Reduce resources remaining

NO

Is job x critical? †

NO

YES

Postpone job x until next day

NO

Can resources be obtained from noncritical jobs already scheduled?

YES

Schedule job x. Make adjustments in other jobs affected. Reduce resources remaining

Have all jobs in list for day D been considered?

YES

NO

Are there jobs remaining to be scheduled?

YES

NO

Go on to next job in list. Increase x by 1.

Go on to next day. Increase D by 1.

STOP. SCHEDULE IS COMPLETE.

*Day D is the day under consideration.
† A job is <u>critical</u> if it has no slack.
‡Job x is the job under consideration.

FIGURE 7-8.

114

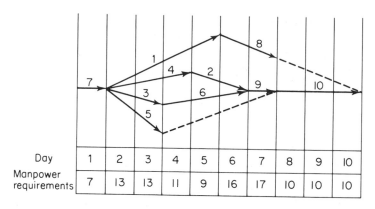

Day	1	2	3	4	5	6	7	8	9	10
Manpower requirements	7	13	13	11	9	16	17	10	10	10

FIGURE 7-9. Schedule Graph, Unlimited Resources

Suppose, however, that only 10 men are available for the project on any one day. How should the project be scheduled so as not to exceed this constraint but still to complete the project as soon as possible? One way to find the shortest feasible schedule would be to enumerate all possible schedules. For example, on day 1 there is just one possible choice of jobs (job 7). On day 2, with four jobs available, there are 13 feasible combinations: four consisting of a single job, six consisting of pairs of jobs, and three consisting of triples of jobs. (The remaining combinations exceed the manpower limit of 10.) Each of these 13 choices represents a different way to begin a schedule, and multiple choices fan out from each of these on succeeding days. The number of all possible schedules is very large, even for this small project.

Day-to-day decisions

The heuristic program diagrammed in Figure 7-8 does not examine all possible schedules; it selects just one combination of jobs for each day, only occasionally retracing its steps to see if a better set could be found. Scheduling day by day (as required by the first heuristic of the program), the program would make the following decisions:

Day 1

Only one job (7) is available to start in this period and there are sufficient men to schedule it.

> Schedule job 7 (slack = 0, calculated relative to jobs on the critical path, which are defined as having no slack); 3 men remain available.

Day 2

Four jobs (1, 3, 4, and 5) can be started on day 2, but there are not enough men to schedule them all. The second heuristic calls for scheduling the jobs with the least slack first.

Schedule job 3 (slack = 0); 7 men remain.
Schedule job 4 (slack = 0); 3 men remain.
Schedule job 1 (slack = 3); 2 men remain.

Job 5 must be delayed, as there are just 2 men unassigned.

Postpone job 5 (slack = 4).

Day 3

We assume that jobs cannot be interrupted once started; partially completed jobs have first call on the available resources.

Continue job 3 (slack = 0); 7 men remain.
Continue job 4 (slack = 0); 3 men remain.
Continue job 1 (slack = 3); 2 men remain.

Since there are still not enough men for job 5, it must be delayed again.

Postpone job 5 (slack = 3).

At this point the schedule graph appears as shown in Figure 7-10. Heavy lines indicate jobs already scheduled; light lines are projected schedules, which still must be checked for feasibility. Note that job 5, which has been postponed 2 days, now has only 2 days slack, or possible slippage, remaining.

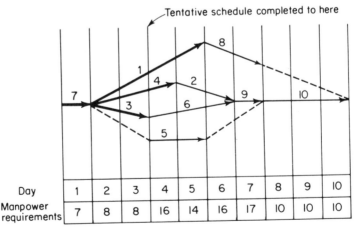

Day	1	2	3	4	5	6	7	8	9	10
Manpower requirements	7	8	8	16	14	16	17	10	10	10

FIGURE 7-10.

Day 4

Continue job 4 (slack = 0); 6 men remain.
Continue job 1 (slack = 3); 5 men remain.
Job 6 has no slack and hence is critical, but only 5 men are still unassigned.

The third heuristic is now brought into play: Are there noncritical jobs still active which could be postponed without delaying the project? Job 1 satisfies this requirement and hence is reassigned to begin later.

> Reschedule job 1; 6 men remain.
> Schedule job 6 (slack = 0); 0 men remain.
> Postpone job 5 (slack = 2).

The schedule graph at the end of day 4 is shown in Figure 7-11.

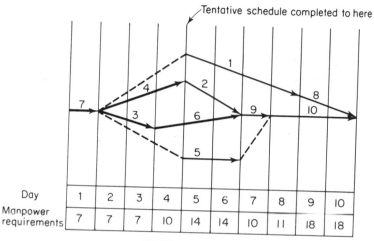

Day	1	2	3	4	5	6	7	8	9	10
Manpower requirements	7	7	7	10	14	14	10	11	18	18

FIGURE 7-11.

Day 5

> Continue job 6 (slack = 0); 4 men remain.
> Schedule job 2 (slack = 0); 2 men remain.
> Schedule job 1 (slack = 0); 1 man remains.
> Postpone job 5 (slack = 1).

Day 6

> Continue job 6 (slack = 0); 4 men remain.
> Continue job 2 (slack = 0); 2 men remain.
> Continue job 1 (slack = 0); 1 men remains.
> Postpone job 5 (slack = 0).

Job 5 is now critical, but there are no active jobs that can be postponed without delaying the project. Note that the projected finish date is delayed a day by job 5's postponement, as shown in Figure 7-12.

Day	1	2	3	4	5	6	7	8	9	10	11	
Manpower requirements	7	7	7	10	9	9	15	6	18	18	10	

FIGURE 7-12.

Day 7

Continue job 1 (slack = 1); 9 men remain.
Schedule job 5 (slack = 0); 4 men remain.
Postpone job 9 (slack = 1).

Day 8

Continue job 5 (slack = 0); 5 men remain.
Postpone job 9 (slack = 0); no noncritical jobs can be rescheduled.
Postpone job 8 (slack = 2).

At the end of day 8, the schedule graph appears as in Figure 7-13.

Remaining period

Program decisions for the remaining 6 days are as follows:

Day 9—Schedule job 9 (slack = 0); 1 man remains. Postpone job 8 (slack = 2).
Day 10—Schedule job 10 (slack = 0); no men remain. Postpone job 8 (slack = 1).
Day 11—Continue job 10 (slack = 0); no men remain. Postpone job 8 (slack = 0).
Day 12—Continue job 10 (slack = 1); no men remain. Postpone job 8 (slack = 0).

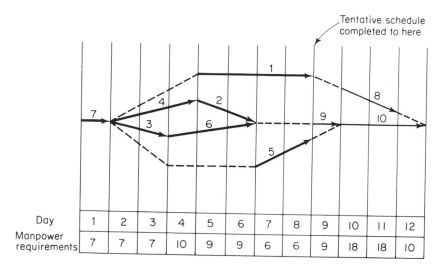

FIGURE 7-13.

Day 13—Schedule job 8 (slack = 0); 2 men remain.
Day 14—Continue job 8 (slack = 0); 2 men remain.

All jobs are now scheduled. The final schedule graph appears in Figure 7-14.

Thus the manpower limit of 10 men per day has resulted in a 4-day increase in the project length, compared with the unlimited resources schedule. In this application the heuristic program has found an optimal schedule. There are other feasible schedules, but none is shorter than 14 days.

FIGURE 7-14. Final Schedule-Limited Resources

It would not be difficult to think up sample projects for which the above program would *not* produce optimum results. Of course, no heuristic program can *guarantee* an optimum schedule, but the above program could be considerably improved by the addition of appropriate heuristics which take into account more information or special circumstances. For instance, it may be possible in some projects to crash or stretch out certain jobs by varying the rate of resource application. Also, some jobs might allow *splitting* —that is, an interruption in their schedule—while others may have to move to completion once started. Resource limits themselves may vary from period to period. An operational scheduling program should take cognizance of these and other factors in order to be generally useful for project scheduling. Project scheduling situations often differ so markedly, however, that special programs must be written or more general programs modified to meet particular needs. Heuristic programming, as a general technique, facilitates such custom tailoring of scheduling procedures.

The SPAR-1 Resource Allocation Model

A number of different resource allocation programs for scheduling large projects have been described in published accounts.[5] One of these, called SPAR-1,[6] illustrates how the basic model that has been discussed can be elaborated with additional heuristics. A brief description of its structure is given here for readers who are interested in such programs and who might be stimulated to try their own hands at heuristic programming. The basic logic of a heuristic scheduling program can be worked out by someone who knows little or nothing about computer programming per se.

In a manner similar to that of the simple model described earlier, SPAR-1 allocates available resources, period by period, to project jobs listed according to their early start times. Jobs are scheduled, starting with the first period, by selecting from the list of those currently available and sorted in order of their total slack (which is based on technological constraints only and normal resource assignments). The most critical jobs have the highest probability of being scheduled first, and as many of these jobs are scheduled as available resources permit. If an available job fails to be scheduled in that period, an attempt is made to schedule it in the next period. Eventually, all

---

[5]For an excellent review of the development of such programs and an extensive bibliography of relevant literature that has been published, see Edward W. Davis, "Project Scheduling Under Resource Constraints—Historical Review and Categorization of Procedures," *AIIE Trans.* (Dec. 1973). Selected articles are cited in the Bibliography at the end of the present volume.

[6]SPAR is an acronym for Scheduling Program for Allocating Resources; see J. D. Wiest, "A Heuristic Model for Scheduling Large Projects with Limited Resources," *Mgt. Science*, **13**, No. 6 (Feb. 1967), B359–B377.

jobs so postponed become critical and move to the top of the priority list of available jobs.

This basic program is modified by a number of additional scheduling heuristics or subroutines generally designed to increase the use of available resources and/or to decrease the length of the schedule. For simplicity in our description of these heuristics, we will refer to "resources" as "men," to the "amount of resources applied to a job" as the "crew size," to a "group of homogeneous resources" as a "shop," and to the "scheduling period" as a "day." Any other units, of course, could be used in place of these.

Crew Size: With each job is associated a normal crew size, or the number of men or other resources normally assigned to the job; a maximum crew size, or the maximum number of men required for crashing the job; and a minimum crew size, or the smallest number of men that can be assigned to the job. Normally, these three crew sizes will differ from each other. But in some cases two or all three of them may be equal, when jobs cannot be stretched out or crashed. The rules for crew size selection are as follows. If a job to be scheduled is critical (the degree of criticality is specified by an input parameter), it is placed on a priority list and given special treatment. If sufficient men are available, the job is scheduled at its maximum crew size; that is, it is crashed. If insufficient men are available to crash the job or even to schedule it at normal crew size, an attempt is made to obtain the required men by means of the borrow and reschedule routines which we describe below. If all efforts fail, however, and the job cannot be scheduled even at minimum crew size, then its early start date is delayed one period and an attempt is made to schedule the job on the following day. Jobs with sufficient positive slack (that is, noncritical jobs) are scheduled at normal crew size if the required number of men are available; but if resources available are insufficient for scheduling even the minimum crew size, the jobs are delayed for consideration until the next day.

Augment Critical Jobs: Repeated attempts are made to speed up critical jobs—including those which become critical after being scheduled—which have crew sizes less than their maximum crew size. Before any new jobs are scheduled on a given day, jobs previously scheduled and still active are examined. If any of these is critical and has a crew size less than its maximum, and if resources are available, the job's crew size is increased as much as possible up to the maximum.

Multi-resource Jobs: Sometimes a job requires a number of different resources, such as men of different skills, machines, money, and so on, each of which may be limited in quantity. For such multi-resource jobs, separate jobs are created for each resource and the jobs are constrained to start on the same day with the same level of resource assignment—that is, normal, minimum, or maximum crew size.

Borrow from Active Jobs: If resources available are insufficient for scheduling some critical job *j*, the model enters into a procedure for searching currently active jobs to see if sufficient men might be borrowed from them for scheduling job *j* on that day. Men are borrowed from a job only when the resultant stretching of the job will not delay the entire project.

Reschedule Active Jobs: Sometimes a critical job *j* could be scheduled if other jobs previously scheduled that use the same resources had been postponed. The model scans the list of currently active jobs and picks out those which could be postponed without delaying the project due date. If sufficient men could be obtained in this way and/or from the borrow routine described earlier, then job *j* is scheduled and the necessary adjustments are made in previous assignments. (This is similar to the third heuristic of our simple model, p. 113.)

The reschedule routine has much the same effect as a "look-ahead" feature. Instead of attempting to look ahead to the future needs of critical jobs (which would be difficult to do in the limited resource case, since jobs are not always scheduled at their early start), SPAR-1 schedules all jobs possible as it moves along from day to day. It repents, so to speak, of previous scheduling errors if jobs are encountered that have more critical need of resources than the jobs to which the resources were assigned at earlier dates.

Add on Unused Resources: After as many jobs as possible are scheduled on a given day, there still may be unused resources in some of the shops for that day. The model compiles a list of active jobs to which these resources might be assigned (that is, jobs which require these resources and which have assigned crew sizes less than the maximum crew size possible). It arranges these jobs in ascending order of their total slack. Proceeding down the list, the model increases the crew size of these jobs until the unused resources or the list of jobs is exhausted. The increment, however, is temporary; jobs supplemented in this way return to their assigned crew size the next day, unless unused resources are also available then.

After going through the above scheduling routines each day, SPAR-1 records the results in a manpower loading table which notes the number of men assigned on each job and in each shop, and it updates the critical path data—that is, the early and late start times, early and late finish times, and total slack. Note that several of the above routines may alter a job's criticality; for example, when the maximum crew size is assigned to a critical job, the shortening of the job may result in its gaining positive slack and perhaps some other job or jobs becoming critical.

SPAR-1 is able to accommodate single or multiple projects, variable crew sizes, jobs that can be split, variable shop limits, shift or nonshift scheduling, and various criteria functions for evaluating a schedule. Probabilistic elements in the program can lead to different schedules with successive applications of the program (in a manner similar to MS²). The best of several schedules can then be selected. Currently written in FORTRAN IV for a 32K machine, SPAR-1 is dimensioned to handle a project with up to 1,200 jobs, 1,000 nodes, and 25 shops. Another version of the model written for a larger computer allows projects up to 6,000 jobs to be scheduled.

Various adaptions of the model have been made for application to particular scheduling problems. For example, in one situation, some jobs could be processed only on machine A, others on machine B, and still others on either of the machines. For the latter group of jobs, the model selects the machine that has idle time, if any, and adjusts the job durations according to the machine chosen (A and B differ in their efficiency). Other changes are possible also. The reader can probably think of scheduling problems, perhaps drawn from his own experience, that would require modifications in the model or perhaps the writing of an entirely new program.

A number of different and interesting approaches have been taken by several authors of heuristic scheduling programs. RAMPS, for example, has a rather elaborate set of heuristics for choosing jobs to be scheduled on a given day. Not only is job slack considered but also such factors as work continuity, cost of idle resources, number of successors to an eligible job, and several others, all of which are given weights to reflect their relative importance. All feasible schedules for each scheduling period are examined, and the one is chosen that rates highest by the weighted criteria factors listed above.

We note again that no heuristic program can promise to yield an optimal project schedule—optimal by such criteria as resource usage, minimum project length, and so on. In fact, it would be impossible in most cases to determine if a given schedule *is* optimal. Analytic procedures, on the other hand, can guarantee such results. Various approaches have been formulated—including linear programming, integer programming, electrical network theory, branch-and-bound techniques, dynamic programming, and others—but none of them are feasible, as yet, for anything but very small projects. For the present and foreseeable future, heuristic programs offer the most promise for dealing with the problem of scheduling large projects with limited resources.

Conceptual Problems of Critical Path Analysis When Resources Are Limited

As mentioned earlier, ordinary critical path scheduling techniques do not take explicit account of job resource requirements or of possible limitations on resource availabilities. Implicitly, they assume that the only constraints on the start time of a job are technological; that is, a job can be started as soon as its predecessors have been completed. With every job started as early as possible, a schedule of early start times is created. Similarly, late start times for jobs are established if every job is delayed as much as possible, given the constraints of its successors and some final project due date. We defined total slack as the difference between a job's early and late start times. It represents a degree of flexibility allowed the scheduler: A job may be delayed for whatever reason, up to the amount of its total slack without delaying the finish date of the project. To illustrate, Figure 7-15 shows a

FIGURE 7-15. Schedule Graphs-Unlimited Resources

simple network project in schedule graph form. Once again the identifying number over each arrow represents its resource requirement, say the number of men needed each day for the job. The top diagram is an early start schedule. All jobs are started as early as their precedence relationships permit. The bottom diagram is a late start schedule, with day 5 taken as the due date. No job could start later in this diagram without violating the ordering constraints or delaying the project. In this first example we have assumed unlimited resources, and a job's slack is measured simply as the difference in start times for the job in the two schedules. Thus job 6 at the top of the diagram has 3 days of slack, jobs 5 and 1 in the middle have 1 day of slack, and job 8 at the bottom has 4 days of slack. All others are slackless.

Slack in a Limited Resource Schedule

Suppose, however, that resources are limited to 10 men per day. Now, the jobs requiring 6, 4, and 8 men cannot all begin at the same time. Several schedules are possible, but the one shown at the top of Figure 7-16 is optimal. There is no feasible schedule which is shorter. Note that job 8 is delayed to the fourth day and that the project duration has been increased to 6 days. Since no job could be started earlier, given the precedence relationships *and* resource constraints, this represents an early start schedule in the case of limited resources. Unlike the unlimited resource case, which had a unique early start schedule, this limited resource schedule is only one of several possible early start schedules.

The schedule at the bottom of Figure 7-16, similarly, is a late start schedule (again, one of several possible schedules), based on a due date of 6. Slack, as in the unlimited resource example, can be measured as the difference between a job's early and late start times. Thus job 2 has 1 day of slack, job 1 has 2 days of slack, and all other jobs are critical, that is, slackless.

Several observations are worth noting:

1. The slack concept, although modified, may still be used and retains its utility as a measure of flexibility in a project schedule.

2. Slack is dependent upon both precedence orderings *and* resource availability.

3. In general, resource limitations reduce the amount of slack in a schedule.

4. Since, in general, the early and late start schedules are not unique, the set of slack values for a project is not unique. Slack is *conditional upon the scheduling rules* for creating early start and late start schedules.

5. While a critical path of technologically connected jobs does not always exist in a limited resources schedule, under certain conditions a "critical sequence" of slackless jobs which span the length of the project can be

Early start schedule

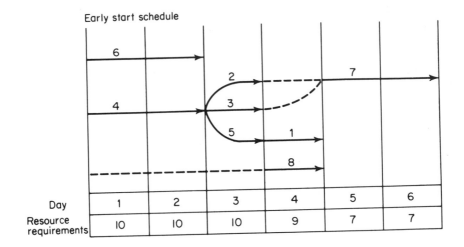

Day	1	2	3	4	5	6
Resource requirements	10	10	10	9	7	7

Late start schedule

Day	1	2	3	4	5	6
Resource requirements	10	10	8	10	7	8

FIGURE 7-16. Schedule Graphs-Limited Resources (10/day)

identified.[7] The jobs are continuous in time, if not in predecessor-successor relationship. One such critical sequence may be seen in the early start schedule of Figure 7-16, consisting of jobs 4, 5, 8, and 7. (Jobs 6 and 3 are slackless jobs parallel to 4 and 5, respectively, and could be named in alternative critical sequences.)

[7]The conditions are described in detail in J. D. Wiest, "Some Properties of Schedules for Large Projects with Limited Resources," *Opns. Res.*, **12**, No. 3 (May-June 1964).

The Late Start Schedule

Heuristic programs such as SPAR-1 generate, in effect, an early start, limited resource schedule. With slight modifications and using the same heuristics, they could also generate late start, limited resource schedules. Or, without modifications, such programs can effect the same results if the network is reversed in its orientation—that is, all jobs have their predecessors and successors reversed[8]—and if scheduling starts with the final day and proceeds backward through time to the first day. Applied in this double fashion, a heuristic program could permit the calculation of limited resource slack, a more reliable measure of schedule flexibility than results from conventional slack calculation.

Value of the Late Start Schedule

The late start schedule has interest beyond its function of permitting the calculation of slack values, however. In many projects the investment of labor and materials in the various activities is quite sizable. If time-adjusted value-of-money concepts are taken into account (as they should be for extended projects), the late start schedule has a marked advantage. The later one can postpone investments in project jobs, the lower will be the present value of such investments (and, by summation, the present value of the whole project). A late start schedule would thus result in the lowest present value, and an early start schedule the highest present value, of job-related project costs.

Given this observation, one might ask if all projects should be scheduled according to late start job times. The answer depends upon the degree of uncertainty of job times. If one were virtually certain of the correctness of job time estimates and if there were little chance of unexpected delays, then the late start schedule would usually be the preferable one. Many kinds of projects come close to these requirements, especially when the project has been done before or is similar to an earlier effort. Examples include the construction of tract homes, the manufacture of large hydroelectric generators or diesel locomotives, and the overhauling of jet aircraft engines. In these and similar projects, there may be elements of uncertainty, but reasonably good time estimates can be made for the majority of activities. The time estimates themselves often contain a safety factor to allow for uncertainties. Investments in such projects may be effectively reduced by scheduling activities at or near their late start times.

[8]A simple transformation of schedule dates is involved. If the schedule is n days long, then day 1 becomes day n, day 2 becomes day $(n-1)$, and, in general, day i becomes day $n + 1 - i$.

Projects with Uncertain Activity Estimates

On the other hand, research and development types of projects are characterized by a high degree of uncertainty, not only in the time estimates for activities but also in the activities themselves. It would be risky to schedule such activities at their late start times, as any underestimates of activity times or unforeseen difficulties would directly lead to a delay in the project completion time. Scheduling such activities at their early start times allows the project manager some time cushion, at least for those activities with slack, to absorb delays in activity completion times or to add additional activities whose need was not anticipated at the time of initial scheduling.

Probably most projects have activities, or jobs, of both kinds—those for which time estimates can be accurately made and those which are highly uncertain. Development projects have more of the latter kind, while some construction and manufacturing projects consist mainly of the former kind. This suggests a possible modification of the scheduling heuristics, or at least an option to be used when desired. In place of, or in addition to, job slack as criteria for a priority ordering of jobs to be scheduled, jobs could be characterized by the degree of certainty associated with their time estimate. Those with the greatest uncertainty would receive highest priority for early scheduling; those with more certain time estimates would tend to be scheduled later, or possibly to be postponed up to their late start times.

Planning Versus Scheduling

Several limited resource project scheduling models are presently operational and have demonstrated their worth to managers in a variety of applications. Not only are they useful in generating day-to-day schedules for guiding a firm's project operations, but they have also proved to be valuable planning tools. Long-range schedules, based on expected project requirements and present or planned manpower and equipment capabilities, may be projected into the future. Bottlenecks in certain resources are likely to be uncovered and plans drawn up for relieving such shortages. Various resource patterns may be tried and the resulting schedules compared. Scheduling models may thus be used to simulate long-range operations under various assumed conditions. Such a capability would be especially useful for a company with long lead times on resource procurement.

Conclusion

Before we close this chapter, it would be well if we summarize and compare the various ways that resources have been incorporated in project network planning and scheduling techniques. We will conclude with a few comments on their operational requirements and some implications for managers. First we list and describe the general approaches, in increasing order of complexity:

Approaches	Capability
Ordinary PERT and CPM	No explicit consideration of resources is made.
Resource scheduling program	For each resource, the program calculates a total resource requirements profile by summing, period by period, requirements for that resource of all activities as they occur in an early start (or any other) schedule. No resource leveling is involved.
Resource leveling program	Using the resource requirements profile of the early start schedule, the program attempts to reduce peak requirements by shifting slack jobs to nonpeak periods. Resource limits are not specified, but peak requirements are leveled as much as possible without delaying the specified due date.
Resource allocation program	Fixed amounts of resources are allocated to available jobs according to certain scheduling heuristics that determine which jobs will be postponed if total requirements for a given period exceed resources available. The completion date of the project may be pushed ahead to keep within specified resource limits.

As can be expected, as we move down the list of programs, the input data requirements grow larger and the computer run time and cost increase correspondingly. For this additional effort and cost, the project manager gains added realism in the model. If certain resources are indeed limited in supply and constitute a serious restriction on the manager's scheduling decisions, the added effort is not only worthwhile but necessary. In other contexts, perhaps, very few real limitations may exist. Additional men, materials, and other resources may be readily obtainable, in which case simpler network models should suffice. We can hardly think of a situation, however, in which a manager should not be aware of the resource implications of a given project schedule, even if resource supplies are plentiful. For this reason, some means of generating resource profiles should be employed, at least for the more important resources.

The extent to which all this information might be used for resource allocation, whether by hand or by sophisticated computer programs, depends on the size and importance of the project, the urgency or "tightness" of the scheduled completion date, the degree to which resource limitations may hinder scheduling, and the availability and cost of data. All of these are factors to be evaluated by the project manager. But the range of choices in terms of scheduling models and computer programs to implement them is far greater than it was a decade or so ago. Since the introduction of project network models, no single problem related to their use has received as much attention in the literature as limited resource scheduling. Many powerful and flexible programs, based on a variety of scheduling heuristics, have been developed and are available commercially. Considerable research effort has been directed at determining which scheduling rules are most effective.[9] Continued development and experiments on the part of both researchers and practitioners will lead, it is hoped, to approaches that are even more effective than those presently available. We are safe in saying, however, that the heuristic approach to project scheduling, aided by the ever-increasing computational power of digital computers, has and will continue to contribute significantly to solving some of the complex planning and scheduling problems of large project management.

Appendix: *Integer Programming Formulation—Project Scheduling with Limited Resources*

Integer programming provides an analytic solution to the problem of project scheduling with limited resources. Using an approach similar to Bowman's for the job shop problem,[10] we may develop a project scheduling model as follows:

Subscripts and their ranges:

s shop (resource) $s = 1, 2, \ldots, m$
d day (time period) $d = 1, 2, \ldots, z$
j job (activity) $j = 1, 2, \ldots, n$
p immediate predecessor of j; $p \in P_j$
  $= $ [all immediate predecessors of j].

Variables:

x_{jd} activity of job j on day d; constrained to the integer values 1 (if job j is active) or 0 (if job j is inactive).

Constants:

a_{sd} men available in shop s on day d
c_{sj} crew size; men of shop s required on job j
t_j time length of job j, in days
T minimum project completion time, given unlimited resources.

[9]See Davis, *op. cit.*
[10]E. H. Bowman, "The Schedule-Sequencing Problem," *Opns. Res.*, **7**, No. 5 (Sept.-Oct. 1959), 621–624.

Constraints:

1. $0 \leq x_{jd} \leq 1$ (and by integer programming techniques, x is constrained to equal either 0 or 1); all jd.

2. Jobs will be performed:

$$\sum_{d=1}^{z} x_{jd} = t_j \qquad j = 1, \ldots, n.$$

3. Capacity of shop will not be exceeded:

$$\sum_{j=1}^{n} c_{sj} x_{jd} \leq a_{sd} \qquad \begin{aligned} d &= 1, \ldots, z \\ s &= 1, \ldots, m. \end{aligned}$$

4. No job will be started before its predecessors are completed:

$$t_p x_{jd} \leq \sum_{i=1}^{d-1} x_{pi} \qquad \text{all } p \in P_j$$

$$d = 1, \ldots, z$$
$$j = 1, \ldots, n, \text{ except beginning jobs.}$$

(The summation term is taken as 0 when $d = 1$.)

5. No jobs will be split:

$$t_j x_{jd} - t_j x_{j(d+1)} + \sum_{i=d+2}^{z} x_{ji} \leq t_j \qquad \begin{aligned} j &= 1, \ldots, n \\ d &= 1, \ldots, z. \end{aligned}$$

Objective function:

minimize $1 \sum_{j=1}^{n} x_{jk} + 4 \sum_{j=1}^{n} x_{j(k+1)} + 16 \sum_{j=1}^{n} x_{j(k+2)}$

$+ \ldots + R_z \sum_{j=1}^{n} x_{jz}$, where k is some number such that

$T < k < z$, and $R_z = 4R_{z-1}$.

The term 4 is somewhat arbitrarily chosen to assure that the model will seek the shortest schedule satisfying the above constraints. We should note that the model does not allow for crashing or stretching a job, nor is allowance made for use of premium cost resources such as overtime. In spite of these simplifications, the problem is a formidable one in terms of sheer size, even for a small project. For example, a project with 50 jobs having 100 precedence relationships and requiring four different resources over a time span of 30 days has 1,500 variables and over 6,500 constraints (not counting slack variables or the additional constraints and variables necessary to assure an integer solution). Many of these equations, of course, are redundant, and many of the variables could be eliminated at the beginning by calculating the early start times for all jobs, assuming unlimited resources. Then all $x_{jd} = 0$ for $1 \leq d < ES_j$. For practical-sized projects, however, even a trimmed-down formulation would exceed the capacity of present computers and in any event, would be an inefficient means of solving the project scheduling problem.

Nevertheless, the desirability of an analytic solution to the problem has attracted the efforts of many researchers. Pritsker, Watters, and Wolfe have published an integer programming model[11] which requires fewer constraints than the one above and which allows greater scheduling flexibility. They reported computational results for a three-project, eight-job sample problem. A variety of implicit enumeration or "branch-and-bound" schemes have also been described in the literature (some of which are noted in our Bibliography). These appear to be more promising, with optimal solutions having been reported for one-resource problems with as many as 50 activities. This is still, of course, a small project in real-world terms. The primary problem is that modest increases in project size translate into discouragingly large increases in computational effort required by even the best of the analytic techniques. Thus even though genuine progress has been made in recent years and studies have given us additional insight into project scheduling, the analytic approaches are still far from handling projects large enough to be of general interest to managers.

[11]A. A. B. Pritsker, L. S. Watters, and P. M. Wolfe, "Multi-project Scheduling with Limited Resources: A Zero–One Programming Approach," *Mgt. Science*, **16**, No. 1 (Sept. 1969), 93–108.

8

Modifications
and Extensions
of Network Models

It is probably inevitable that the development of new management techniques such as PERT and CPM will be followed by efforts to modify or elaborate on the techniques. No matter how general the model or broad its applications, there will be situations in which it does not quite apply or is not completely satisfactory in its present form. Efforts will then be made to extend its usefulness by incorporating additional features and capabilities. Sometimes the model stimulates researchers or practitioners to think of how a like approach might be used to solve similar (or even dissimilar) problems; and major modifications in the original model result from attempts to adapt it to new applications.

Such a course of development has certainly been true in the case of PERT and CPM. We have already described the extension of PERT into a cost accounting system (Chapter 6) and the incorporation of resource constraints in network scheduling models (Chapter 7). In both these cases, the concept of a project network remained unchanged: it still consisted of a collection of partially ordered jobs, all of which had to be performed in accordance with certain fixed precedence constraints (and, in Chapter 7, resource constraints) before the project was completed.

This chapter deals with extensions of the model in which the concept of the network itself is modified. Some of the assumptions on which the network model is based have been criticized as inappropriate or insufficient in certain project planning and scheduling situations. For example, the single precedence relationship used in the network ("a job must be finished before its successors can begin") is considered by some managers to be too restrictive. They prefer the flexibility afforded by the inclusion of other types of relationships (such as "job *A* cannot be finished before job *B* is begun" or "job *A* cannot be started before job *B* has been started"). Such modifications in the model extend the meaning of precedence relationships but still accept the premise that a project network represents an identifiable collection of jobs all of which are necessary for completion of the project.

Others have observed that not all projects are so readily specifiable, that in some cases the jobs which potentially comprise a project cannot all be identified and "networked" at the time a project is planned (or even when it is begun). Thus there is some uncertainty about the network itself, both with respect to what jobs will be included and what their precedence relationships should be. These elements of uncertainty go far beyond those considered in the PERT model, which deals only with uncertainties in job durations, and they are much more difficult to deal with. Nevertheless, some interesting attempts have been made to incorporate such considerations in the basic context of a project network model.

In this chapter we will first look at network models with expanded types of precedence relationships. Then we will examine an effort to modify project networks for use, essentially, as decision trees for purposes of guiding management decisions in the preplanning stage of project management. Finally, we will consider some rather elaborate schemes for incorporating uncertainty in the structure of a network model and discuss the kind of information that can come out of such an approach.

Precedence Networking

There is only one type of precedence relationship allowed in typical PERT or CPM programs, as implied in the arrow diagram: A job leading into a node must be completed before any job emanating from the node may begin. This is called a *finish to start* (*FS*) relationship. That is, a given job must finish before any successors may start. Three additional types of relationships, however, are possible: *finish to finish* (*FF*), *start to start* (*SS*), and *start to finish* (*SF*). These other relationships are incorporated in an extension of PERT and CPM called *precedence networking* (*PN*). Not only does PN permit these alternative relationships, but it allows for a lead-lag quantity to be associated with any of them, a minimum time period that must separate start and/or finish points specified in the relationship.

These ideas may best be represented schematically in the form of a *precedence network*, which resembles an AON diagram with activities on nodes and precedence relationships shown as arrows. Now, however, we have to further define the relationships as *FS*, *SS*, and so on, and show the amount of the lead-lag factor. The relationship symbol may be subscripted, if desired, to clarify the jobs being related (for example, $F_A S_B$); but if the symbol is attached to an arrow, such information is obvious from the network. In the diagrams in the table, job A is always in precedence relationship to job B. Both jobs are shown as rectangles to facilitate the graphic representation of a job's start (left side of rectangle) and finish (right side of rectangle). The "flow" of jobs in terms of succeeding precedence relationships is, in general, from left to right. A precedence symbol with the amount of lead-lag (together called the *lead-lag factor*) and a verbal definition accompany each diagram. Time periods are assumed to be in days.

Precedence Network	Precedence Relationships (Lead-Lag Factor)	Definition
$A \longrightarrow B$	$FS = n$	Finish to start: job B cannot start until n days after job A is finished.
A / B	$SS = n$	Start to start: job B cannot start until n days after job A is started.
A / B	$FF = n$	Finish to finish: job B cannot finish until n days after job A is finished.
A B	$SF = n$	Start to finish: job B cannot finish until n days after job A is started.

The most commonly encountered relationship (and the *only* one in traditional CPM networks) is $FS = 0$, meaning that job B can start immediately after job A is finished. If B is to lag A by some number of days (for example, to allow for delivery time), this is conventionally accomplished by inserting a "pseudo job" between A and B, whose length is the desired lag period. The same effect is more easily accomplished in a precedence network by assigning a value to the lead-lag factor, such as $F_A S_B = 5$. Job B now must lag A by 5 days. That is, B can start no sooner than 5 days after A finishes.

$F_A S_B$ implies an absolute precedence of A to B: *All* of A must be completed before *any* of B can begin. In the event that it is technologically permissible for B to start after A is *partially* completed, then in conventional networks A could be divided into *two* jobs: A_1, which is the part of A that *must* precede B, and A_2, that part which can proceed in parallel with B:

But this adds to the job list and necessitates special programming to assure that A_1 and A_2 are regarded as a single job not to be interrupted, once started, in both forward- and backward-pass calculations.

The same effect can more easily be accomplished in precedence net-working by using the *SS* factor. For example, if the part of job A that *must* precede job B is 4 days long, the lead-lag factor $S_A S_B = 4$ will accomplish this result without splitting A and creating a new job. To cite a real-world example, suppose that in a construction project, job A is "Pour cement drive-way" and job B is "Level and smooth cement." Then obviously B cannot begin until A has, but it need not wait (in fact, *should not wait* if the driveway is a long one) until A has been completed. The appropriate precedence rela-tionship is $S_A S_B = 0$, which implies that B's start time is limited only by the start of A.

FF, the third relationship above, places no restrictions on the start of job B but requires that its finish time be no earlier than A's finish time. For example, in the construction of a home, job A might be "Lay carpet" and job B might be "Final clean-up." Some of B, such as cleaning outside windows and washing bathroom fixtures, could be done while the carpet is being laid or even before; but if picking up scraps from the carpet-laying job is part of B, then presumably B cannot be completed before A is.

It might be argued that B should then be split into two parts: B_1, which can proceed in parallel with A if desired; and B_2 (pick up carpet scraps), which cannot start until A is completed. But even then job A is not an absolute predecessor of B_2: picking up carpet scraps could presumably commence in some rooms where carpet has been laid even before all of job A is completed. The last scraps, however, cannot be picked up until the last carpet is laid, which means that A and B_2 are best described by an *FF* relationship. And in some situations, there may be reasons for not wanting to split a job at all, even if an *FS* relationship might be achieved, if the job is an integral activity that cannot be separated.

For example, "Pour cement driveway" conceivably could start at one end of the driveway while another crew was still working on "Erect cement forms" at the other end. But the cement pouring cannot be split into two jobs. Once pouring begins, it has to proceed without interruption until the last shovel-full has been put into place and smoothed (which, of course, cannot occur until all the forms are placed). *FF* would thus be the proper relationship to use to describe these two activities.

In some cases, two jobs may have dual relationships, as is true in our earlier example, where A was "Pour cement" and B was "Level and smooth."

Not only is *A* in *SS* relationship to *B*, but since the job of leveling and smoothing cement cannot be completed until all cement is poured, *A* is also in *FF* relationship to *B*:

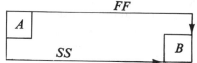

One must be careful not to create loops in a precedence network. The same is also true in ordinary networks, but the likelihood of creating a loop is higher in a precedence network because of the additional relationships allowed. Quite reasonable-sounding verbal descriptions of a project, when reduced to precedence symbols, can lead to looping conditions in the network. For example, suppose that job *C* must start before job *D* does, but that *D* must finish before *C* is completed. Then the two jobs have dual relationships *SS* and *FF* but with the direction of the latter reversed:

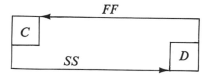

As we observed in Chapter 2, if loops exist in a network the job list cannot be put in topological order; and such ordering must be achieved before network calculations can be performed. In the example above, *D* cannot be scheduled until *C* is, and *C* cannot be scheduled until *D* is.

SF, the last relationship, is not typically included in the literature of precedence networking, presumably because the need for it seldom arises. It is included here to complete the four logical ways of connecting starts and finishes of two jobs and can be used in a manner similar to the other three relationships if the precedence logic of a project requires it.

Computer programs have been written which incorporate in various ways the major features of precedence networking described above. Besides the usual input of project data, the programs permit any additional precedence relationships to be specified for any job, along with lead–lag times if desired. As we noted, such delays could be effected by introducing additional jobs in the network, separating the jobs where a lag is desired; but the computer programs provide a convenient means of accomplishing the same purpose without enlarging the project network.

Forward- and backward-pass algorithms for precedence networks are outlined and briefly discussed in the Appendix to this chapter. They can be used directly to perform hand calculations on small networks, or they may be developed into a computer program for use on larger networks. An example problem is also given and discussed in the following pages.

While the additional precedence relationships outlined above complicate the CPM model, they do allow more flexibility in project modeling and permit a network representation of projects which do not really fit the simpler model. It is true that these additional precedence relationships may be accommodated in a conventional arrow diagram, at least to some degree, by splitting jobs into multiple segments. But this can greatly enlarge the arrow network,[1] and it requires special programming to recognize the split jobs as, in fact, single jobs. The precedence network is smaller, easier to develop, simpler to calculate, and clearer to interpret, both in terms of the network itself and schedules based upon it. It is not surprising that many companies using CPM have switched to precedence networking. Unfortunately, though, relatively little has appeared in the published literature describing the extent or success of efforts to use PN as a guide to potential users. Commercially available software packages and their accompanying literature provide some information, but the potential user is largely left to gain his experience firsthand.

Example: Laying Cement Slabs for Three Condominium Units

Our example takes as its setting the construction of a large condominium project, in which a number of essentially identical housing units are built sequentially. To keep the problem manageable, we will follow three units only and be concerned with just the laying of cement slabs. (In practice, of course, a network would be developed for *all* construction activities and *all* condominium units in the project.) Our main purpose is to illustrate PN concepts rather than to portray accurate job breakdowns and time durations.

Assume, then, that five jobs must be performed for each unit:

Clear lot and grade for slab	8 elapsed working hours
Place concrete forms	12 elapsed working hours
Lay sewer lines	16 elapsed working hours
Install reinforcement steel	9 elapsed working hours
Pour concrete and smooth	4 elapsed working hours

We shall number these jobs sequentially, unit by unit, so that jobs 1 through 5 refer to unit 1, jobs 6 through 10 to unit 2, and jobs 11 through 15 to unit 3. Job 7, for example, is "Place concrete forms, unit 2" and job 15 is "Pour concrete, unit 3."

[1]In an example reported by Keith Crandall, an arrow diagram required 71 activities to describe the same logic as a 15-job precedence network. See "Project Planning with Precedence Lead/Lag Factors," *Project Mgt. Quart.*, **4,** No. 3 (Sept. 1973).

Precedence relationships are given in verbal form, as they might be described by a contractor or job foreman. These are reduced to their equivalent symbolic representations (lead-lag factors), from which the network can be developed.

Description	Symbolic Representation		
	Unit 1	Unit 2	Unit 3
1. The lots must be cleared and graded before concrete forms or sewer lines can be placed.	$F_1S_2 = 0$ $F_1S_3 = 0$	$F_6S_7 = 0$ $F_6S_8 = 0$	$F_{11}S_{12} = 0$ $F_{11}S_{13} = 0$
2. Concrete forms or sewer lines can be placed at the same time, but sewer lines must be finished at least 2 hours before concrete forms are finished, to allow the final forms to be placed over sewer connections between the building and exterior lines.	$F_3F_2 = 2$	$F_8F_7 = 2$	$F_{13}F_{12} = 2$
3. Installation of reinforcement steel can begin after the concrete forms and sewer lines jobs are both 7 hours underway. It cannot be finished until the sewer lines are completed or until 1 hour after concrete forms are completed.	$S_2S_4 = 7$ $S_3S_4 = 7$ $F_2F_4 = 1$ $F_3F_4 = 0$	$S_7S_9 = 7$ $S_8S_9 = 7$ $F_7F_9 = 1$ $F_8F_9 = 0$	$S_{12}S_{14} = 7$ $S_{13}S_{14} = 7$ $F_{12}F_{14} = 1$ $F_{13}F_{14} = 0$
4. Two hours must be allowed for inspection of the first four jobs before cement pouring can begin.	$F_4S_5 = 2$	$F_9S_{10} = 2$	$F_{14}S_{15} = 2$
5. Crews for the clear and grade jobs must complete their work at one site before moving on to the next. The same is true for the installation of reinforcement steel. But the placement-of-concrete-forms jobs may overlap up to 2 hours from site to site, as may the pour-concrete jobs. Laying sewer lines may overlap up to 6 hours.	$F_1S_6 = 0$ $S_2S_7 = 10$ $S_3S_8 = 10$ $F_4S_9 = 0$ $S_5S_{10} = 2$	$F_6S_{11} = 0$ $S_7S_{12} = 10$ $S_8S_{13} = 10$ $F_9S_{14} = 0$ $S_{10}S_{15} = 2$	

Figure 8-1 displays the precedence network defined by the job list and relationships described above. Since the symbols are shown on the precedence arrows, we do not have to graphically represent the "start" and "finish" portions of the job rectangles as we did earlier. And a single arrow

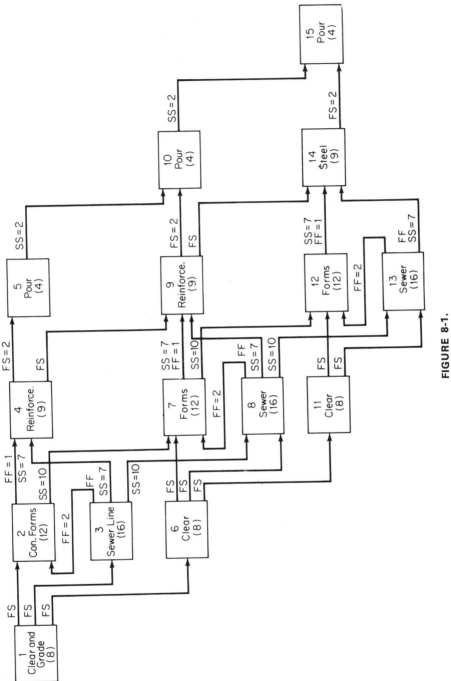

FIGURE 8-1.

can represent more than one precedence relationship, as may be observed. Numerical values of lead-lag factors are also shown. Symbols with no numbers attached have lead-lag factors of zero.

Using the PN algorithms described earlier, we can now calculate the early and late start schedules. In Figure 8-2 we show these two schedules for

FIGURE 8-2.

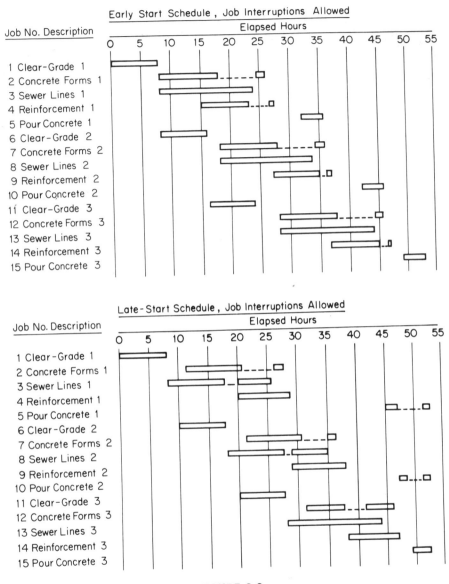

FIGURE 8-3.

the case where no interruptions are allowed. Figure 8-3 shows the schedules that result when that restriction is relaxed. In both figures the schedules are displayed in Gantt chart form.

A few observations should be noted. First, the early start schedule with interruptions is slightly shorter (53 hours) than the no-interruptions schedule (56 hours). This will not always be true, but allowing interruptions is one means of making the schedule a little less constrained and should lead, at least in some cases, to shorter schedules.

In conventional network calculations, we measured total slack as either $(LS–ES)$ or $(LF–EF)$. As long as jobs are not interrupted once started, the results will be identical. But notice what happens in the schedules of Figure 8-3, where some jobs are split. Total slack calculations for the first five jobs yield the following results:

Job No.	LS–ES	LF–EF
1	0	0
2	3	2
3	0	2
4	5	2
5	16	20

Total slack figures are the same only for job 1. Similar results hold for the other 10 jobs. Whenever a job is interrupted, and the period of interruption differs in the early and late start schedules, the two methods of calculating total slack will yield different figures. This means, of course, that the slippage allowed in the two halves of a split job is not always the same. For example, the first half of job 5 could be delayed up to 16 hours from its early start time without delaying the project finish, while the second half could be delayed up to 20 hours. And the effects of delaying a PN job are more complicated than in a conventional network, because of the more complex precedence relationships. Delaying the first segment of job 2, for example, will affect the start times (and hence the first segments) of jobs 4 and 7. Delaying job 2's second segment will delay job 4's second segment. (These are just the effects on immediate successors of course; more distant successors will be affected in chain-reaction style depending on other precedence relationships.)

Finding the critical path in a PN is not as simple as in conventional networks. Previously, we defined the critical path as a connected sequence of jobs from the beginning to the end of the project network, all of which have zero slack. A "connected sequence" was clearly identifiable, since all job connections were "finish-to-start." We further stated that all zero-slack jobs were on a critical path (or perhaps more than one such path), and that delaying the start of any critical job would delay the project completion date.

In precedence networks the job connections are not so simple; and although we can identify zero-slack jobs, they do not always fit in a neat finish-to-start sequence. To illustrate, in Figure 8-2 we can identify the following critical (zero-slack) jobs: 1, 2, 3, 7, 8, 12, 13, 14, and 15. By determining which precedence relationships are binding in both the early and late start schedules, we can construct three critical paths, as illustrated in Figure 8-4. At the top of the figure we show a PN diagram of critical jobs and critical precedence relationships only. Three different paths from start to finish can be delineated in this partial network. To further clarify the nature of these critical paths, we draw them separately in Gantt chart form. Critical

FIGURE 8-4.

jobs are shown as bars, while binding precedence constraints appear as arrows. Durations of jobs and lead-lag factors are indicated by the horizontal time scale.

Obviously these critical paths appear quite different from those we have seen before. It is still true that each critical job has zero slack, and that if any such job is delayed, the project will be delayed correspondingly. But there are differences, too. We previously observed that a critical path may be shortened by reducing the duration of any of its jobs. In path A of Figure 8-4, that statement holds true for jobs 1, 13, 14, and 15; but shortening jobs 3 and 8 has no effect on the length of the critical path, since the precedence relationships affect only the start times of these jobs. For this reason we are tempted to leave these jobs (3 and 8) off critical path A, retaining only their initial nodes for purposes of connecting the start-to-finish path of jobs and precedence arrows. The dashed precedence arrows look much like jobs themselves, having length and precedence relationships but requiring no resources.

So far so good. But notice job 12. Shortening that job has the anomalous effect of *lengthening* the critical path, due to the particular structure of the network.[2] The same can be said for job 2 in path B and job 7 in path C. Conversely, lengthening these jobs would shorten their respective critical paths. But to reduce the *project* duration, *all* critical paths must be shortened simultaneously. After examining Figure 8-4, we conclude that the latter can be accomplished in this case only by crashing job 1, 14 or 15, or by reducing, if feasible, the length of critical lead-lag factors. On the other hand, the project finish date will be delayed if any one of jobs 1, 3, 8, 13, 14, or 15 takes longer than expected or if any one of jobs 2, 7, or 12 is shortened.

As we observed above, when job interruptions are allowed, the split segments of a given job may have different amounts of slack; and this opens the possibility that critical paths in such a network may consist, in part, of job segments. To illustrate we turn to Figure 8-5, which shows the same information as Figure 8-4 but for the case where job interruptions are permitted. The PN network at the top indicates only one critical path through the network, and this is shown again in Gantt chart form for greater detail. Note that only the first segments of split jobs 3 and 8 are drawn, as the latter segments are not critical. Similarly, only the last segment of jobs 12 and 14 are shown, since the first segments have positive slack. None of these jobs, however, could be used for shortening the critical path. Project length could only be reduced by crashing job 1, 13 or 15, or by reducing the length of critical lead-lag factors. Because job interruptions are allowed, the anomalous effects noted in Figure 4 do not occur.

---

[2]This will occur whenever a critical job is in FF relationship with its predecessor and SS relationship with its successor, and when job interruptions are not allowed.

FIGURE 8-5.

It should be obvious, even from this small example, that the use and interpretation of PDM networks with other than FS precedence relationships requires considerable care. The simple, straightforward observations we have made regarding critical paths and jobs in ordinary CPM networks do not always apply in PDM. In such networks, the type of precedence relationships which occur along the critical path must also be taken into account, a price that is paid for the greater flexibility of the PDM model.

Decision Networks

It is generally true that several alternative methods exist for completing at least some jobs in a project. During the planning phase, the "best" of existing alternatives is chosen for inclusion in the final project list of jobs. A project network, then, reflects many decisions concerning which jobs (or job methods) were rejected and which were accepted in the planning process. All these decisions precede the scheduling process, since the calculations of early and late start or finish times presume a given collection of jobs whose durations and precedence relationships are completely specified.

Several observers have criticized this separation of the planning and scheduling phases. The selection of jobs that go into the final project obviously affects schedule results, since the alternative jobs may have not only different durations but different precedence relationships with other jobs in the network. Choosing one job from among several alternatives may also necessitate the inclusion of other jobs (which might not have been required at all in the network had a different alternative been selected.)

It seems reasonable, then, that the scheduling implications of alternative jobs be considered before a final choice is made. One extension of the project network model, called *Decision CPM*, was designed to facilitate such analysis.[3] In that model the project graph contains not only jobs which *must* be performed, along with their durations and precedence relationships, but also sets of alternative jobs with similar information. Each such set contains mutually exclusive job methods, one of which is ultimately to be selected. The project graph is displayed in AON form, with modifications. As before, jobs are shown as circular nodes; but jobs that belong to alternative job sets are preceded by triangles, called *decision nodes*, as illustrated in Figure 8-5.

Job J_0, an ordinary job, precedes job sets J_1 and J_2 and ordinary jobs J_3 and J_4. Job set 1 contains three jobs ($J_{1,1}, J_{1,2}$, and $J_{1,3}$), one of which must ultimately be selected. In this case, no matter which is chosen, J_5 is the successor. The two jobs in job set 2, however, have different successors. If $J_{2,1}$ is selected, J_4 will then be performed. If $J_{2,2}$ is chosen, however, $J_{2,1}$ is eliminated from the network. In order that the path containing J_4 is not broken, an additional link from J_0 to J_4 must be included. Similarly, since J_3 precedes $J_{2,2}$ and $J_{2,2}$ precedes J_6, the direct link between J_3 and J_6 is redundant if $J_{2,3}$ is chosen but must be included if the event $J_{2,1}$ is selected instead. Link J_6–J_9 is necessary for the same reason. Job J_{10} *must* be performed, regardless of the choice at decision node J_7, but J_{11} is required only if $J_{7,3}$ is chosen.

As a consequence of the three decision nodes, each with multiple choices, we can enumerate 18 different ways of choosing from among the alternative jobs (3 from J_1 × 2 from J_2 × 3 from J_3). That is, the decision network in Figure 8-5 implies 18 different ways of completing the project. For example, if the choices were $J_{1,1}, J_{2,1}$, and $J_{7,1}$, the network would reduce to that shown in Figure 8-6A. If, however, the choices were $J_{1,2}, J_{2,2}$, and $J_{7,3}$, the resulting network would be as in Figure 8-6B. In a similar manner, all 18 alternative networks could be developed.

[3]See W. Crowston and G. L. Thompson, "Decision CPM: A Method for Simultaneous Planning, Scheduling and Control of Projects," *Opns. Res.*, **15**, No. 3 (May-June 1967), 407–426.

FIGURE 8-6A.

FIGURE 8-6B.

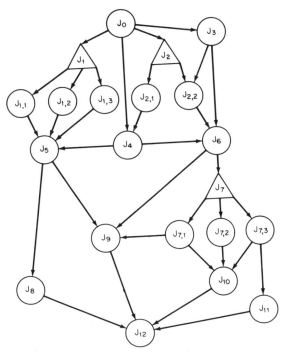

FIGURE 8-6.

On what basis would we choose from among these alternatives? Generally, we would prefer the lowest-cost alternative. If we could obtain the usual estimates for job durations, and in addition could obtain estimates for total job costs and time-related project overhead costs, we could calculate the duration of the project and then the total project cost (sum of all job costs plus project overhead cost based on project duration). A simple comparison would yield the lowest cost alternative, but, as always, other factors not included in this analysis would also have to be weighed before the final choice would be made.

It should be noted that, even with our small example problem, we came up with a fair number of alternative schedules to consider. Although 18 alternatives is not an unreasonable number to evaluate, even by hand, what would happen in a much larger project? If a project graph had m decision nodes, the first with n_1 choices, the second with n_2 choices, and so on, then there could be as many as $n_1 \times n_2 \times n_3 \times \cdots \times n_m$ different alternative projects to consider. The actual number might be less if some decision nodes were conditional upon choices at earlier decision nodes, but the combinatorial nature of the problem could nevertheless lead us to a rather sizable number of alternatives for consideration. Suppose, for example, that there were 20 decision nodes, each with 3 alternative choices, and suppose further that the decision nodes were independent of each other (no two on the same path through the network). Then there would be 3^{20} different projects to consider—almost $3\frac{1}{2}$ billion. Even a high-speed computer would not help much here. If each project could be evaluated in $\frac{1}{10}$ second, it would still take over 11 *years* to complete the enumeration of all $3\frac{1}{2}$ billion projects—obviously an infeasible approach.

As is generally true with large combinatorial problems, some means has to be found to reduce the number of alternatives actually considered, either by a branch-and-bound method or a heuristic approach. (We ran into a similar situation in Chapter 7 when examining the limited resource scheduling problem.) Crowston and Thompson describe one such heuristic procedure in their article. Although they do not guarantee that their procedure will lead to an optimal solution, their method does achieves what is presumed or hoped to be a "good" solution with a reasonable amount of computational effort.

Whether a complete enumeration approach (for small problems) or a heuristic procedure (for larger problems) is used, the method does provide a reasonable means of combining the planning and scheduling phases of project management. We should note that the CPM model of Chapter 5 is in some sense a combination planning–scheduling model: for each job, alternative durations are considered, along with their costs, in arriving at an optimum overall schedule. But in the present context, the job alternatives are discrete, the time–cost trade-offs usually cannot be expressed in functional form, and more significantly, the alternatives may affect the very structure of the network itself, which is not true in the CPM model. Thus Decision CPM permits analysis of a wider and less rigidly structured class of project management programs.

Probabilistic Networks

Both of the extensions to network models discussed so far are "deterministic" in nature. That is, they do not involve probabilistic elements. The different types of precedence relationships are specified by the persons who analyze the project, not by any random elements that may occur. Likewise, in Decision CPM, the "best" job from among an alternative set is rationally selected by management rather than being determined by a chance mechanism beyond management's control. In the PERT model (Chapter 4) we did consider some elements of uncertainty that may exist—specifically with respect to job durations. But there are other areas of uncertainty in project management, particularly with regard to the project network. Not only may job times be variable, but the network itself may change as a result of some unforeseen circumstance or outcome.

For example, one activity in a missile-development project might be "Test propulsion system." Depending on the outcome of the test, the project may proceed as planned or the engineers might be sent "back to the drawing boards" for redesign, refabrication, and retesting of the system. The possibility for such looping paths is not included in the basic PERT or CPM models—in fact, it is prohibited. The network must be acyclic, which means that no cycles or loops can occur. Additionally, PERT/CPM networks require that *all* jobs must be successfully completed; no allowance is made for possible failures. These are serious limitations, for there are many project situations in which an activity may have several unpredictable outcomes, including outright failure, and the nature of that part of the project which follows depends heavily on the particular outcome that occurs. Examples include bidding situations, test programs, feasibility studies, and research programs in which multiple approaches are attempted.

In order to expand the modeling capabilities of PERT and CPM to include such problems, a number of researchers have proposed expanded, more general networking systems.[4] Most of these make use of what are called

[4]For example, see R. Freeman, "A Generalized Network Approach to Project Activity Sequencing," *IRE Trans. Eng. Mgt.*, EM-7 (Sept. 1960); H. Eisner, "A Generalized Network Approach to the Planning and Scheduling of a Research Project," *Opns. Res.*, 10, No. 1 (Jan.-Feb. 1962); S. E. Elmaghraby, "An Algebra for the Analysis of Generalized Activity Networks," *Mgt. Science*, 10, No. 3 (Apr. 1964); A. A. B. Pritsker and W. W. Happ, "GERT: Graphical Evaluation and Review Technique, Part I: Fundamentals," *J. Indust. Eng.*, 18, No. 5 (May 1966).

probabilistic nodes, which differ considerably from ordinary project network nodes (events). In the latter case, every node is eventually reached or *released* —specifically, when all jobs leading into the node have been completed. Similarly, all jobs emanating from the node may start after the node is released, and all of them must eventually be completed.

By contrast, probabilistic networks allow the possibility that certain nodes may be released when one or more (but not necessarily all) jobs leading into them are completed. Such networks also allow the possibility for probabilistic exits from the node, in which case only one of several emanating jobs is actually taken. Thus jobs themselves may be probabilistic, occurring with some stated probability, which may be less than 1.

The additional flexibility in probabilistic networks is gained by defining several types of nodes. In GERT,[5] the most extensively developed and widely studied system employing probabilistic networks, nodes are considered to have an input and an output side, each characterized by certain logical relations with respect to connecting jobs. Two types of output sides are used, which determine the type of *branching* that occurs from the node. *Deterministic branching* is used when all activities emanating from a node will be undertaken. *Probabilistic branching* is used when only one of several emanating activities is to be performed.

Symbols for the output sides of nodes are as follows:

Symbol	*Meaning*
j ◗	Deterministic branching node. Upon release of node j, all jobs emanating from the node will be initiated.[6]
j ▷	Probabilistic branching node. Upon release of node j, *one* of the emanating activities will be initiated, according to the probabilities given.

Several types of input sides of nodes are used, and these specify the conditions that control *nodal release*, or the point when branching from a

---

[5]Since its introduction (see Pritsker and Happ, *op. cit.*), GERT has been revised and considerably extended. Its most recent general version, GERT III Z, is described here. (Details may be found in *The GERT III Z User's Manual* by A. A. B. Pritsker and C. E. Sigal, Pritsker & Associates, Inc., West Lafayette, Indiana, 1974). Specialized versions include Q-GERT, for analyzing queueing and logistics problems, and P-GERT, for project planning using precedence networks. For additional references, see the Bibliography.

[6]*Release* is controlled by activity completions on a node, as explained below.

node can begin. In general, the input side specifies how many incoming activity completions are required for the first release of the node as well as for subsequent releases. Since cycles or feedback loops may exist in a GERT network, the possibility exists that the same activity could be completed several times and trigger release of a node. If *different* activity completions are desired for nodal release, this can be signaled by an AND capability, symbolized on the input side of the node by *A*. The user can also specify that, when a node is released, any unfinished jobs connecting to the node are halted. He does this by labeling the node with an *H* capability. If both *A* and *H* capabilities are desired, the symbol *U* is utilized. This will require a node to have different activities completed in order to meet the specified number for nodal release, *and*, when it is released, all on-going jobs entering the node are halted.

These notions concerning the input sides of nodes may be summarized as follows:

Symbol	Meaning
m / n	The first nodal release will occur when there have been m incident activity completions. Subsequent releases require n completions.
m / A / n	The first nodal release requires that m *different* incident activities be completed. Subsequent releases require n such completions.
m / H / n	The first nodal release will occur with m incident activity completions. All other on-going incident activities will be halted at that point. Subsequent releases require n completions, with the same halting condition.
m / U / n	The first nodal release requires m *different* incident activities to be completed. All other on-going incident activities will be halted at that point. Subsequent releases require n such completions, with the same halting conditions.

These symbols for input and output sides may be combined to form eight different types of nodes. A few examples should help to clarify their use and meaning.

Symbol	Meaning
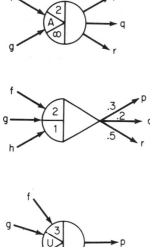	This is the node of conventional arrow diagrams. Jobs *f* and *g* must both be completed before the node is released, at which point jobs *p*, *q*, and *r* can begin (and must ultimately be finished). The ∞ on the input side indicates that the node cannot be rereleased; it is not involved in any cycles or feedback loops.
	Any two completions among jobs *f*, *g*, and *h* will release the node the first time. Since the node may be in a feedback loop, it is possible for the same job to be completed twice and thus release the node, though completion of any two from among jobs *f*, *g*, and *h* would accomplish the same thing. Upon nodal release, one of the three jobs *p*, *q*, and *r* will start, according to the probabilities shown. Should the node reoccur in a feedback loop, only one of the incident jobs need be completed to release the node.
	Three different jobs from among *f*, *g*, *h*, and *i* must be completed to release the node both on first and subsequent passes. When any three are completed, work in process on the fourth (if any) is halted. Upon nodal release, job *p* will begin.
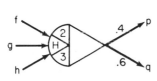	Any two completions of incident jobs will release the node on the first pass. Three completions are required on subsequent passes. Completions need not be for different jobs. After nodal release, on-going work on any other incident job is halted, and either job *p* or *q* (but not both) will commence, according to the probabilities shown.

The other four possible node types are defined similarly. Note that *A* and *U* capabilities require that the number of incident jobs be at least as great as the number of completions required on either first or subsequent passes. Similarly, the *U* capability is not used unless the number of incident jobs is greater than required completions on first or subsequent passes.

Used as required, these eight nodes greatly extend the usefulness and generality of network techniques for analyzing complex, probabilistic systems. And "systems" need not be limited to projects but can include repetitive operations, continuous production lines, and other on-going processes. The simple example that follows, although hardly suggesting the scope or complexity of systems that might be modeled, illustrates the use of probabilistic networks in a familiar context: contractual bidding.

Suppose that the Space Armor Company has an opportunity to bid on three different contracts, each calling for the design, testing, and construction of reentry shields for a group of space vehicles to be used in various research programs. Contract 1 is for the largest and most profitable system, followed in order by contracts 2 and 3. The company has the engineering capacity to design and test any two of the three, but construction capacity is sufficient to complete only one contract by the due dates anticipated. After some consideration, management decides to prepare bids for contracts 1 and 2, and then, if both of these bids are rejected, to bid on contract 3. If the company is successful in both contracts 1 and 2, the construction of the simplest of the two systems will be subcontracted.

Based on past experience and an assessment of their competititive position in the industry, management estimates the probabilities of successfully bidding the three contracts as follows:

Contract	Probability of Successful Bid
1	.3
2	.5
3	.4

In addition, because of the complexity of the first contract, there is a 10 per cent chance that the bid will be neither accepted or rejected but returned for revision or modification. Management feels that the probabilities associated with outcomes on the second go-around would be the same, including the likelihood of another return for revision.

Each system must be subjected to a thorough testing. Minor problems that show up here may be easily corrected; but "failure" of the test requires that the system be completely redesigned (at about the same expense in time and money as before) and retested. Management's best estimates of probabilities associated with the testing program are as follows:

Contract	Probability of Successful Test
1	.6
2	.8
3	.9

There are several ways of displaying the above project in a GERT-type probabilistic network, including that shown in Figure 8-7. Some of the nodes have been numbered to facilitate discussion of the network. Note that

FIGURE 8-7.

node 2 is reached only if bids 1 and 2 are *both* rejected, in which case the parts of the network from node 1 to node 9 and from node 3 to node 9 may be ignored, along with connecting branches. Node 2 is not released if node 1 or node 3 (or both) is released. Node 6 is released only if both bids 1 and 2 are accepted, which means that construction of system 2 must be subcontracted. Node 5 will be released only if bid 1 is the only one accepted. (Its predecessors include a path from bid 1 accepted and another from bid 2 rejected.) Likewise, node 7 represents acceptance of bid 2 only, and node 8 is reached only if bid 3 is accepted. Thus nodes 5, 6, 7, and 8 all represent mutually exclusive events, so node 9 is released when one and only one of the paths leading into it is attained.

Because we wanted to keep the example simple, the graph is a highly aggregated model of the company's project. But any part of it could be expanded if additional detail were desired. A design branch, for example, could be divided into many branches and nodes—a kind of subproject of its own. The test outcomes could be expanded beyond the simple dichotomies that we have shown, which would permit a revision in the somewhat unrealistic assumption implied by our graph that the "failure" cycle could continue indefinitely (although with small probability). The point is, of course, that the probabilistic features of the graph permit the modeling of a much wider range of projects than is possible with the more restrictive assumptions of normal PERT- or CPM-type networks. Our little example project above could not have been represented at all by such networks, nor could any project in which the outcomes of one or more events is probabilistic in nature —so that not all jobs in the network will necessarily be undertaken.

If the events have different outcomes, it follows that there may be more than one possible outcome for a project as a whole. In our example there are five possible outcomes, only one of which may occur:

1. System 1 is delivered.
2. System 2 is delivered.
3. Systems 1 and 2 are delivered.
4. System 3 is delivered.
5. No systems are delivered, as all bids were rejected.

The probability of each outcome may be determined from the branch (job) probabilities and the structure of the network. For example, the probability of outcomes (1) and (3) is $\frac{1}{6}$ each, outcome (2) is $\frac{1}{3}$, outcome (4) is $\frac{2}{15}$, and outcome (5) is $\frac{1}{5}$.[7] Although these probabilities were simple to determine,

---

[7]The probability that bid 1 will ultimately be accepted (perhaps after revision) is $.3/(.3 + .6) = \frac{1}{3}$. The joint probability of this occurrence *and* the rejection of bid 2 is $\frac{1}{3} \times \frac{1}{2} = \frac{1}{6}$. Probabilities for outcomes 2 through 5 are similarly calculated.

similar calculations in a large, complex network could become rather difficult. Pritsker and Elmaghraby both discuss the algebra of probabilistic networks, including means of transforming networks to equivalent representations, making exclusive use of input nodes requiring only one activity completion for release.[8] If durations of jobs (which may be either fixed or probabilistic, as in PERT) are given, then expected project duration for each of the possible outcomes may be calculated. The model becomes a means of simulating a project to determine possible outcomes and their probabilities, and indeed Pritsker has developed a computer simulation language especially well suited to the kind of analysis that we have been discussing.[9] Its purpose (as is true of most simulation languages) is to facilitate the modeling and analysis of complex project systems. The interested reader is referred to the growing body of literature concerning GERT, some of which is included in our Bibliography.

To Use or Not to Use

Relatively little information is available concerning the extent to which any of the above modifications of project network models have found applications. Beyond the expository articles describing the methods, a few additional articles have appeared detailing their applications (particularly this is true of GERT). But such articles are infrequent, especially as compared with the hundreds of articles in trade journals and other application-oriented publications that followed the introduction of PERT and CPM. Of course, the models described above are more specialized and more complex. Fewer opportunities for their use would arise than for the simpler network models. And their use requires a great deal more sophistication on the part of the user than is true for PERT and CPM (which themselves were not always well understood by project managers). So it is not surprising that reports of applications are slow in coming.[10]

Thus potential users will have limited guidance based on the experience of other users. They will necessarily be experimenting to some extent. Whether such experiments are worth attempting must be answered by each potential user, depending on the nature of the project and the types of problems involved. Are the simpler PERT and CPM models inadequate for the

[8]Such graphs become signal-flow graphs and enable the well-developed theory of SFGs to be applied to the analysis of probabilistic project networks.

[9]See, for example, *The GASP IV Simulation Language* (New York: John Wiley & Sons, Inc., 1974).

[10]Edward W. Davis, in an extensive survey of large construction companies, found no examples of applications of the models described in this chapter. He describes his survey in "CPM Use in TOP 400 Construction Firms," *J. Construction Div., ASCE,* **100** (Mar. 1974).

particular situation? Does he want greater flexibility in the planning stage? (Decision CPM might facilitate the consideration of various alternative procedures.) Are there major uncertainties regarding the outcomes of some activities that could vitally affect that part of the project that follows them? (Probabilistic networks might provide a more realistic model.) Is the manager capable of understanding and using the models, and does he have staff people who can implement them? Is the project of sufficient size and importance to warrant the expense of more complicated modeling? Would the experience gained be useful for future projects?

Only the project manager can answer these and other relevant questions; and it will be the aggregate answers of many project managers who will determine how useful the newer models are as tools of management.

Appendix: *Precedence Networking Algorithms*

Two cases are outlined below, one in which job interruptions are not allowed and the other in which they are. The former case is simplest. When several precedence conditions impinge on a job, the most restrictive of these, whether it affects the start or finish time, determines when the job will be scheduled. The job, when started, proceeds to its finish without a break.

The latter case looks separately at the constraints on a job's start time and those on its finish time. In the forward pass, a job's start time is determined by FS and SS relationships; and the finish time is determined by the FF (and SF, if used) relationship, along with job duration. If the early start and early finish so determined differ by more than the job's duration, then the job is split according to rules outlined in the algorithm. Analogous procedures hold for the backward pass.

Symbols used for early and late start and finish times closely follow those used in earlier chapters, and precedence symbols are the same as described above. These are summarized as follows:

ES_j	Early start time of job j
EF_j	Early finish time of job j
LS_j	Late start time of job j
LF_j	Late finish time of job j
t_j	Duration of job j
F_iS_j	Minimum interval between the finish of job i and the start of job j
S_iS_j	Minimum interval between the start of job i and the start of job j
F_iF_j	Minimum interval between the finish of job i and the finish of job j

a_j Length of the first segment of an interrupted job during the forward pass

b_j Length of the last segment of an interrupted job during the backward pass

In the algorithm below, subscript j is used for the job being evaluated. Predecessor jobs are subscripted with i and successor jobs with k. Thus arc ij represents a predecessor relationship (used in forward-pass calculations) and jk represents a successor relationship (used in backward-pass claculations).

First Case: Job Interruptions Not Allowed

Forward pass

ES: For jobs with no predecessor relationships: set $ES_j = 0$. All other jobs: for each predecessor arc ij, calculate ES_j as follows:

Predecessor Type	Calculation
F_iS_j	$ES_j = EF_i + F_iS_j$
S_iS_j	$ES_j = ES_i + S_iS_j$
F_iF_j	$ES_j = EF_i + F_iF_j - t_j$

Finally, set ES_j equal to the *maximum* of all the ES_j's calculated above.

EF: For all jobs: $EF_j = ES_j + t_j$

T: Project duration $T = \max_{\text{all } j} (EF_j)$

Backward pass

LF: For jobs with no successor relationships: set $LF_j = T$. All other jobs: for each successor arc jk, calculate LF_j as follows:

Successor Type	Calculation
F_jS_k	$LF_j = LS_k - F_jS_k$
F_jF_k	$LF_j = LF_k - F_jF_k$
S_jS_k	$LF_j = LS_k - S_jS_k + t_j$

Finally, set LF_j equal to the *minimum* of all the LF_j's calculated above.

LS: For all jobs: $LS_j = LF_j - t_j$

Second Case: Job Interruptions Allowed[11]

Forward pass

> *ES:* For jobs with no *FS* or *SS* precedessor relationships, set ES_j = 0. All other jobs: For each predecessor arc *ij*, calculate ES_j as follows:

Predecessor Type	Calculation
$F_i S_j$	$ES_j = EF_i + F_i S_j$
$S_i S_j > a_i$	$ES_j = EF_i + S_i S_j - t_i$
$S_i S_j \leq a_i$	$ES_j = ES_i + S_i S_j$

Finally, set ES_j equal to the *maximum* of all ES_j's calculated above.

> *EF:* For all jobs, calculate $$EF_j = ES_j + t_j \tag{1}$$
>
> For jobs with $F_i F_j$ relationships, also calculate $$EF_j = EF_i + F_i F_j \tag{2}$$
> for each $F_i F_j$
>
> Finally, set EF_j equal to the *maximum* of the EF_j's in (1) and (2):
>
> If (1) is a maximum, set $a_j = t_j$
> If (2) is a maximum, set $a_j = t_j - F_i F_j$, using that $F_i F_j$, which yielded the maximum EF_j in (2).

> *T:* Project duration $$T = \max_{\text{all } j} (EF_j)$$

Backward pass

> *LF:* For jobs with no *FS* or *FF* successor relationships, set $LF_j = T$. All other jobs: For each successor arc *jk*, calculate LF_j as follows:

Successor Type	Calculation
$F_j S_k$	$LF_j = LS_k - F_j S_k$
$F_j F_k > b_k$	$LF_j = LS_k - F_j F_k + t_k$
$F_j F_k \leq b_k$	$LF_j = LF_k - F_j F_k$

Finally, set LF_j equal to the *mimimum* of all LF_j's calculated above.

[11]The algorithm follows the job-splitting rules suggested by Keith C. Crandall in "Project Planning with Precedence Lead/Lag Factors," *Project Mgt. Quart.*, **4,** No. 3 (Sept. 1973).

LS: For all jobs, calculate $\qquad LS_j = LF_j - t_j \qquad\qquad$ (1)

For jobs with S_jS_k relationships,
also calculate $\qquad\qquad LS_j = LS_k - S_jS_k \qquad$ (2)

$\qquad\qquad$ for each $\quad jk$ arc

Finally, set $LS_j = minimum \ LS_j$ from (1) and (2):

If (1) is a minimum, set $\quad b_j = t_j$

If (2) is a minimum, set $\quad b_j = t_j - S_jS_k$, using
that S_jS_k, which yielded the *minimum LS_j* in
(2).

Effect of Job-Splitting Rules

The effect of the rules above in the forward pass is to start each job as soon as allowed by its *FS* or *SS* predecessor relationships, and to finish it as soon as allowed by its duration or by its *FF* predecessor relationships. If the early finish is determined by an *FF* relationship, say F_iF_j, and not by the duration, then the job will be interrupted. The split will be such that the first portion is a_j days long and the last portion F_iF_j days long, with the last segment commencing at EF_i (the point at which predecessor job i just finishes).

Similarly, in the backward pass, each job finishes as late as allowed by the *FS* or *FF* successor relationships, and starts as late as allowed by its duration or by its *SS* successor relationships. If late start is determined by the latter, say S_jS_k, and not by the duration, then the job will be split. The first portion will be S_jS_k days long, ending just at the point successor job k begins (LS_k); and the second portion will be b_j days long.

These rules for determining how the split will occur are somewhat arbitrary (as would be true of any other rules). The split can, of course, be made at any point within the range of the determined start and finish times of the job. But the rules above have the advantage that they preserve a "continuity of flow" from the end of one job to the remaining portion of a successor. For example, in an early start schedule, if jobs i and j are related by an F_iF_j and job j is split, then just as job i ends, job j recommences for its final F_iF_j days. This would allow commonly used resources (if any) to be shifted directly from job i to job j, to complete the latter. Of course, this says nothing about the initial portion of job j and how it relates—in time or in resource usage—with job i. Other rules for splitting jobs might focus on this initial portion according to some other rationale. In practice, of course, the project manager has the option of splitting an interruptable job at any point between its scheduled start and finish times, as long as the job starts and finishes within its precedence constraint. The preceding routine yields the range within which such splitting can take place, and the user has the freedom to schedule actual work segments within these limits, or to use job slack for even further flexibility.

Slack in a Precedence Network

When job interruptions are not allowed, total slack in a precedence network is identical to ordinary CPM networks and can be calculated from either LS_j-ES_j or LF_j-EF_j. But when job interruptions are allowed, the two methods may yield different results. Slippage from the early start schedule to the late start schedule may be different for the initial portion of a split job than for the final portion. That is, the initial portion may have different slack (calculated as LS_j-ES_j) than the final portion (calculated as LF_j-EF_j). This results from the fact that the former is affected by SS constraints and the latter by FF constraints, and the effects can very well be different. Allowing job splits, although it slightly complicates the notion of slack, actually increases flexibility in scheduling, as it identifies portions of jobs that might be delayed more than would be possible if interruptions were not allowed.

9

Problems and Prospects
in Applications
of PERT/CPM

More than two decades have passed since critical path scheduling was first introduced—enough time so that we can look back with a measure of objectivity and appraise what happened during its early and rather hectic introductory period. We do so with the intent of considering the lessons that can be learned for the benefit of today's managers who make use of PERT and CPM.

As is true of many new techniques (or new commercial products of any kind), there was a lot of initial ballyhooing for PERT and CPM. Interest was greatly accelerated when the federal government, particularly the Department of Defense, jumped on the PERT bandwagon and began requiring PERT capability of major defense contractors. Converts—willing or unwilling—were numerous. Since the model was basically simple, it could be learned readily; and instant experts offered themselves in great numbers as consultants. Published literature abounded, with articles appearing everywhere—from trade magazines to learned projessional journals. Many students won master's and doctoral degrees with theses based on project scheduling models. PERT entered the English language not only in its original form but also as a verb ("the project was *perted*"), an adjective (*pertable* and *pertorial*), an adverb (*pertwise*), and in various noun derivatives (*pertor, pertee, pertocracy,* etc.).[1]

---

[1]See M. Krakowski, "PERT and Parkinson's Law," *Interfaces,* **5,** No. 1 (Nov. 1974).

And as might be predicted, while the intensive promotion built interest and enthusiasm to a high peak, it could not be maintained. Inevitably, there followed a period of decline, a slump in interest, a falling-out of the unwilling converts. Some became disillusioned because they were promised too much, or expected too much, and the models did not solve all their project management problems. (Whether promoted as such or because users hope they will be so, new management techniques are too frequently viewed as panaceas for the aches and ills of managers.) Other users who adopted PERT and CPM when they became fashionable just as quickly dropped them when fashions changed. Academics who were quick to ride the ascending star of PERT/CPM were just as quick to heap scorn during its eclipse.[2] Articles on the subject in professional journals decreased in number, replaced by an occasional satirical piece.[3] In some circles, to admit use of PERT became an embarassment. Vazsonyi reported an incident in which a major aerospace company was preparing a proposal for a multibillion-dollar Air Force project. The planning and control system was admittedly sound and attractive, but some aspects vaguely resembled PERT, which apparently offended a high-ranking Air Force official. He urged the company to change the wording so that the proposed system would appear as "un-PERT-like" as possible.

The reaction to the excessive promotion of PERT and CPM was probably inevitable. The "bandwagon effect" applies to both getting on and getting off. But while an adjustment in management's attitude was necessary and desirable to bring expectations in line with realities, there has probably been an overreaction among some managers and reporters. Like a car with bad shock absorbers, an excessive "high" has been followed by an excessive "low." When balance and perspective are finally restored, managers will be able to view more objectively what network models can (and cannot) contribute to project management. Separated from wall-to-wall PERT charts, massive computer printouts, rooms full of CRT terminals and other gadgets, and perhaps even from the stereotyped PERT and CPM acronyms, the basic, simple models can significantly assist managers in some, although not all, aspects of project management. As Vazsonyi describes the "post-PERT" phase: "The acronyms and associated false images are discarded, but the underlying sound concepts, such as events, activities, technological sequence, slack, network analysis, are retained and added to the permanent and useful framework of management knowledge on how to plan, control, and schedule massive programs."[4]

---

[2] For an example of such change of heart, forthrightly told, see A. Vazsonyi's "L'Historie de la grandeur et de la décadence de la méthode PERT," printed (in English) in *Mgt. Science*, **16**, No. 8 (Apr. 1970), B449–B455.

[3] For an amusing example, read Krakowski, *op. cit.*

[4] *Op. cit.*

So with less ballyhooing but greater understanding, project network models continue to be used by project managers—not only for "massive programs" but for projects of various types and dimensions. Several recent surveys confirm that PERT and CPM have become well established in the repertory of techniques used by modern managers. One of these surveys, conducted by Edward Davis among the top 400 construction firms in the United States, showed 80 per cent of the respondent firms using critical path methods, up from 47 per cent usage rate among the same firms prior to 1965.[5]

In another survey, this one among manufacturing firms, Norman Gaither found that PERT and CPM ranked above all other quantitative decision-making tools in terms of the percentage of firms who used them.[6] Sampling 500 companies located in seven South-Central states, he found about half of them using one or more operations research techniques; and among those which did, 69 per cent reported using PERT with 67 per cent using CPM. (The next most used tools were linear programming, 57 per cent; statistical analyses, 56 per cent; and computer simulation, 52 per cent.)

Not all users of project network techniques are satisfied with the results. Davis noted that 16 per cent of the construction firm respondents in his survey reported they had been unsuccessful in achieving the various advantages attributed to CPM compared to 61 per cent who reported "moderate success" and 15 per cent who said they had been "highly successful"). What makes the difference? What contributes to success or disappointment among the users? At this point it would be appropriate for us to examine such questions and to appraise the models from a more detached and comprehensive perspective than was possible when we were examining their structure and operation at close range. Now that we know *how* they work and something about their extensions, we are in a better position to ask: "Are they as useful as claimed? In what situations are they appropriate, and when are they inappropriate? Will they really help a manager to plan and schedule a project? How can he influence the degree of their success in use?"

These are important questions, and they should be answered before we complete our book. The basic models are straightforward: Network calculations, although tedious for large projects, are not complex; and the results follow logically from the assumptions upon which the models are built. However well thought out the models are, though, we want to know if they are accurate representations of that portion of the real world they attempt to model. No model is any better than the assumptions that underlie

[5]Edward W. Davis, "CPM Use in Top 400 Construction Firms," *J. Construction Div., ASCE,* **100** (Mar. 1974).

[6]Norman Gaither, "The Adoption of Operations Research Techniques by Manufacturing Organizations," *J. Decision Sciences,* **6**, No. 4 (Oct. 1975).

it; so a logical place for us to begin our evaluation is with the PERT/CPM assumptions. From a consideration of these, and of how closely they approximate real-world conditions, we shall turn to some operational problems of applying PERT and CPM, and note some of the observations and criticisms of practitioners—those who have had experience in applying the models to project management.

The PERT and CPM Assumptions

Many assumptions, explicit or implicit, underlie the network models, and our list here is by no means exhaustive. But there are a few which, we believe, are particularly relevant to our evaluation. Not necessarily in order of importance, they include the following:

1. *A project can be subdivided into a set of predictable, independent activities.* ("Independence" here refers to the separateness of the activities in an operational sense rather than in a time-ordered technological sense. That is, a clear beginning and ending point for each activity can be identified, and activities whose predecessors are completed can be started and stopped independently of each other.)

Two aspects of this assumption have been challenged by observers and practitioners. First is the assumption that activities comprising a project can be known beforehand. Although this is not unreasonable for certain projects that involve well-established technology and operations, for some projects, such as research and development programs involving state-of-the-art developments, this is not necessarily true. All problems cannot be anticipated in advance; therefore, activities necessary for their solution cannot be planned and included in a project network. To some extent the network must develop or change as the project proceeds. Concerning such projects, Eyring has argued that PERT may even be dysfunctional as a planning model for research-and-development managers in that the mere attempt to list the activities necessary to complete a research project may tend to remove the flexibility the manager needs to shift directions and procedures as new problems and possibilities arise in the course of the project's completion. The skillful manager, he claims, is not one who can set down a plan and follow it faithfully but one who can rapidly respond to new information as it develops by shifting resources to more promising avenues of endeavor, even if it means scrapping an original plan.[7] To the extent, then, that a project cannot be

[7]Henry B. Eyring, "Evaluation of Planning Models for Research and Development Projects" (D.B.A. thesis, Harvard University, June 1963). In his thesis Eyring presents an interesting and thoughtful analysis of both conceptual and practical problems encountered in applying network planning models to research-and-development projects.

laid out with reasonable assurance in the planning stage, PERT and CPM are not as useful and appropriate as might be desired, although they still can be employed to project rough estimates of project duration based on current "best-guess" constructions of the project network (or of possible alternative networks).

The second aspect of the assumption concerns the identification of separate independent activities. In practice, while the assumption is often valid, not all activities can be so clearly identified. Where one activity ends and another begins is sometimes a matter of arbitrary choice, and some functions necessary for a project, such as the general management function or a support function such as legal counsel, fit somewhat awkwardly into the definition of an activity.

Occasionally, also, two activities which appear on separate parallel paths in the network *must* be performed at the same time; they are not operationally independent, in spite of the way they appear on the network.[8]

2. *The precedence relationships of project activities can be completely represented by a noncyclical network graph in which each activity connects directly into its immediate successors.*[9] For many projects, this assumption is valid, but in certain situations it is not. In the first place, not all precedence relationships can be anticipated before a project begins; this is especially true for research-and-development types of projects which involve new technology and unknown problems. Second, predecessor relationships are assumed to be firm—that is, a given job must be completed in its entirety before any successor jobs can begin. Frequently, however, predecessor relationships are "soft." Although completion of one job may be desirable before any successors begin, it is possible to somewhat relax the strict requirement and begin the successors earlier if necessary.[10] And third, while a network

[8]Part of this difficulty is due, however, to the problems associated with aggregating large detailed networks. When activities are broken into sufficiently small units of work, predecessor relationships can be shown with considerable accuracy. But if a "big picture" view of the network is desired, without the clutter of thousands of arrows and nodes, activities must be grouped together into higher-level aggregate tasks. Usually, this requires that some of the precedence connections between small tasks be ignored and that only the major technological relationships be retained. Critical path calculations based on aggregate networks may thus be somewhat distorted.

[9]A connection through a dummy activity is still considered direct. By noncyclical, we mean that no part of the network loops back on itself. A loop, or cycle, would exist, for example, if the following precedence relationships were given: Job 1 is a predecessor of job 2, job 2 is a predecessor of job 3, and job 3 is a predecessor of job 1.

[10]"Soft" predecessor relationships may be handled in one of several ways. One method is to redefine the jobs and identify those portions which are truly necessary before successors can begin. Equivalently, a series of jobs that previously were scheduled in strict sequence might be overlapped to some degree:

implies a known and fixed ordering of activities, in practice, some precedence relationships (and activities themselves) are contingent upon the outcome of previous activities. For example, if a test phase for a new missile guidance system is successfully completed, the next activity may be to manufacture the system. But if the test fails, the system may go back to the drawing boards. Neither PERT nor CPM allows for *conditional* activities and precedence orderings of this type. All activities in the network *must* be performed, and in the order shown.

We have already reported on the efforts of several researchers to modify the basic models by incorporating the possibility of alternative outcomes of certain events.[11] In the GERT model, for example, probabilistic event nodes facilitate the representation of projects in which there may be more than one outcome of a given event, and in which some activities may occur more than once (in a feedback loop) or perhaps never at all. Although the models have not been as widely used as PERT and CPM, they are interesting and worthy of review by the manager faced with projects that do not fit the traditional PERT/CPM mold.

3. *Activity times may be estimated—either as single-point estimates or as three-point PERT estimates—and are independent of each other.* Critical path calculations depend upon given time estimates for all activities. Such calculations, naturally, are only as good as the time estimates upon which they are based; some time estimates may be rather gross if the projects involve new technology or highly uncertain outcomes.[12] The problem is not unique with PERT and CPM, of course; most scheduling methods require time inputs. But PERT and CPM are especially sensitive to these estimates because so much of the output of the models depends upon activity times, for example

---

The second approach has been called *fast-track scheduling* (or *multitrack scheduling*, or *phased design and construction*) in the construction industry, where it has been employed as a means to shorten total project time. The same effect could be achieved, of course, with precedence networking by using start-to-start relationships in place of finish-to-start where overlapping is desired (see Chapter 8).

[11]See Chapter 8 and the references to probabilistic networks, particularly Pritsker's GERT model.

[12]Hence the term GIGO commonly cited by PERT users: "garbage in, garbage out."

various slack measures for activities and events, early and late start times for activities and events, identification of the critical path, and the expected mean and variance of activity and project durations.

Also important to PERT/CPM is the assumption of independence of activity durations. Both identification of the critical path and estimation of its length require that durations of critical path activities may be added directly. In practice, however, activity times are not always independent of each other. It is not uncommon for an activity to have to be accelerated as a result of delay in the completion of one or more of its predecessors. Also, as we noted in Chapter 7, resource limitations may cause time dependencies of activities sharing the same resources. Scheduling one activity may cause another otherwise independent activity to be stretched out (or postponed) because of a lack of sufficient common resources.

To some extent, both types of time dependencies may be accounted for in the planning–scheduling phase of project management. With the results of network calculations based on an initial set of time estimates, a manager may examine the path of critical activities and determine if one or more of these might be expedited to shorten the critical path (as discussed in Chapter 3). With these adjustments the network is recalculated, and the process is repeated until a satisfactory schedule is reached. Similarly, if resource conflicts are observed, activity start times may be adjusted or durations changed along the lines suggested in Chapter 7. In this way, time dependencies are anticipated and planned for before the project begins. Of course, when activities are not performed as planned, adjustments have to be made as the project proceeds. But, once again, this is not a problem unique to PERT and CPM. Indeed, one of the useful aspects of the models is their ability to *project* the effects of unanticipated delays as these are encountered, and thus to guide managers in making the most appropriate schedule adjustments.

For all projects, however, time estimates are still largely subjective in nature, and depend both on the vagaries of the humans who produce these estimates and on the environment within which they operate. Some people are inclined to be more cautious (or should we say pessimistic, conservative, or realistic?) than others and tend toward more generous time estimates. Especially might this be true if the estimator is also the one who performs or supervises the activity when it occurs and who would be held responsible for a time overrun. The system of rewards within which contractors operate might also influence their estimates for bidding purposes. Cost-plus contracts might well lead to underestimated times to enhance the probability of receiving the contract, while incentive-type contracts might lead to the opposite bias.

All these factors are of obvious concern to the manager who must make decisions based on activity time estimates supplied to him. King and others[13] have suggested that project managers establish a "supernetwork" in addition to the basic network and time estimates which are openly displayed for all to see. The supernetwork is the manager's private guide and incorporates *adjusted* time estimates based upon the manager's knowledge of past experience and the behavior of estimators. If reasonable adjustments can be made, the modified network would represent a more realistic and effective guide for planning and control purposes. Initial research efforts at developing adjustment models seem promising, but there is much to learn about estimating behavior before such models may be considered useful and reliable tools for project managers.

4. Already discussed in Chapter 4 are the assumptions of the probabilistic PERT model: *Activity duration is assumed to follow the beta distribution; the standard deviation of the distribution is assumed to be one-sixth of its range; the mean is approximated by* $\frac{1}{6}(t_o + 4t_m + t_p)$; *and the variance in length of a project is assumed to be equal to the sum of the variances of activites on the critical path.* The theoretical problems of these assumptions have been examined thoroughly by MacCrimmon and Ryavec.[14] They concluded that the PERT formulas could lead to absolute errors in t_e and S_t on the order of 30 and 15 per cent, respectively, in rather extreme cases, and about 5 to 10 per cent in more reasonable situations. Other formulas have been proposed which reduce the statistical errors. Moder and Rodgers[15], for example, suggest using the 5 and 95 percentile estimates for t_o and t_p rather than the 0 and 100 percentiles (the end points) of classical PERT. With such estimates ($t_{.05}$ and $t_{.95}$, say), activity standard deviation is best estimated by $S_t = (t_{.95} - t_{.05})/3.2$, which they show to have much less negative bias than the usual PERT estimate. Perry and Greig,[16] using the 5 and 95 percentile estimates along with the "most likely" estimate t_m, prove that the expected activity duration calculated from $t_e = (t_{.05} + .95t_m + t_{.95})/2.95$ has an esti-

[13]See W. R. King and T. A. Wilson, "Subjective Time Estimates in Critical Path Analysis," *Mgt. Science*, **13**, No. 5 (Jan. 1967), 307–320; and W. R. King, D. M. Wittevrongel, and K. D. Hezel "On the Analysis of Critical Path Time Estimating Behavior," *Mgt. Science*, **14**, No. 1 (Sept 1967), 79–84. One interesting result of their studies was that, for the projects studied, the accuracy of time estimates did not improve over a period of time, that is, ". . . no significant changes in accuracy were observed either for preactivity estimates (as the beginning of the activity approached) or for estimates of the remaining duration of an activity (as the proportion of the activity remaining became smaller)" (from page 80 of the second article). This would seem to somewhat simplify the development of adjustment models, as the time element might be ignored.

[14]K. R. MacCrimmon and C. A. Ryavec, "An Analytical study of the PERT Assumptions," *Opus. Res.*, **12**, No.1 (Jan.-Feb. 1964), 16–37.

[15]J. J. Moder and E. G. Rodgers, "Judgment Estimates of the Moments of PERT Type Distributions," *Mgt. Science*, **15**, No. 2 (Oct. 1968).

[16]C. Perry and I. D. Greig, "Estimating the Mean and Variance of Subjective Distributions in PERT and Decision Analysis," *Mgt. Science*, **21**, No. 12 (Aug. 1975).

mation error usually around 1 or 2 per cent and never more than 5 per cent for almost any reasonable distribution—considerably under the errors noted above for the conventional PERT t_e.

Although every reasonable effort should be made to reduce statistical errors by methods such as those above, we need to maintain some perspective of the problem. In practice, apparently, the errors due to faulty assumptions and not-so-rigorous statistics are small compared to the errors in time estimates themselves. PERT was developed for, and has generally been applied to, research and development types of projects with all their attendant uncertainties. Errors in time estimates of 10 or 20 per cent are common, and actual times that are twice the original estimates are not unknown. Given this setting, most statistical problems associated with the PERT assumptions become irrelevant in a practical sense. Time estimates are the major source of error by a large margin (which is not to say, of course, that statistical errors should be ignored if, indeed, they can be reduced).

Possible problems associated with the PERT procedure of picking a single critical path and calculating the expected length and variance of the project based on this path alone are solvable, as we noted in Chapter 4, if one is willing to apply the simulation techniques suggested by Van Slyke and Klingel (cited in that chapter). Admittedly, the approach may be impractical in terms of computer capacity for very large, detailed projects. But if applied to smaller or aggregated networks, simulation could supply the manager with very useful statistical information concerning the major phases of his project. And, if desired, the method could be used on individual subsystems of the project to yield similar information for more detailed activities in the network. The cost of such studies could well be small compared to costs stemming from serious errors of judgment as a result of PERT's biased estimates of completion time distributions.

Associated with the uncertainties of activity durations has been the difficulty of even obtaining three time estimates per activity, as required by the PERT model. Project managers who request such estimates have often been told, "It is difficult enough to give *one* time estimate for an activity we've never done before, let alone *three*. The extreme values are especially problematical. What do you mean, for example, by 'pessimistic time'? If *everything* went wrong, we might never finish the activity. How pessimistic are we supposed to be in coming up with a pessimistic time?" Answers to questions like these are difficult to give. Guidelines are necessarily vague. It is not surprising that engineers, project leaders, foremen, or others who supply the estimates often come up with rather arbitrary values, as evidenced by the large number of such estimates as 2–4–6 or 50–60–70. Such figures, of course, are of little value, and network calculations based on them tend to give an impression of greater precision than is justified.

As a result many, perhaps most, users of PERT have ceased using three time estimates per activity and require estimators to give only one figure—supposedly the best guess or expected duration for each activity. To be sure, there are other reasons for this practice. The sheer logistics of data handling for large projects with thousands of activities led to a desire for simplification in the model. And then, too, many managers untrained in statistical methods did not understand the meaning of expected value or "standard deviation of project length." There seemed to be little point in generating data that would be neither understood nor used.

In many ways this is regrettable. PERT represents an earnest, if not completely rigorous, attempt to cope with uncertainties in project management by a simple, rather straightforward application of statistical theory. Despite some minor conceptual difficulties, it represents a step forward in dealing with a particular complex problem, and is certainly an improvement over models that deal with the problem deterministically—as if there were no uncertainties involved. In recent years, especially, managers have shown an appreciation for, and increasing understanding of, quantitative tools of decision making. Even though a knowledge of statistical methods as a whole requires a good deal more training than most managers have had, still the basic notions used in PERT are not beyond their ability to comprehend. It is unfortunate that the statistical elements of the PERT model were apparently tossed out before they could be proved—or improved—in the practice of project management.

5. The CPM model also has its special assumptions. One is: *The duration of an activity is linearly (and inversely) related to the cost of resources applied to the activity.* The assumption is a plausible one, and even if the linearity part of it is inaccurate, extensions of the CPM model allow for other functional relationships to be handled, as we indicated in Chapter 5. The problem with the cost-optimizing CPM model is not conceptual, however, but practical. Cost–time trade-off relationships are difficult to obtain in many instances, either because data are not available or because estimates are too bothersome or expensive to compile. The problem is similar to that described above for PERT. When asked for trade-off curves for each activity, engineers or foremen (or whoever supplies the information) frequently give somewhat arbitrary estimates, usually because they do not *know* what the actual relationships are. As a result, most applications of CPM to date have been without the cost-optimizing feature. Thus CPM and PERT, in practical application, have tended to lose their distinctive features and to become essentially the same model.

Although it is true that there is much of value in CPM to the manager aside from the cost-optimizing feature, we can still argue, as we did for PERT, that deemphasis of its distinctive feature is unfortunate. Even if accurate cost–time data are not available, best guesses, unless completely arbitrary, are useful information and should help a project manager to arrive at better decisions on the average than no guesses at all. Most often those closely associated with a project or with particular activities will have some feeling for the nature of work that must be completed and can give at least a rough estimate of how much an activity could be expedited with certain additional resources. Even two points on a cost–time trade-off curve can supply the basic information needed for the optimizing calculations. Additional information, such as nonlinearities or discontinuities in the function, is useful, of course, and should help to yield more realistic results. Rough but reasonable estimates can be used to supply the project manager with a general idea of the cost–time trade-off relationships for the project as a whole —information that is certainly valuable to him. On the other hand, if only single time estimates are given for each activity, the manager has no way of knowing if a schedule exists with costs lower than the one based on normal activity times. While the difficulty of obtaining the required data should be recognized, so should the potential benefits of using that data in the CPM model.

Need for Top Management Support

In the survey of 400 top construction firms cited earlier, Davis explored the reasons for differences in attitudes toward network techniques and concluded that the chief factor in the success or failure of CPM and PERT was the measure of support they received from top management and from the people who used the system. A thoughtful comment by one of the executives in the survey seems to pinpoint a key to successful application of network methods (or, for that matter, of any management tool): CPM is a very effective tool in our company for getting the job completed on time in the most efficient manner. But it requires a lot of work and top management support. Most construction people we've seen who aren't benefiting from CPM don't really understand this—and they'll continue to find fault with its use.[17]

There are several reasons why top management support is crucial. First of all, CPM and PERT are relatively new approaches to project planning and scheduling and there is bound to be resistance in any organization to major changes in old and comfortable ways of doing things. If a CPM/PERT system is initiated by top management or with their clear approval, it has greater assurance of acceptance and success than if a lower-level agency attempts its installation. As we noted earlier, CPM and PERT techniques cut across organizational lines, not only in terms of activity identification, but also in managerial responsibilities. No one department is responsible for

[17]Davis, *op. cit.*, p. 49.

seeing that a project is kept on schedule. Activities on the critical path, or even a single critical activity, may involve several different departments. Thus there is vital need for top-level guidance and coordination. The system cannot be segmented and turned over to various parts of an organization for implementation. Nor can an existing agency of some department, like production control or operations research, be assigned responsibility for coordinating the whole system. A CPM/PERT group, if organized, should preferably report to top management rather than at some lower level within a subsection of the organization.

Top management consideration of expenses involved in a network is also needed. For a large project such expenses are not trivial; sometimes they run to several hundred thousand dollars. The Air Force has estimated that PERT costs have averaged between 0.1 and 0.5 per cent of total project costs, with the higher figure more typical of research and development programs. Expenditures of this magnitude merit top level analysis and control, especially during the start-up period of building a CPM/PERT capability.[18]

Also needed from top management is guidance concerning the standards of data collection and reporting. All agencies in an organization should supply data in a consistent from to facilitate processing, and output reports should be standardized in format and level of detail to facilitate their use not only within the firm but by customers or contractors. By their nature, CPM and PERT are capable of producing reams of various output reports, and there is a temptation to overuse this capability and to overstructure the project information and control system. In an extensive study of PERT/CPM users,[19] Murphy et. al. noted with concern an increasing emphasis within some corporations on the creation of ". . . elaborate and detailed reporting and control systems (which lead to) excessive delays, red tape, superficial reports, and inadequate information flows." They found some cases in which PERT/CPM techniques were overused and overdetailed, creating excessive control and tending to detract from project effectiveness. It is top management's responsibility to supply guidelines for the design of a project planning and control system, to ride herd on its development, to specify the kinds of information and report summaries that would be most useful at various levels in the organization, and to make sure that the system does not become an overelaborated, overcontrolling, and self-defeating report-writing mill.

[18]Expected returns from such expenditures should be of even greater magnitude, and equally deserving of management's attention and analysis. Savings from network techniques—in better coordination, reduced delays, more accurate forecasts, fewer crash programs, and so on—are less easily identified than direct dollar costs and are often apparent only from the manager's projectwide viewpoint.

[19]David C. Murphy, Bruce N. Baker, and Dalmar Fisher, "Determinants of Project Success," Management Institute, Boston College (1974). Prepared for the National Aeronautics and Space Administration.

Above all, to successfully use project network models, managers must recognize their strengths and limitations and not be overly reliant on the models for managerial purposes. As Murphy concludes in his study,

An implicit assumption in the (network) techniques is that they will be used by intelligent men, in a reasonable manner, for a reasonable purpose. All too often this is not the case. It's not that the techniques are not good, it's that they are not used properly, for the proper purpose, in the proper manner, with the proper precautions, and the proper understandings of their limitations and legitimate uses.

Managers, like anyone else, like to find simple solutions to complex problems. PERT and CPM are essentially simple tools, which explains in part the tendency of some project managers to overrely on them, with the inevitable disillusionment that follows. Fortunately, managers are becoming more discriminating and more sophisticated in their use of quantitative management techniques, including project network models.

Decision Making at Various Levels of Management

One of the attractive features of PERT and CPM is that they are useful tools for management at various levels within an organization and at different times within the life cycle of a project. Further, ways in which the models are used and the information derived from them are dependent upon both the particular stage of the project and the organization level of a firm. For example, for maximum benefits, network techniques should be applied during the early planning stages of a program. Many users of PERT and CPM have observed that primary benefits from using the techniques came in that stage, mostly because networking forced the integration of project planning. Planners are required to specify not only all the activities necessary to complete a project but also their technological dependencies. Network calculations then lay out clearly the implications of these interdependencies and aid the planners in finding problems that might otherwise be overlooked in large, complex projects. For example, one defense manufacturer found, as a result of using networks, that a prior plan required two missiles to be erected and launched on the same platform on the same day. And many examples of this nature may be cited.

At the planning level of project management, networks are usually constructed at an aggregate, nondetailed level, mainly to allow top management to study the feasibility and general outlines of a proposed project. When broad approval for a project has been given, these networks can be drawn with greater detail and more precision for purposes of scheduling and control.[20] Time scheduling of activities and resources follows from such networks, and they allow department or group managers to measure subsequent progress against plans and to take appropriate action when needed.

Further down the organizational ladder, the network graph is useful to foremen and others at the operating level in helping them to understand the sequencing of jobs and the necessity of pushing those that are critical. They can more readily see the relationships of activities for which they are responsible and predecessor or successor activities which fall in other areas or departments.

Conclusion

For large, nonrepetitive operations or projects, CPM, PERT, and related network techniques are useful aids, indeed, for project managers. As a summary to our exposition of CPM and PERT, we note some of their features and characteristics that make them powerful and flexible tools for decision making:

1. As discussed immediately above, they are useful at several stages of project management—from the early planning stages, when various alternative programs or procedures are being considered; to the scheduling phase, when time and resource schedules are laid out; and finally in the operational phase, when used as a control device to measure actual versus planned progress.

2. They are straightforward in concept and easily explainable to the layman with no background in network theory. Data calculations, although tedious for large projects, are not difficult. Basic critical path data may be hand-calculated with reasonable speed for projects with up to 500 or 600 activities. Computer programs are readily available for larger projects.

3. The network graph displays in a simple and direct way the complex interrelations of activities which comprise a project. Managers of various subdivisions of the project may quickly perceive from the graph how their portion affects, and is affected by, other parts of the project. It is an effective tool of communication.

[20]The size of a project may affect the usefulness of CPM/PERT for scheduling purposes. After trying unsuccessfully to use PERT for scheduling the Dyna-Soar Program, the Boeing Company concluded that the technique could not be used for detailed scheduling of large programs. Computer technology has advanced considerably since that time, however, and present computers and programs are capable of handling much larger networks. The logistics of handling networks with tens of thousands of activities still present problems of data gathering and information processing, however.

4. Network calculations pinpoint attention to the relatively small subset of activities in a projcet which are critical to its completion. Managerial action is thus focused on exceptional problems, contributing to more reliable planning and more effective control.

5. The network, from its original form in the planning stage through various modifications as the project progresses, forms a valuable documentation device for the project and its development. Further, it can be used to provide a simple and graphic means of displaying responsibility for various activities within a project.

6. CPM enables the manager to reasonably estimate total project costs for various completion dates. These various trade-off possibilities, along with other decision criteria, enable him to select an optimum or near-optimum schedule.

7. CPM and PERT are applicable to many types of projects—from aerospace development projects to large construction and maintenance jobs, from new product introduction programs to missible countdown procedures. Moreover, they may be applied at several levels within a given project, from a single department working on a subsystem to multiplant operations within a large corporation.

8. Combined with resource scheduling and allocation routines, critical path programs help managers to project resource requirements for any given schedule and to make decisions on how best to allocate scarce resources among competing activities.

9. As simulation tools, they enable the manager to project into the future the effects of planned or unanticipated changes and to take appropriate action when such projections indicate the need for it. For example, the manager can quickly study the effects of crash programs and can anticipate in advance potential resource bottlenecks that might result from shortening certain critical jobs.

When wisely used by a project manager who understands their strengths and limitations, CPM and PERT can be effective amplifiers of his managerial skills.

Bibliography

The literature on network planning and scheduling techniques has continued to expand rapidly. Not surprisingly, the following bibliography has also grown from that in the original edition. But we have been guided by the same purpose: to compile a representative rather than comprehensive list of references. As before, we have categorized the entries according to general content or purpose, in order to make the list somewhat more useful to the reader.

First listed are general sources, mostly of an expository nature, whose major purpose is to acquaint the reader with the basic network techniques. Most of these are articles which have appeared in a wide variety of journals and magazines. We have attempted to select explanatory rather than descriptive articles, omitting, for the most part, short news articles of from one to four pages from newspapers and trade journals. Following the articles is a list of books primarily devoted to project management and network analysis. Some of these are "how-to-do-it" books (for example, those by Miller, The Federal Electric Corporation, and Martino), while others contain material of theoretical interest (those by Battersby, Kelley, and Moder and Phillips).

The next major heading is "Theory: Analyses and Extensions of Network Scheduling Techniques," followed by a number of subtopics. Entries in this section are drawn mainly from technical journals and were typically authored by persons more interested in theoretical rather than practical aspects of the techniques. Their purpose has been to analyze critically rather than to describe the models and to suggest modifications or extensions of conceptual interest. The subheadings reflect what we feel have been some of the major areas of analysis and research. Not all articles fit neatly into our categories, however, and some of our placement decisions may seem a little arbitrary. Fulkerson's article, "A Network Flow Computation for Project Cost Curves," for example, obviously straddles our categories, "Cost-Time-Performance Relationships" and "The Network: Theory, Interpretations, *Complexity, Decomposition, Divisible Activities*," though we placed it in the former.

The final section, "Managerial and Operational Aspects," lists articles with a more practical slant—those describing particular applications of PERT and CPM or evaluating such applications from a managerial viewpoint. Operational rather than theoretical strengths and weaknesses of the models are stressed. The section closes with a list of bibliographical sources which will guide the interested reader to more articles—and perhaps more bibliographies!

A. General

Original descriptions

Kelley, James E., Jr., and Morgan R. Walker, "Critical Path Planning and Scheduling," *Proceedings of the Eastern Joint Computer Conference,* Boston, Mass. (1959), pp. 160–173.

PERT, Program Evaluation Research Task, Phase I Summary Report, Special Projects Office, Bureau of Ordinance, 7, Department of the Navy, Washington, D. C. (July, 1958), pp. 646–669.

Expository articles

Archibald, R. D., "PERT and the Role of the Computer," *Computers and Automation,* 12, 7 (July, 1963), pp. 26–30.

Battersby, A., "Network Flow Analysis," *The Accountant,* 147, 4574 (1962), pp. 184–186; and 147, 4575 (1962), pp. 228–231.

Boulanger, D. G., "Program Evaluation and Review Technique," *Advanced Management,* (July-August, 1961).

Burgher, P. H., "PERT and the Auditor," *The Accounting Review,* 39 (1964), pp. 103–120.

Fazar, W., "Program Evaluation and Review Technique," *American Statistician,* 13, 2 (April, 1959), p. 10.

———, "Navy's PERT System," *Federal Accountant,* 11 (December, 1961), pp. 123–136.

————, "The Origin of PERT," *The Controller*, (December, 1962), pp. 598–602, 618–621.

Fondahl, J. W., "A Non-Computer Approach to the Critical Path Method for the Construction Industry," Technical Report No. 9, Construction Institute, Stanford University (1962).

————, "Methods for Extending the Range of Non-Computer Critical Path Applications," Technical Report No. 47, Construction Institute, Stanford University (1964).

Glaser, L. B., and R. M. Young, "Critical-path Planning and Scheduling," *Chemical Engineering Progress*, 57,11 (November, 1961), pp. 60–65.

Levy, F. K., G. L. Thompson, and J. D. Wiest, "The ABC's of the Critical Path Method," *Harvard Business Review*, 41, 5 (September-October, 1963), pp. 98–108.

Malcolm, Donald G., John H. Roseboom, Charles E. Clark, and Willard Fazar, "Applications of a Technique for Research and Development Program Evaluation," *Opns. Res.*, 7, 5 (September-October, 1959), pp. 646–669.

————, "PERT: A Designed Management Information System," *Industrial Management*, 3 (June, 1961), pp. 23–32.

————, "PERT: An Automated R[esearch] and D[evelopment] Management Information System," *Proc. 12th Annual National American Institute of Industrial Engineers Conference* (1961), pp. 77–89.

Martino, R., "New Way to Analyze and Plan Operations and Projects Will Save You Time and Cash," *Oil/Gas World*, 3 (September, 1959), pp. 38–46.

Miller, R. W., "How to Plan and Control with PERT," *Harvard Business Review*, 40, 2 (March-April, 1962), pp. 93–104.

Neuwirth, S. I., and J. Zelnick, "Introduction to PERT," *J. Accountancy*, 115, 5 (May, 1963), pp. 83–87.

Norden, P., "On the Anatomy of Development Projects," *IRE Trans. Eng. Mgt.*, 7, 1 (March, 1960), pp. 34–42.

Paige, H. W., "How PERT-Cost Helps the General Manager," *Harvard Business Review*, 41, 6 (November-December, 1963), pp. 87–95.

Roper, Don E., "Critical Path Scheduling," *J. Indust. Eng.* XV, 2 (March-April, 1964).

Schoderbeck, P. P. and L. A. Digman, "Third Generation, PERT/LOB," *Harvard Business Review*, 45, 5 (September-October, 1967), pp. 100–110.

Sobczak, T. U., "A Look at Network Planning," *IRE Trans. Eng. Mgt.*, 9, 3 (September, 1962), pp. 113–116.

Usry, M. F., "PERT/Cost and the Capital Expenditure Control Program," *J. Accountancy*, 115, 3 (March, 1963), pp. 83–86.

Whitehouse, G. E., "Project Management Techniques," *Industrial Engineering*, 5, 3 (March, 1973), pp. 24–29.

Expository books

Archibald, R. D., and R. L. Villoria, *Network-Based Management Systems (PERT/CPM)*. New York: John Wiley and Sons, Inc., 1967.

Baboulene, B., *Critical Path Made Easy*. London: Duckworth Press, 1970.

Baker, Bruce N., and R. L. Eris, *An Introduction to PERT/CPM*. Homewood, Ill.: Richard D. Irwin, Inc., 1964.

Battersby, A., *Network Analysis for Planning and Scheduling*. London: Macmillan & Company, Ltd., 1967.

Burman, P. J., *Precedence Networks for Project Planning and Control*. London: McGraw-Hill Co., 1972.

Federal Electric Corporation, *A Programmed Introduction to PERT*. New York: John Wiley & Sons, Inc., 1963.

Hajek, Victor G., *Project Engineering*. New York: McGraw-Hill Book Company, 1965.

Hansen, B. J., *Practical PERT*. Washington, D. C.: American Aviation Publication, 1964.

Horowitz, J., *Critical Path Scheduling*. New York: The Ronald Press, 1967.

Kelley, J. E., Jr., *Critical Path Scheduling*, Vol. 11 of the SIAM Series in Applied Mathematics. New York: John Wiley & Sons, Inc. (forthcoming).

Learning Systems Italiana, Spa., *PERT, Program Evaluation and Review Technique*. Rome: Edizione Centro Europeo Coordinamento Istruzione Lavoro, 1965.

Levin, R. I. and C. A. Kirkpatrick, *Planning and Control with PERT/CPM*. New York: McGraw-Hill Book Co., 1966.

Lockyer, K. G., *An Introduction to Critical Path Analysis*. New York: Pitman Publishing Corp., 1964.

Martino, R. L., *Finding the Critical Path*. New York: American Management Association, 1964.

————, *Applied Operational Planning*. Project Management and Control Series, Vol. II, New York: American Management Association, 1964.

McLaren, K. G. and E. L. Buesnel, *Network Analysis in Project Management*. London: Cassell and Co., 1969.

Miller, R.W., *Schedule, Cost and Profit Control with PERT*. New York: McGraw-Hill Co., 1963.

Moder, J. J. and C. R. Phillips, *Project Management with CPM and PERT*. New York: Reinhold Publishing Corp., 1970.

Morris, L. N., *Critical Path Construction and Analysis*. Oxford: Pergamon Press, 1967.

Muth, J. F. and G. L. Thompson (eds.), *Industrial Scheduling*. Englewood Cliffs, N. J.: Prentice-Hall, Inc., 1963.

O'Brien, J. J., *CPM in Construction Management*. New York: McGraw-Hill Book Company, 1965.

Secretary of Defense and National Aeronautics and Space Administration, *DOD and NASA Guide, PERT Cost Systems Design*. Washington, D.C.: Government Printing Office, June 1962.

Shaffer, L. R., J. B. Ritter, and W. L. Meyer, *Critical Path Method*. New York: McGraw-Hill Book Company, 1965.

USAF PERT-TIME System Description Manual, Vol. 1, September, 1963.

Woodgate, H. S., *Planning by Network*. London: Business Publications Limited, 1964. Second Ed., Brandon Systems Press, 1968.

B. Theory: Analyses and Extensions of Network Scheduling Techniques

The network: theory, interpretations, complexity, decomposition, divisible activities

Bildson, R. A,. and J. R. Gillespie, "Critical Path Planning—PERT Integration," *Operations Research*, 10, 6 (November-December, 1962), pp. 909–912.

Charnes, A. and W.W. Cooper, "A Network Interpretation and a Directed Subdual Algorithm for Critical Path Scheduling," *J. Indust. Eng.*, XIII, 4 (July-August, 1962), pp. 213–219.

Corneil, D. G., C. C. Gotlieb, and Y. M. Lee, "Minimal Event-Node Network of Project Precedence Relations," *Commun. ACM*, 16, 5 (May, 1973), pp. 296–298.

Davis, Edward W., "Project Network Summary Measures, Constrained Resource Scheduling," *AIIE Trans.*, 7, 2 (June, 1975), pp. 132–142.

Elmaghraby, S. E., "The Theory of Networks and Management Science: Part II,"*Management Science* 17, 2 (October, 1970), pp. B54–B71.

Jewell, W. S., "Divisible Activities in Critical Path Analysis," *Opns. Res.*, 13, 5 (September-October, 1965), pp. 747–760.

————, "Divisible and Movable Activities in Critical Path Analysis," *Opns. Res.*, 19, 2 (March-April 1971), pp. 323–348.

Kaimann, Richard A., "Coefficient of Network Complexity," *Mgt. Science*, 21, 2 (October, 1974), pp. 172–177.

————, "Defining the Complexity of a Project Management Network," *Project Management Quarterly*, 6, 4 (December 1975), pp. 32–34.

MacCrimmon, K. R., and C. A. Ryavec, "Analytical Studies of the PERT Assumptions," *Operations Research*, 12, 1 (January-February, 1964), pp. 16–37.

Parikh, S. C. and W. S. Jewell, "Decomposition of Project Networks," *Mgt. Science*, 11, 3 (January, 1965), pp. 444–459; and "Note" by R. W. Blanning and A. G. Rao, 12, 1 (September, 1965), pp. 145–148.

Phillips, D. T. and P. A. Jensen, "The Out-of-Kilter Algorithm," *Industrial Engineering*, 6, 2 (February, 1974), pp. 36–44.

Statistical considerations and problems; activity time estimates

Abernathy, W. J., "Subjective Estimates and Scheduling Decisions," *Management Science*, 18, 2 (October, 1971), pp. 80–88.

Charnes, A., W. W. Cooper, and G. L. Thompson, "Critical Path Analysis Via Chance Constrained and Stochastic Programming," *Opns. Res.*, 12, 3 (May-June, 1964), pp. 460–470.

Clark, C. E., "The PERT Model for the Distribution of an Activity Time," *Opns. Res.*, 10, 3 (May-June, 1962), pp. 405–406.

Clingen, C. T., "A Modification of Fulkerson's PERT Algorithm," *Opns. Res.*, 12, 4 (July-August, 1964), pp. 629–632.

Donaldson, W. A., "The Estimation of the Mean and Variance of a 'PERT' Activity Time," *Opns. Res.*, 13, 3 (May-June, 1965), pp. 382–385 and "Note" by H. Coon, pp. 386–387.

Elmaghraby, S. E., "On the Expected Duration of PERT-Type Networks," *Mgt. Science*, 13, 5 (January 1967), pp. 299–306.

Fulkerson, D. R, "Expected Critical Path Lengths in PERT Networks," *Opns. Res.*, 10, 6 (November-December, 1962), pp. 808–817.

Grubbs, F. E., "Attempts to Validate Certain PERT Statistics or 'Picking on PERT'," *Opns. Res.*, 10, 6 (November-December, 1962), pp. 912–915.

———, "Corrigenda," *Opns. Res.*, 11, 1 (January-February, 1963), p. 156.

Hartley, H. O. and A. W. Wortham, "A Statistical Theory for PERT Critical Path Analysis, *Mgt. Science*, 12, 10 (June 1966), pp. 469–481.

Healy, T., "Activity Subdivision and PERT Probability Statements," *Opns. Res.*, 9, 3 (May-June, 1961), pp. 341–348. Comments by C. Clark, *Opns. Res.*, 9, 3 (May-June, 1961), p. 348. Comments by H. Millstein, *Opns. Res.*, 9, 3 (May-June, 1961), p. 349. Comments by J. Roseboom, *Opns. Res.*, 9, 6 (November-December, 1961), p. 909.

Hershauer, J. C. and G. Nabielsky, "Estimating Activity Times," *J. Systems Management*, 23, 9 (September, 1972), pp. 17–21.

Jewell, W. S., "Risk-Taking in Critical Path Analysis," *Mgt. Science*, 11, 3 (January, 1965), pp. 438–443.

Karns, Lanny A. and Lloyd A. Swanson, "The Effects of Activity Time Variance On Critical Path Planning," *Project Mgt. Quarterly*, 4, 4 (December 1973), pp. 17–25.

King, W. R. and P. A. Lukas, "An Experimental Analysis of Network Planning," *Mgt. Science*, 19, 12 (August 1973), pp. 1423–1432.

————, and T. A. Wilson, "Subjective Time Estimates in Critical Path Analysis," *Mgt. Science*, 13, 5 (January, 1967), pp. 307–320.

————, D. M. Wittevrongel, and K. D. Hezel, "On the Analysis of Critical Path Time Estimating Behavior," *Mgt. Science*, 14, 1 (September, 1967), pp. 79–84.

Klingel, A. R., Jr., "Bias in PERT Project Completion Time Calculations for a Real Network," *Mgt. Science*, 13, 4 (December, 1966), pp. B-194 to B-201.

Kotiah, T. C. T. and N. D. Wallace, "Another Look at the PERT Assumptions," *Mgt. Science*, 20, 1 (September 1973), pp. 44–49.

Lindsey, J. H. II, "An Estimate of Expected Critical-Path Lengths in PERT Networks," *Opns. Res.*, 20, 4 (July-August, 1972), pp. 800–812.

Lukaszewicz, J., "On the Estimation of Errors Introduced by Standard Assumptions Concerning the Distribution of Activity Duration in PERT Calculations," *Opns. Res.*, 13, 2 (March-April, 1965), pp. 326–327.

MacCrimmon, K. R. and C. A. Ryavec, "An Analytical Study of the PERT Assumptions," *Opns. Res.*, 12, 1 (January-February, 1964), pp. 16–37.

Moder, Joseph J. and E. G. Rodgers, "Judgment Estimates of the Moments of PERT Type Distributions," *Mgt. Science*, 15, 2 (October, 1968), pp. B76–B83.

Perry, C. and I. D. Greig, "Estimating the Mean and Variance of Subjective Distributions in PERT and Decision Analysis," *Mgt. Science*, 21, 12 (August 1975), pp. 1477–1480.

Ringer, Larry J., "Numerical Operators for Statistical PERT Critical Path Analysis, *Mgt. Science*, 16, 2 (October 1969), pp. B136–B143.

————, "A Statistical Theory for PERT in Which Completion Times of Activities are Inter-dependent," *Mgt. Science*, 17, 11 (July 1971), pp. 717–723.

Van Slyke, R. M., "Monte Carlo Methods and the PERT Problem," *Opns. Res.*, 11, 5 (September-October, 1963), pp. 839–860.

Welsh, D. J. A., "Errors Introduced by a PERT Assumption," *Opns. Res.*, 13, 1 (January-February, 1965), pp. 141–143.

Cost-time-performance relationships

Berman, E. B., "Resource Allocation in a PERT Network under Continuous Activity Time-Cost Functions," *Mgt. Science*, 10, 4 (July, 1964), pp. 734–745.

Bildson, R. A. and J. R. Gillespie, "Critical Path Planning—PERT Integration," *Opns. Res.*, 10, 6 (November-December, 1962), pp. 909–912.

Burgess, A. R. and J. B. Killebrew, "Variation in Activity Level on a Cyclical Arrow Diagram," *J. Indust. Eng.*, XIII (March-April, 1962), pp. 76–83.

Clark, C., "The Optimum Allocation of Resources Among the Activities of a Network," *J. Indust. Eng.*, XII (January-February, 1961), pp. 11–17.

Elmaghraby, S. E., "The Determination of Optimum Activity Duration In Project Scheduling," *J. Indus. Eng.*, 19, 1 (January 1968), pp. 48–51.

—— and S. Arisawa, "Optimal Time-cost Trade-offs in GERT Networks," *Mgt. Science*, 18, 11 (July 1972), pp. 589–599.

Falk, James E. and Joel L. Horowitz, "Critical Path Problems with Concave Cost-time Curves," *Mgt. Science*, 19, 4 (December, 1974), pp. 446–455.

Fulkerson, D., "A Network Flow Computation for Project Cost Curves," *Mgt. Science*, 7, 2 (January, 1961), pp. 167–178.

———, "Scheduling in Project Networks," The RAND Corporation, RM-4137-PR (June, 1964).

Goyal, S. K., "A Note on a Simple CPM Time-Cost Tradeoff Algorithm," *Mgt. Science*, 21, 6 (February, 1975), pp. 718–722.

Kelley, J., "Critical-Path Planning and Scheduling: Mathematical Basis," *Opns. Res.*, 9, 3 (May-June, 1961), pp. 296–320.

Lamberson, L. R. and R. R. Hocking, "Optimum Time Compression in Project Scheduling," *Mgt. Science*, 16, 10 (June 1970), pp. B597–B606.

Malcolm, D. G., "Reliability Maturity Index (RMI)—An Extension of PERT into Reliability Management," *J. Indust. Eng.*, XIV (January-February, 1963), pp. 3-12.

McGee, A. A. and M. D. Markarian, "Optimum Allocation of Research/Engineering Manpower within a Multi-Project Organizational Structure," *IRE Trans. Eng. Mgt.*, 9 (1962), pp. 104–108.

Meyer, W. L. and L. R. Shaffer, "Extensions of the Critical Path Method Through the Application of Integer Programming," Department of Civil Engineering, University of Illinois (July, 1963).

Paige, H. W., "How PERT/Cost Helps the General Manager," *Harvard Business Review*, 41, 6 (November-December, 1963), 87–95.

Siemens, Nicola, "A Simple CPM Time-Cost Trade-off Algorithm", *Mgt. Science*, 17, 6 (February, 1971), pp. B354–B363.

Precedence, probabilistic, and decision networks

Clayton, E. R., and L. J. Moore, "PERT vs. GERT," *Journal of Systems Management*, 22, 2 (February, 1972), pp. 11–19.

Crandall, Keith C., "Project Planning with Precedence Lead/Lag Factors," *Project Mgt. Quarterly*, 4, 3 (September, 1973), pp. 18–27.

Crowston. W. and G. L. Thompson, "Decision CPM: A Method for Simultaneous Planning, Scheduling and Control of Projects," *Opns. Res.*, 15, 3 (May-June, 1967), pp. 407–426.

Eisner, H., "A Generalized Network Approach to the Planning and Scheduling of a Research Project," *Opns. Res.*, 10, 1 (January-February, 1962), pp. 115–125.

Elmaghraby, S. E., "An Algebra for the Analysis of Generalized Activity Networks," *Mgt. Science*, 10, 3 (April, 1964), pp. 494–514.

Freeman, R., "A Generalized Network Approach to Project Activity Sequencing," *IRE Trans. Eng. Mgt.*, 7, 3 (September 1960), pp. 103–107.

Fulkerson, D. R., "Expected Critical Path Lengths in PERT Networks," *Operations Research*, 10, 6 (November-December, 1962), pp. 808–817.

Pritsker, A. A. B., "GERT Networks," *The Production Engineer* 48, 10 (October, 1968), pp. 499 -506.

———, "Precedence GERT," RM 71–14, Industrial Engineering, Purdue University (December, 1971).

———, "The Status of GERT," in H. Lombaers (Ed.), *Project Planning by Network Analysis*. Amsterdam-London: North-Holland Publishing Co., 1970, pp. 170–177.

——— and W. W. Rapp, "GERT: Graphical Evaluation and Review Technique, Part I: Fundamentals," *J. Indust. Eng.*, XVII, 5 (May, 1966). Part II: "Probabilistic and Industrial Engineering Applications," XVII, 6 (June, 1966).

Van Slyke, R. M., "Monte Carlo Methods and the PERT Problem," *Operations Research*, 11, 5 (September-October, 1963), pp. 839-860.

Whitehouse, G. E., "Extensions, New Developments and Applications of GERT," Ph.D. thesis, Arizona State University (August, 1965).

Whitehouse, G. I., and A. A. B. Pritsker, "GERT: Part III—Further Statistical Results: Counters, Renewal Times, and Correlations," *AIIE Transactions*, 1, 1 (March 1969), pp. 45–50.

Limited resource scheduling methods

Blair, R. J., "Critical Path Resources Simulation and Scheduling," *IRE Trans. Eng. Mgt.* 10, 3 (September, 1963), pp. 100–103.

Carruthers, J. A., and A. Battersby, "Advances in Critical Path Methods," *Operational Research Quarterly*, 17, 4 (December, 1966), pp. 359–380.

Davis, Edward W., "An Exact Algorithm for the Multiple Constrained-Resource Project Scheduling Problem," Ph.D. thesis, Yale University (May 1968).

———, "Project Network Summary Measures Constrained-Resource Scheduling," *AIIE Transactions*, 7, 2 (June, 1975), pp. 132–142.

———, "Project Scheduling under Resource Constraints—Historical Review and Categorization of Procedures," *AIIE Transactions*, 5, 4 (December, 1973).

————, "Resource Allocation in Project Network Models—A Survey," *J. Indust. Eng.*, XVII, 4 (April, 1966), pp. 177–188.

———— and George E. Heidorn, "An Algorithm for Optimal Project Scheduling under Multiple Resource Constraints," *Mgt. Science*, 17, 12 (August, 1971), pp. B803–B816.

———— and James H. Patterson, "A Comparison of Heuristic and Optimum Solutions in Resource Constrained Project Scheduling," *Mgt. Science*, 21, 8 (April 1975), pp. 944–955.

————, "Resource-based Project Scheduling: Which Rules Perform Best?", *Project Mgt. Quarterly*, 6, 4 (December, 1975), pp. 25–31.

De Witte, L., "Manpower Leveling of PERT Networks," *Data Processing for Science/Engineering*, 2, 2 (1964), p. 29.

Dike, S. H., "Project Scheduling with Resource Constraints," *IEEE Transactions on Engineering Management*, EM-11, 4 (1964).

Fendley, L. G., "Toward the Development of a Complete Multiproject Scheduling System," *J. Indus. Eng.*, 19, 10 (October, 1968), pp. 505–515.

Gorenstein, S., "An Algorithm for Project (Job) Sequencing with Resource Constraints," *Opns. Res.*, 20, 4 (July-August, 1972), p. 835.

Hastings, N. A. J., "On Resource Allocation in Networks," *Operational Research Quarterly*, 23, 2 (June, 1972).

Herroelen, Willy S., "Resource-Constrained Project Scheduling—The State of the Art," *Oper. Res. Quarterly*, 23, 3 (September, 1972), pp. 261–275.

Hooper, P. C., "Resource Allocation and Levelling," Proceedings of the Third CPA Symposium, Operational Research Society, London (1965).

Johnson, T. J. R., "An Algorithm for the Resource-Constrained Project Scheduling Problem," Ph.D. thesis, School of Management, Massachusetts Institute of Technology (August, 1967).

Kelley, James E., Jr., "The Critical Path Method: Resources Planning and Scheduling," Chapter 21 in *Industrial Scheduling*, eds. J. F. Math and G. L. Thompson. Englewood Cliffs, N. J.: Prentice-Hall, Inc., 1963.

Knight, R. M., "Resource Allocation and Multi-Project Scheduling in a Research and Development Environment," Ph. D. Thesis, School of Management, Massachusetts Institute of Technology (June, 1966).

Lambourn, S., "Resource Allocation and Multiproject Scheduling (RAMPS), A New Tool in Planning and Control," *Computer Journal*, 5, 4 (January, 1963), pp. 300–304.

Levy, F. K., G. L. Thompson, and J. D. Wiest, "Multi-Ship, Multi-Shop, Workload Smoothing Program," *Naval Research Logistics Quarterly*, 9, 1 (March, 1962), pp. 37–44.

Martino, R. L., *Resource Allocation and Scheduling*, Project Management and Control Series, Vol. III. New York: American Management Association, 1965.

Mason, A. T., and Colin L. Moodie, "A Branch and Bound Algorithm for Minimizing Cost in Project Scheduling," *Mgt. Science*, 18, 4 (December, 1971), pp. B158–B173.

Mize, J. H., "A Heuristic Scheduling Model for Multi-Project Organizations," Ph. D. thesis, Purdue University, August, 1964.

Moshman, J., J. Johnson and Madalyn Larsen, "RAMPS: A Technique for Resource Allocation and Multiproject Scheduling," Proceedings of the 1963 Spring Joint Computer Conference.

Pascoe, T. L., "An Experimental Comparison of Heuristic Methods for Allocating Resources," Ph. D. thesis, Engineering Dept., Cambridge University, 1965.

Patterson, J. H., "Alternate Methods of Project Scheduling with Limited Resources," *Naval Res. Logistics Quarterly*, 20, 4 (December, 1973), pp. 767–784.

Patterson, James H. and Walter D. Huber, "A Horizon-varying, Zero-one Approach to Project Scheduling," *Mgt. Science*, 20, 6 (February, 1974), pp. 990–998.

Patton, George T., "Optimal Scheduling of Resource Constrained Projects," Ph. D. thesis, Stanford University (August, 1968).

Petrovic, R., "Optimality of Resource Allocation in Project Planning," *Opns. Res.*, 16, 3 (May-June, 1968), pp. 559–568.

Pritsker, A. A. B., Lawrence J. Watters and Philip M. Wolfe, "Multi-Project Scheduling with Limited Resources: A Zero-One Programming Approach," *Mgt. Science*, 16, 1 (September, 1969), pp. 93–108.

Schrage, Linus, "Solving Resource-Constrained Network Problems by Implicit Enumeration—Nonpreemptive Case," *Opns. Res.*, 18, 2 (March-April, 1970), pp. 263–278.

———, "Solving Resource-Constrained Network Problems by Implicit Enumeration," *Opns. Res.*, 20, 3 (May-June, 1972), pp. 668–677.

Sunaga, Teruo, "A Method of the Optimal Scheduling for a Project with Resource Restrictions," *J. Operations Research Society of Japan*, (March, 1970).

Verhines, D. R., "Optimum Scheduling of Limited Resources," *Chemical Engineering Progress*, 54, 3 (March, 1963).

Wiest, J. D., "The Scheduling of Large Projects with Limited Resources," Ph. D. thesis, Carnegie Institute of Technology, 1963.

———, "Some Properties of Schedules for Large Projects with Limited Resources," *Opns. Res.*, 12, 3 (May-June, 1964), pp. 395–418.

———, "A Heuristic Model for Scheduling Large Projects with Limited Resources," *Mgt. Science,* 13, 6 (February, 1967), pp. B359–B377.

———, "A Heuristic Scheduling and Resource Allocation Model for Evaluating Alternative Weapon System Programs," RAND Corp. Report No. RM-5769-PR, (August, 1969).

Woodgate, H. S., "Planning Networks and Resource Allocation," *Datamation*, 14, 1 (January, 1968), pp. 36–43.

Man-computer interactive project scheduling

Gustafson, Carl E., "Computer Assisted Interactive Resource Scheduling System," NASA Spec. Publ. 326 (1973) for Symp. on Significant Accomplishments in Technology, pp. 143–146.

Leahy, John P., "A Man-Machine CPM System for Decision Making in the Construction Industry, Construction Research Series No. 9, Department of Civil Engineering, University of Illinois, Urbana (1967).

Miller, Robert W., "How to Plan and Control with PERT," *Harvard Business Review*, 40, 2 (March-April, 1962), pp. 93–104.

Paulson, Boyd C., "Man-Computer Concepts for Project Management," The Construction Institute, Technical Report No. 148, Stanford University (August, 1971).

Paulson, Boyd C., "Man-Computer Concepts for Planning and Scheduling," *J. Constr. Div.* ASCE, 98, CO2 (September, 1972), pp. 275–286.

Wiest, Jerome D., "Computer Graphics for Project Management," *Proceedings of the Seminar-Symposium*, Project Management Institute, St. Louis, 1970.

Computational considerations; computer programming

Brindley, Reynaud C., "Some Problems in Using Computers in Project Planning by Network Analysis," *Project Planning by Network Analysis*, Proc. 2nd Int. Congress, Amsterdam (October, 1969), pp. 330–339.

Goldberg, C. R., "An Algorithm for the Sequential Solution of Schedule Networks," *Opns. Res.*, 12, 3 (May-June, 1964), pp. 499–502.

Jenett, Eric, "Availability of CPM Programs," *Project Management Quarterly*, 1, 2 (July 1970), pp. 10–13.

Kahn, A. B., "Skeletal Structure of PERT and CPA Computer Programs," *Communic. of ACM*, 6, 8 (August, 1963), pp. 473–479.

———, "Topological Sorting of Large Network," *Communic. of ACM*, 5, 11 (November, 1962), pp. 558–562.

Lass, S. E., "PERT Time Calculations Without Topological Ordering," *Communic. of ACM*, 8, 3 (March, 1965), pp. 172–174.

Lasser, D., "Topological Ordering of a List of Randomly-Numbered Elements of a Network," *Communic. of ACM*, 4, 4 (April, 1961), pp. 167–168.

Matozzi, M., "How to do CPM Scheduling Without an Arrow Diagram," *Eng. News-Record*, 170 (May 9, 1963), pp. 30–31.

Matye, T. and G. Rich, "PERT/PEP Planning and Programming on [Electric Accounting Machines]," *J. Machine Accounting*, 12 (July, 1961), pp. 6–13.

Moder, J. J., "How to Do CPM Scheduling Without a Computer," *Eng. News-Record*, 170 (March 14, 1963), pp. 30–36.

Montalbano, M., "High Speed Calculation of the Critical Paths of Large Networks," *IBM Systems Journal*, 6, 3 (1967), pp. 163–191.

Phillips, C. R., "Fifteen Key Features of Computer Programs for CPM and PERT," *J. Indust. Eng.*, XV (January-February, 1964), pp. 14–20.

Prostick, J., "Loop Tracing in PEP/PERT Networks," (abstract), *Communic. of ACM*, 4, 7 (July, 1961), p. 304.

Solomon, N. B., "Automated Methods in PERT Processing," *Computers and Automation*, 14, 1 (January, 1965), pp. 18-22.

C. Managerial and Operational Aspects

Applications; system design

Ameiss, Albert P., and Warren A. Thompson, "PERT for Monthly Financial Closing," *Management Advisor*, 7, 1 (January-February, 1974), pp. 30–37.

Antill, J. M. and R. W. Woodhead, *Critical Path Methods in Construction Practice*, 2nd Ed. New York: Wiley Interscience, 1970.

Bellas, C. J., and A. C. Samli, "Improving New Product Planning with GERT Simulation," *California Management Review*, 15, 4 (Summer, 1973), pp. 14–21.

Benson, B., *Critical Path Methods in Building Construction*, Englewood Cliffs, N. J.: Prentice-Hall, Inc., 1970.

Benson, L. A. and R. F. Sewall, "Dynamic Crashing Keeps Projects Moving," *Computer Decisions*, 4, 2 (February, 1972), pp. 14–18.

Berkwitt, George J., "Management Rediscovers CPM," *Dun's Review*, 97, 5 (May, 1971), pp. 57–59.

Beutel, M. L., "Computer Estimates Costs, Saves Time, Money," *Eng. News-Record*, 170 (February 28, 1963), pp. 26–30.

Borklund, William, "Why Polaris Is Winning Its Race Against Time," *Armed Forces Journal*, (December, 1958).

Brennan, J., ed., *Applications of Critical Path Techniques*. London: The English Universities Press, 1968.

Bruegman, D. C., "Using Critical Path at a University," *J. Systems Management*, 24, 1 (January, 1973), pp. 22–25.

Butler, R. A., "Systems Design with PERT," *J. Data Management*, 3, 6 (June, 1965), pp. 22–25.

Calica, A. B., "Project Network Algorithms for Use in Shop Loading and Sequencing," *IBM Systems Journal*, 4, 3 (1965).

Carr, R. I., and W. L. Meyer, "Planning Construction of Repetitive Building," *J. Constr. Div.* ASCE, 100, 3 (September, 1974), pp. 403–412.

Childs, M. R., "Does PERT Work for Small Projects?" *Data Processing,* 4 (1962), pp. 32–35.

Collins, F. T., *Practical Applications and Examples of CPM and PERT.* Eugene, Ore.: Know-How Publications, 1964.

Croft, F. M., "Putting a Price Tag on PERT Activities," *J. Indus. Eng.,* (March, 1970), pp. 19–21.

Davis, E. W., "CPM Use in the Top 400 Construction Firms," *J. of the Construction Division,* ASCE, 100, CO1 (March, 1974), pp. 39–49.

DeCoster, Don T., "PERT/Cost, The Challenge," *Management Services,* (May-June, 1964).

Fazar, W., "Advanced Management Systems for Advanced Weapon Systems," *Conf. Proc. 5th Nat. Convn. on Military Electronics* (1961), 32–43.

———, "Progress Reporting in the Special Projects Office," *Navy Mgmt. Review,* 4 (April, 1959), pp. 9–15.

Fohdahl, J., "Can Contractors Own Personnel Apply CPM Without a Computer?", *The Constructor,* (November, 1961), pp. 56–60.

Gisser, P., "Taking the Chances Out of Product Introductions," *Industrial Marketing,* 50, 5 (May, 1965), pp. 86–91.

Glasser, L. and R. Young, "Critical Path Planning, and Scheduling: Application to Engineering and Construction," *Chem. Eng. Progress,* 57 (November, 1961), pp. 60–65.

Gorham, W., "An Application of a Network Flow Model to Personnel Planning," *IRE Trans. Eng. Mgt.,* 10, 3 (September, 1963), pp. 113–123.

Hallbauer, R. M., "CPM Facilitates Project Planning and Cost Control," *Cost and Management,* 39, 4 (April, 1965), pp. 167–175.

Hamdy, M., "Problems Encountered in the Application of Network Analysis Techniques in Project Implementation in Developing Countries and Pertinent Recommendations," *Project Planning by Network Analysis,* Proc. 2nd Int. Congress, Amsterdam (October, 1969), pp. 54–70.

Hanson, R. S., "Moving the Hospital," *Industrial Engineering,* 4, 11 (November, 1972), pp. 32–38.

Hardesty, T. Frank, "Poor Mans PERT," *Supervisory Management,* 17, 3 (March, 1972), pp. 15–18.

Kaimann, Richard A., "PERT—Review Possibilities," *J. OS Systems-Management,* 23, 6 (June, 1972), pp. 39–41.

Kaimann, R. and W. Lundberg, "How to PERT for HUD," *Government Data Systems,* 2, 3 (May/June, 1972), pp. 21–22; 31, 38.

Kelley, J., "Critical-Path Planning and Scheduling: Case Histories," (abstract), *Opns. Res.,* 8 (1960), B109.

Kurzeja, J. T., "When Work Schedules Need Computers," *Hydrocarbon Process. and Petrol. Refiner,* 44, 4 (April, 1965), pp. 171–174.

Lock, D., *Project Management.* London: Gower Press, 1969.

Lombaers, H. J. M., *Project Planning by Network Analysis.* Amsterdam:

North-Holland Publishing Co. (1969). A collection of fifty-five papers presented at the 2nd International Congress on Network Analysis in Holland, October, 1969.

Malcolm, D. G., "Reliability Maturity Index—An Extension of PERT Into Reliability Management," *J. of Industrial Engineering*, XIV, 1 (January-February, 1963).

"Management Rediscovers CPM," *Dun's Review*, May, 1971.

Mark, E. J., "How Critical Path Method Controls Piping Installation Progress," *Heating, Piping, and Air Condit.*, 9 (September, 1963), pp. 121–126.

Michaels, A. J., "Establishing a PERT System," *Management Accounting*, 53, 4 (October, 1971), pp. 26–32.

Moder, Joseph J., R. A. Clark, and R. S. Gomez, "Applications of a GERT Simulator to a Repetitive Hardware Development Type Project," *AIIE Transactions*, 3, 4 (December, 1971).

Moses, S., "CPM Opens a Pool Ten Months Early; West Hartford, Conn.," *American City*, 79, 12 (December, 1964), pp. 78–79.

Naaman, Antoine E., "Networking Methods for Project Planning and Control," *J. Constr. Div.* ASCE, 100, 3 (September, 1974), pp. 357–372.

Newnham, D. E., *et al.*, "A PERT Control Center for Management of Major Ballistic Missile Modifications Programs," *J. Indus. Eng.* XVI, 4 (July-August, 1965).

Odom, Ralph G. and E. Blystone, "A Case Study of CPM in a Manufacturing Situation," *J. Indust. Eng.*, XV, 6 (November-December, 1964).

Page, J. C., and J. F. Stolle, "Space Age Technique to Launch New Products," *Sales Management*, 93 (July 3, 1964), pp. 23–27.

Paulson, Boyd C. Jr., "Project Planning and Scheduling: Unified Approach," *J. Constr. Div.*, ASCE, 99, CO1 (July, 1973), pp. 45–58.

Pearce, W. G., "Canadian National Railways' Experience with Critical Path Methods," *Applications of Critical Path Techniques*. London: The English Universities Press Ltd., 1968.

Pearlman, J., "Engineering Program Planning and Control Through the Use of PERT," *IRE Trans. Eng. Mgt.*, 7, 12 (December, 1960), pp. 125–134.

Peart, A. T., *Design of Project Management Systems and Records*. London: Gower Press, 1971.

Peer, Shlomo, "Network Analysis and Construction Planning," *J. Constr. Div.* ASCE, 100, 3 (September, 1974), pp. 203–210.

Peterson, R. J., "CPM Helps an A-E Consultant Schedule Manpower," *Eng. News-Record*, 170 (June 27, 1963), pp. 22–25.

Phelps, H. S., "What Your Key People Should Know about PERT," *Management Review*, 51, 10 (October, 1962), pp. 44–51.

Reed, R., "Plan Handling Systems with Network Diagrams," *Industrial Engineering* (January, 1969), pp. 27–31.

Reeves, E., "Critical Path Speeds Refinery Revamp," *Canadian Chem. Processing*, 44 (October, 1960), pp. 74–76.

Robinson, I. G., "4 Simple Steps—The PERT Approach to Plant Layout," *Factory* (September, 1965), pp. 104–105.

Rozmus, F., "Critical Path Method—Application to Electrical Industry," *Electr. Eng.* (Melb) 51; three parts: April, 1974, pp. 20–24; May, 1974, pp. 23–26; June, 1974, pp. 25–28.

Sadow, R. W., "How PERT Was Used in Managing the X-20 (Dyna-Soar) Program," *IEEE Transactions on Engineering Management*, FM-11, 4 (December, 1964), pp. 138–154.

Saitow, Arnold R., "CSPC: Reporting Project Progress to the Top," *Harvard Business Review*, 46, 1 (January-February, 1969).

Samli, A. C., and C. Gellas, "The Use of GERT in the Planning and Control of Marketing Research," *Journal of Marketing Research*, 8, 8 (August, 1971), pp. 335–339.

Schroeder, Richard G., "GERT: An Aid to Managerial Accounting," *Managerial Planning*, 22, 4 (January-February, 1974), pp. 35–37.

Schwinger, Pinhas, "The Uses of PERT in a Developing Economy," *Managerial Planning*, 20, 3 (November-December, 1972), pp. 26–33.

Self, R. Harvey, "Project Management in Construction: Fast-Tracking," *Project Mgt. Quarterly*, 5, 2 and 3, (1974), pp. 22–24.

Smith, A., "Control of a Large Programming Project Using Network Based Cost Analysis," *Project Planning by Network Analysis*, Proc. 2nd Int. Congress, Amsterdam (October, 1969), pp. 381–386.

Strenski, James B., "PERT Charting Public Relations," *Public Relations Jrnl*, 31, 2 (February, 1975), pp. 22–23.

Thornley, G., Ed., *Critical Path Analysis in Practice*, New York: Barnes and Noble, Inc., 1968. A collection of 18 papers on project control, written by practitioners and representing a "state-of-the-art" survey of uses of critical path analysis in the United Kingdom, 1960-1966.

Vaughen, B. W. and G. V. Kedrowsky, "SYNCOM Event Schedule Networks—The Best of PERT," *IRE Trans. Eng. Mgt.*, 10, 3 (September, 1963), pp. 104–112.

Wahl, R. P., Jr., "PERT Controls Budget Preparation," *Public Management*, 46 (February, 1964), pp. 29–33.

Walton, H., "Experience of Application of Critical Path Method to Plant Construction," *Operations Research Quarterly*, 15, 1 (March, 1964), pp. 9–16.

Whitehouse, G. E., *Systems Analysis and Design Using Network Techniques*, Englewood Cliffs, N. J.: Prentice-Hall, Inc., 1973.

Wong, Y., "Critical Path Analysis for New Product Planning," *J. Marketing*, 28, 4 (October, 1964), pp. 53–59.

Woodgate, H. S., The Planning Network as a Basis for Resource Allocation, Cost Planning and Project Profitability Assessment," *Proceedings, Fall Joint Computer Conference* (1967).

Evaluations and critiques

Avots, I., "The Management Side of PERT," *California Mgt. Review*, 4, 2 (Winter, 1962), pp. 16–27.

———, "Why Does Project Management Fail?", *California Mgt. Review*, 12, 1 (Fall, 1969).

Barmby, J. G., "The Applicability of PERT as a Management Tool," *IRE Trans. Eng. Mgt.*, 9, 3 (September, 1962), pp. 130–131.

Bennigson, Lawrence, "The Strategy of Running Temporary Projects," *Innovation*, 24 (September, 1971), pp. 32–41.

Boulanger, D., "Program Evaluation and Review Technique (PERT): A Case Study Application With Analysis," *Advanced Mgt.*, 26 (July-August, 1961), pp. 7–12.

Boverie, R. T., "The Practicalities of PERT," *IRE Trans. Eng. Mgt.*, 10, 1 (March, 1963), pp. 3–5.

Crowston, W., and G. L. Thompson, "Decision CPM: A Method for Simultaneous Planning Scheduling and Control of Projects," Operations Research, 15, 3 (May, 1967), 407–426.

Dooley, A., "Interpretations of PERT," *Harvard Business Review*, 42, 6 (November-December, 1964), pp. 160–168.

Eyring, Henry B., "Evaluation of Planning Models for Research and Development Projects," D. B. A. thesis, Harvard University, June, 1963.

———, "Some Sources of Uncertainty in Engineering Design Projects," The RAND Corporation, RM-4503 (September, 1965).

Frambes, R., "Next Big Step for PERT," *Aerospace Mgt.*, 4 (October, 1961), pp. 77–78.

Fry, B. L., "SCANS—System Description and Comparison with PERT," *IRE Trans. Eng. Mgt.*, 9, 3 (September, 1962), pp. 122–129.

Geddes, P., "How Good is PERT?" *Aerospace Mgt.*, 4 (September, 1961), pp. 41–43.

Gleason, W. J., Jr., and J. J. Ranieri, "First Five Years of the Critical-Path Method," *J. Construct. Division, Proc. Am. Soc. Civil Engin,*. 90, C01, Proceeding Paper No. 3892 (March, 1964), pp. 27–36.

Greenlaw, Paul S., "Management Science and Personnel Management," *Personnel Journal*, 52, 11 (November, 1973), pp. 946–953.

Grubbs, F. E., "Attempts to Validate Certain PERT Statistics or Picking on PERT," *Operations Research*, 10, 6 (November- December, 1962), pp. 912–915.

Hawthorne, R., "PERT and PEP: Useful Tools or Timewasters?" *Space/Aeronautics*, 36 (August, 1961), pp. 56–58.

Hill, L. S., "Communications, Semantics, and Information Systems," *J. Indust. Eng.*, XVI, 2 (March-April, 1965), pp. 131–135.

———, "Perspective: Some Possible Pitfalls in the Design and Use of PERT Networking," *J. Acad. Management*, 8, 2 (June, 1965), pp. 139–145.

———, "Management Planning and Control of Research and Technology Projects," The RAND Corporation, RM-4921-PR (June, 1966).

———, "Some Cost Accounting Problems in PERT Cost," *J. Indust. Eng.*, XVII, 2 (February, 1966), pp. 87–91.

Holtz, J. N., "An Analysis of Major Scheduling Techniques in the Defense Systems Environment," RAND Corp. Report No. RM-4697-PR (October, 1966).

Jenett, Eric, "Experience With and Evaluation of Critical Path Methods," *Chemical Engineering*, 73, 3 (February 10, 1969), pp. 96–106.

Krakowski, Martin, "PERT and Parkinson's Law," *Interfaces*, 5, 1 (November, 1974), pp. 35–40.

Mintz, S. and J. Taul, "Towards a Simplified Decision Making Criteria for PERT-Type Systems: The [Value Index Predictor] Index" (abstract), *Opns. Res.*, 9 (1961), B130.

Murphy, D. C., B. N. Baker, and D. Fisher, "Determinants of Project Success," School of Management, Boston College (1974); prepared for National Aeronautics and Space Administration.

Murray, J. E., "Consideration of PERT Assumptions," *IRE Trans. Eng. Mgt.* 10, 3 (September, 1963), pp. 94–99.

Paige, Millard W., "How PERT-COST Helps the General Manager," *Harvard Business Review*, 41, 6 (November-December, 1963), pp. 87–95.

Pocock, J. W., "PERT an as Analytical Aid for Program Planning—Its Payoff and Problems," *Opns. Res.*, 10, 6 (November-December, 1962), pp. 893–903.

Roman, D. D., "The PERT Systems: An Appraisal of Program Evaluation Review Technique," *J. Acad. Management*, 5, 1 (April, 1962), pp. 57–65.

Schoderbeck, P. P., "A Study of the Applications of PERT," *J. Acad. Management*, 8, 3 (September, 1965), pp. 199–210.

———, P. P., "Overcoming Resistance to PERT," *Business Topics*, 14, 2 (Spring, 1966), pp. 50–56.

———, "PERT/Cost: Its Values and Limitations," *Management Services*, 3, 1 (January-February, 1966), pp. 29–34.

Simon, C., "Standardization: The Key to Making PERT Work," (abstract), *Opns. Res.*, 9 (1961), B140.

Stewart, John M., "Making Project Management Work," *Business Horizons*, 8, 3 (Fall, 1965), pp. 54–68.

Thompson. R. E., "PERT—Tool for R and D Project Decision Making," *IRE Trans. Eng. Mgt.*, 9, 3 (September, 1962), pp. 116–121.

Thompson, V., "PERT: Pro and Con About This Technique," *Data Processing*, 3 (October, 1961), pp. 40–44.

Vazsonyi, Andrew, "L'Histoire de Grandeur et de la Décadence de la Méthode PERT," *Mgt. Science*, 16, 8 (April, 1970), pp. B449–B455.

Welsh, D. J A., "Errors Introduced by a PERT Assumption," *Operations Research*, 13, 1 (January-February, 1965), pp. 141–143.

Bibliographies on network techniques

Bigelow, C. G., "Bibliography on Project Planning and Control by Network Analysis: 1959–1961," *Opns. Res.*, 10, 5 (September-October, 1962), pp. 729–732.

Davis, Edward W., ed., *Project Management: Techniques, Applications and Managerial Issues.* Publication No. 3 in the monograph series, Production Planning and Control Division, American Institute of Industrial Engineers, Inc., 1976.

Dooley, A. R., "Interpretations of PERT." *Harvard Business Review*, 42, 2 (March-April, 1964), pp. 160–162.

Fry, B. L., "Selected References on PERT and Related Topics," *IRE Trans. Eng. Mgt.*, 10, 3 (September, 1963), pp. 150–151.

Lerda-Olberg, S., "Bibliography on Network-Based Project Planning and Control Techniques: 1962–1965," *Opns. Res.*, 14, 5 (September-October, 1966), pp. 925–931.

U. S. Air Force, PERT Orientation Center, *Bibliography: PERT and Other Management Systems and Techniques*, Washington, D. C., June, 1963.

Exercises

To test your understanding of the concepts presented throughout this book, you may wish to work some or all of the problems printed below. They have been grouped according to chapter, with three or more problems drawn from Chapters 2, 3, 4, 5, and 7. Answers to the problems immediately follow this section.

Chapter 2

1. As a college student, your project is College Education, with graduation marking the end event.

   Draw a network representing the project. Include necessary courses with their precedence relationships (where course requirements are relevant), special examinations, projects, research, thesis writing, and so forth, required for the degree.

2. You are preparing to leave on an extended business or vacation trip.

   Set down in network form the jobs that must be done before you go.

3. You are planning to undertake one of the following projects: Remodel Kitchen, Add New Bedroom, or Move to New House.

   Draw the network of activities that you anticipate would be required.

4. The Wonder Widget is manufactured in six steps, labeled A through F. Because of its size and complexity, the Wonder Widget is produced one

at a time. Mr. Green, the production control manager, thinks that network scheduling techniques might be useful in planning future production. He asked the foreman in charge of Widgets about the six steps required in production and the order in which the steps took palce. He recorded the following information:

> *A* is the first step and precedes *B* and *C*
> *C* precedes *D* and *E*
> *B* follows *D* and precedes *E*
> *F* follows *E*
> *D* is a successor of *F*

a. Draw an activity-on-node diagram for Mr. Green. Do you see any problems with the resulting network?
b. On checking with the foreman again, Mr. Green corrects his last note to read, "*D* is a *predecessor* of *F*." Draw a new AON diagram for the revised project. Simplify the diagram by removing any redundant predecessor arrows.
c. After pondering the network and rechecking with the foreman, Mr. Green concluded that *B* was really a predecessor of *D* rather than vice versa. Draw a revised AON network incorporating this new change.
d. Draw an arrow-diagram representation of the network in part c. How many dummy activities did you use in your network?

5. A work project consists of 12 activities, labeled *A* to *L*. When the work manager was asked to specify the order in which jobs had to be done, he answered as follows: Job *A* comes first and precedes *B*, *C*, and *D*. Both *B* and *C* must be done before *E* starts, and *C* and *D* must precede *F*, but *G* and *H* can start as soon as *D* is completed. Job *I* succeeds *D*, *E*, *F*, and *G*; and jobs *J* and *K* can start when *G*, *H*, and *I* are all completed. Job *L* comes after *J* and *K*.
a. Using a precedence matrix as described in the Appendix to Chapter 2, assist the works manager to eliminate redundancy in his list of precedence relationships. List the *immediate* predecessors for each job.
b. Draw an AON diagram, using as few precedence arrows as necessary to show correct precedence relationships.
c. Draw an arrow-diagram representation of the same project, using as few dummy jobs as necessary to show correct precedence relationships and unique node identification of activities.

6. Presentation of a stage play involves a number of activities which precede the opening night "curtain-up" call. Thus such a presentation may be regarded as a project and analyzed by network techniques. Listed below in random fashion is a collection of activities that must be completed

before the first public performance. Others might be included, but assume that the list is essentially complete.

a. Draw a network for the project, indicating the precedence relationships which you feel are necessary. Quite likely there is no unique ordering of activities upon which all persons would agree; differences of opinion will exist. But decide on that ordering which seems most logical to you. Either an arrow or an activity-on-node diagram may be used.

Activities for Project on Stage

Design of scenery
Tryouts for actors
Selection of stage manager
Publicity—posters, mail advertisements
Selection of director
Initial rehearsals
Arrangements for hall
Selection of play
Selection of business manager
Final dress rehearsal
Constructing and painting scenery
Sale of tickets
Opening night performance
Publicity—newspaper story
Advanced rehearsals (with props)
Making or renting costumes
Obtaining props (set furnishings, items used by actors, etc.)
Erection of scenery

7. Phil Moody, project manager, was interest in developing a network for a 20-job project under his responsibility. He labeled the jobs A to J and for each job listed all its predecessors as best as he could determine:

Job	Immediate Predecessors	Job	Immediate Predecessors
A	—	K	G
B	—	L	F, G, K
C	—	M	H, I
D	A, B	N	H, I, J, L
E	A, B, C	O	J, K, L
F	A, B, C	P	M, N
G	C	Q	O, P
H	D, E	R	J, K, L, O
I	D, E, F	S	N, Q, R
J	F, G	T	O, S

Moody suspected that some predecessors he listed were redundant (implied by other predecessors), and he was not sure how to develop a network from his list of jobs and predecessors.

a. Which (if any) predecessors shown could be eliminated without affecting the network logic?

b. Assist Mr. Moody by drawing an arrow diagram for this project, using as few dummy jobs as possible.

c. Draw an AON diagram from the original project list (including redundant predecessors), and determine to your satisfaction that the redundant predecessor arrows could be removed without changing the network logic.

Chapter 3

1. A small maintenance project consists of the following 10 jobs, whose precedence relationships are identified by their node numbers:

Job	Alternative (Initial Node, Final Node)	Estimated Duration (days)
a	(1, 2)	2
b	(2, 3)	3
c	(2, 4)	5
d	(3, 5)	4
e	(3, 6)	1
f	(4, 6)	6
g	(4, 7)	2
h	(5, 8)	8
i	(6, 8)	7
j	(7, 8)	4

a. Draw an arrow diagram representing the project.

b. Calculate early and late start and finish times for each job.

c. How much slack does job (3, 5) have? Job (4, 6)? Job (7, 8)?

d. Which jobs are critical?

e. If job (2, 3) were to take six days instead of three, how would the project finish date be affected?

f. Do any jobs have free slack? If so, which ones and how much?

2. Each weekday morning Mr. Brady and his wife and children complete a set of activities which are necessary to start Mr. Brady on his way to the office. An analysis of the project Getting Mr. Brady to Work reveals the following list of relevant activities, their durations, and their predecessor relationships:

Activity	Description	Duration (minutes)	Immediate Predecessors
Performed by Mr. Brady			
1	Alarm goes off	0	—
2	Get up, shut off alarm, and turn up heat	2	1
3	Return to bed until house warms up	10	2
4	Get up, shave, and shower	22	3
5	Get dressed	10	4, 13
6	Eat breakfast	20	5, 15
7	Brush teeth	3	6, 20
8	Put on tie and coat	4	7
9	Pick up briefcase, hat, and lunch	2	8, 17
10	Kiss wife goodbye	1	9, 18
11	Walk to bus stop	4	10
12	Catch bus	0	11
Performed by Mrs. Brady			
13	Get up, iron shirt for husband	16	3
14	Wake up children	3	13
15	Prepare breakfast	20	14
16	Eat breakfast	20	15
17	Pack lunch	10	16
18	Comb hair, put on lipstick	3	7, 17
Performed by children			
19	Get up	5	14
20	Use bathroom	37	4, 19

a. Draw an arrow diagram complete with dummy activities for the project Getting Mr. Brady to Work.

b. For each activity calculate early start and finish times, late start and finish times, total slack, and free slack, based on minimum completion time.

c. Mark the critical path and state its length.

d. How early must the alarm go off if Mr. Brady is to catch a 7:30 A.M. bus?

e. If Mr. Brady wanted to obtain more sleep by having the alarm go off later and still catch his bus, would it help for him to:

   1. Take less time showering?
   2. Eat faster?
   3. Have his shirts done at the laundry?
   4. Buy his lunch at work?
   5. Wait until he got to work to brush his teeth?
   6. Complain about the time his children take in the bathroom?
   7. Run for the bus?

  f. Is there any time when Mr. Brady could read the newspaper for a few minutes without delaying his arrival at the bus stop—without setting the alarm for an earlier time? Similarly, is there any time when Mrs. Brady could read the newspaper?

  g. Draw an activity-on-node diagram for the project and mark the critical path. How does the number of precedence-relation arrows of this graph compare with the number of activity arrows, including those for dummy activities, of the diagram for (a)?

3. The major jobs to be completed in building a particular type of house are as follows, with their necessary predecessors and estimated duration times:

Job	Description	Immediate Predecessors	Duration (days)
1	Start: obtain building permit	—	1
2	Clear lot and grade for slab	1	2
3	Place concrete forms, reinforcement rods, sewer lines	2	2
4	Pour slab	3	1
5	Erect wooden frame, including roof	4	5
6	Fasten exterior sheathing	5	2
7	Install rough plumbing	5	3
8	Install rough wiring	5	2
9	Insulate outside walls	6, 7, 8, 27	1
10	Sheetrock and plaster inside walls	9	3
11	Do rough carpentry, including window and door frames	5	5
12	Do finish carpentry: cabinets, trim moldings, paneling	10, 11	10
13	Sand, stain, and varnish wood paneling and cabinets	12	3
14	Lay Formica counter surfaces in kitchen	13	1
15	Install tubs and shower basins	10, 11	1
16	Lay bathroom tile	15	2
17	Install remaining plumbing fixtures	14, 16	1
18	Sand and paint interior walls and trim	17	5
19	Lay flooring (wood and vinyl)	18	2
20	Wallpaper selected surfaces	18	2
21	Install kitchen appliances	18	1
22	Install hot water heater	7	1
23	Install heating and cooling ducts	5	3
24	Install furnace and air conditioner	8, 23	1
25	Complete exterior trim	6	3
26	Lay brickwork (exterior walls plus inside fireplace)	25	5

Job	Description	Immediate Predecessors	Duration (days)
27	Shingle roof	5	2
28	Attach gutters and downspouts	26, 27	2
29	Paint exterior trim	28	2
30	Place insulation in attic	10, 26	1
31	Grade, lay forms for walks and driveways	26	1
32	Pour walks and driveway	31	1
33	Finish grading	32, 37	1
34	Landscape yard	33	2
35	Install electrical outlets, switches, lighting fixtures	20, 21, 22, 24	1
36	Final hookup of electrical system	35	1
37	Clean up interior and exterior, including yard	19, 29, 30, 35	1
38	Lay carpeting	37	2
39	Attach cabinet fixtures	18	1
40	Finish : close out house	34, 36, 38, 39	1

a. Draw an activity-on-node diagram, labeling each node.

b. Draw an arrow diagram. Include necessary dummy jobs. Which representation do you prefer? Why?

c. Using either diagram, calculate early start and finish times, late start and finish times, and total slack for each job.

d. Identify the critical path. What is the minimum length of the project?

e. Which jobs may be delayed without delaying the early start time of any other job? State the amount of free slack of these jobs.

f. If you were the contractor, how would you reduce the construction time by 3 days? By 10 days?

g. Do you foresee any problems of workmen interfering with each other's activities? (Assume an early start schedule.)

Chapter 4

1. If the critical path of a project is 20 months long with a standard deviation of 4 months, what is the probability that the project will be completed within:

   a. 20 months?

   b. 18 months?

   c. 24 months?

2. PERT calculations yield a project length of 60 weeks, with variance of 9. Within how many weeks would you expect the project to be completed with probability .95? (That is, what is the project length that you would

expect to be exceeded only 5 per cent of the time if the project were repeated many times in an identical manner?)

3. A father notes that when his teenage daughter uses the telephone, she takes no less than 5 minutes for a call and sometimes as much as 1 hour. Fifteen-minute calls are more frequent than calls of any other duration. If daughter's phone call were an activity in a PERT project:
    a. What would be the phone call's expected duration?
    b. What estimate would you give for its variance?
    c. In scheduling the project, how much time would you allocate for the phone call?

4. A small project is composed of seven activities whose time estimates are listed in the following table. Activities are identified by their beginning (*i*) and ending (*j*) node numbers.

Activity		Estimated Duration (weeks)		
i	*j*	Optimistic	Most Likely	Pessimistic
1	2	1	1	7
1	3	1	4	7
1	4	2	2	8
2	5	1	1	1
3	5	2	5	14
4	6	2	5	8
5	6	3	6	15

a. Draw the project network and identify all paths through it.
b. Find the expected duration and variance for each activity.
c. Calculate early and late occurrence times for each node. What is the expected project length?
d. Calculate total slack for each activity.

5. Answer the following questions, based on your results from Problem 4:
    a. What is the variance and standard deviation of the project length?
    b. What is the probability that the project will be completed
        (1) At least 3 weeks earlier than expected?
        (2) No more than 3 weeks later than expected?
    c. If the project due date is 18 weeks, what is the probability of *not* meeting the.due date?
    d. What due date has about a 90 per cent chance of being met?

6. The following table lists the jobs of a network along with their time estimates:

| Job | | Duration (days) | | |
i	j	Optimistic	Most Likely	Pessimistic
1	2	3	6	15
1	6	2	5	14
2	3	6	12	30
2	4	2	5	8
3	5	5	11	17
4	5	3	6	15
6	7	3	9	27
5	8	1	4	7
7	8	4	19	28

a. Draw the project network.

b. Calculate the length and variance of the critical path.

c. What is the approximate probability that jobs on the critical path will be completed by the due date of 41 days?

d. What is the approximate probability that jobs on the next most critical path will be completed by the due date?

e. What is your estimate of the probability that the entire project will be completed by the due date? Explain.

7. Refer to the arrow diagram developed in the Mr. Brady problem (Chapter 3, number 2).

   a. Perform *event-oriented* calculations, labeling each event node with its early and late occurrence times.

   b. From the event occurrence times, develop the following data for each activity: ES, EF, LS, LF, TS, FS.

8. (For those familiar with computer programming.) Using the activity expected times developed for the project in Problem 4 of this chapter, follow through the computer program at the end of Chapter 4 and hand-calculate the network data as a computer would do it. Does the program appear to be event-oriented or activity-oriented (or both)?

9. Given the following project network, with arrows as activities and the numbers by each arrow representing job durations in days:

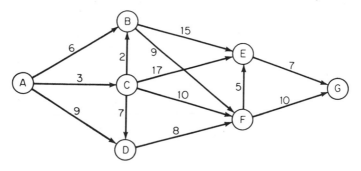

a. Calculate the early and late *node* occurence times, and label each node in the network with its "*ET, LT*." Identify the critical path.

b. For each activity, find its early start, early finish, late start, late finish, total slack, and free slack, all based on the node occurence times calculated in a).

c. Suppose that the variance of jobs along the critical path is 100. What is the probability that the project will be completed within 26 days? What important assumptions underlie this calculation?

Chapter 5

1. In the following project, activities are represented by arrows, and the number above each activity is both its identification and its normal duration (in days).

a. Determine the minimum length of the project, and identify the activities on the critical path.

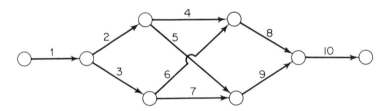

b. Assume that each activity, except 1 and 2, can be shortened up to 2 days at a cost per day equal to the activity number. For example, activity 6 normally takes 6 days but could be shortened to 5 days for a cost of $6, or to 4 days for an additional cost of $6. Determine the least-cost 26-day schedule. Show the new durations of activities which have been shortened and the total cost of shortening the schedule.

2. A small maintenance project consists of the jobs in the following table. With each job is listed its normal time and a minimum, or crash, time (in days). The cost in dollars per day of crashing each job is also given.

Job		Normal Duration (days)	Minimum (Crash) Duration (days)	Cost of Crashing ($/day)
i	*j*			
1	2	9	6	20
1	3	8	5	25
1	4	15	10	30
2	4	5	3	10
3	4	10	6	15
4	5	2	1	40

a. What is the normal project length and the minimum project length?
b. Determine the minimum crashing costs of schedules ranging from normal length down to, and including, the minimum length schedule. That is, if L = length of normal schedule, find the costs of schedules which are $L, L - 1, L - 2$, and so on, days long.
c. Overhead costs total $60 per day. What is the optimum length schedule in terms of both crashing and overhead costs? List the scheduled durations of each job for your solution.

3. A maintenance foreman has given the following estimate of times and costs for jobs in a motor-overhaul project:

Job		Predecessors	Normal Duration (hours)	Cost ($)	Minimum Duration	Cost ($)
A	Remove and disassemble motor	—	8	80	6	100
B	Clean and paint frame	A	7	40	4	94
C	Rewind armature	A	12	100	5	184
D	Replace bearings	A	9	70	5	102
E	Assemble and install motor	B, C, D	6	50	6	50

Assume that the jobs can be done at either normal or fast pace, but not at any pace in between. Plot the relationship between project completion time and minimum total project cost.

4. In Problem 3 assume that a linear cost relationship exists between job duration and job cost, and that a job may be scheduled not only at the normal and minimum durations but at any integer duration in between. With overhead costs at $25 per hour, plot the cost–time relationship.

5. Refer to the arrow diagram of Problem 9 of Chapter 4. Assume that each job in the network can be shortened 1 day at a cost equal to its normal duration. Show which jobs would be shortened to optimally obtain schedules that are 1, 2, 3, and 4 days shorter than the one calculated in Problem 9. Calculate the total crashing costs in each case.

Chapter 7

1. The project represented in the following table is to be scheduled within a resource limit of 12 men. All the men are capable of working on any of the jobs. If not asigned on a particular day, a man is idle but still draws pay. Each job must be assigned a crew of men corresponding to one of the three possible crew sizes listed in the table. No in-between assignments may be made, and the crew size must remain fixed for a job until it is finished. Job duration equals man-days divided by crew size for any

crew size chosen. Schedule the project so as to minimize idle man-days over its active span.

Job		Resource	Crew Size (*men*)		
i	*j*	Requirement (*man-days*)	Minimum	Normal	Maximum
1	2	32	2	4	8
1	3	48	4	6	8
2	3	40	4	5	8
2	4	12	2	3	4
4	5	30	3	5	6
3	5	54	3	6	9

2. Schedule the project described in the following table, subject to a resource constraint of 16 men. Any man can work on any job. For a given job, any crew size within, and including, the stated limits may be selected, if it is evenly divisible into the resource requirement. (For example, job *b* requires 24 man-days. A crew size of 2, 3, 4, or 6 is permissible, but 5 is not.) Crew sizes do not affect efficiency. Schedule length is to be minimized within resource and technological constraints.

Job	Immediate Predecessors	Resource Requirements (*man-days*)	Range of Permissible Crew Sizes	
			Minimum	Maximum
a	—	45	5	15
b	*a*	24	2	6
c	*a*	96	4	12
d	*a*	50	2	10
e	*d*	30	2	10
f	*c*	60	4	12
g	*c*	12	1	6
h	*b*	35	5	7
i	*f*	42	3	14
j	*g, e*	24	3	8
k	*i, j*	20	2	10

3. The situation is the same as in Problem 2 with two changes:
   a. Any crew size between the stated limits is permissible (except for fractional assignments). Once a job is started, its crew size must remain fixed; but if the man-days are not evenly divisible by the selected crew size, the last day scheduled for the job will require fewer than the full crew of men.
   b. The overall resource limit may be established anywhere between the limits of 10 and 22 men. Once established, this limit must remain constant over the project schedule period. You are to schedule the project with the least number of idle man-days.

Answers

Chapter 2

4. a.

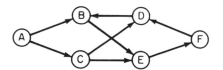

Network contains a cycle (*B* precedes *E*, *E* precedes *F*, *F* precedes
D, and *D* precedes *B*) and redundant arrows (see below).

b.

Note that several redundant predecessor relationships are removed.
("*A* precedes *B*" is implied by "*A* precedes *C*, *C* precedes *D*, and *D*
precedes *B*." Likewise, "*C* precedes *E*" and "*D* precedes *F*" are
redundant.)

c.

d.

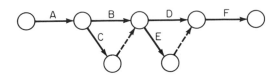

For purposes of network logic, dummy activities are not required in this problem; but two dummies (dashed arrows) have been added to preserve the unique identification of activities by their nodes.

5. a.

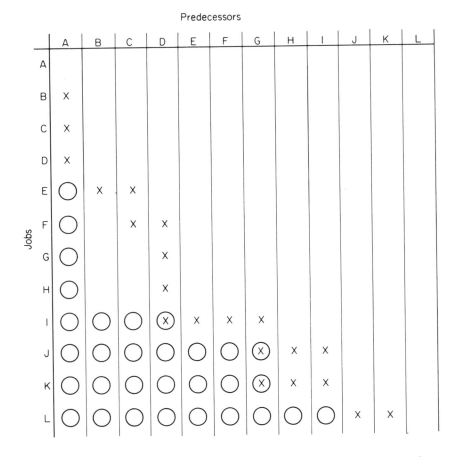

Predecessors

Jobs	A	B	C	D	E	F	G	H	I	J	K	L
A												
B	X											
C	X											
D	X											
E	(O)	X	X									
F	(O)		X	X								
G	(O)			X								
H	(O)			X								
I	(O)	(O)	(O)	(X)	X	X	X					
J	(O)	(O)	(O)	(O)	(O)	(O)	(X)	X	X			
K	(O)	(O)	(O)	(O)	(O)	(O)	(X)	X	X			
L	(O)	(O)	(O)	(O)	(O)	(O)	(O)	(O)	(O)	X	X	

The circled X's represent redundant immediate predecessors and can be removed. The remaining X's are the immediate predecessors for each job listed.

b.

c.

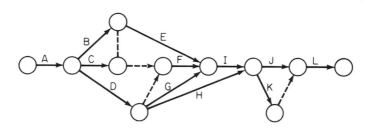

6. a. One possible ordering of activities is shown in the AON diagram:

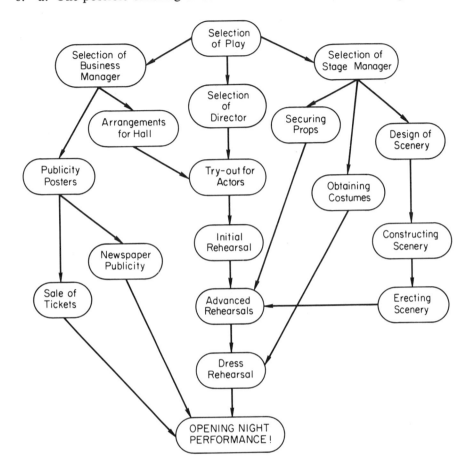

7. a.

Jobs	Redundant Predecessors
L	G
O	K
R	J, K, L
S	N
T	O

b.

c.

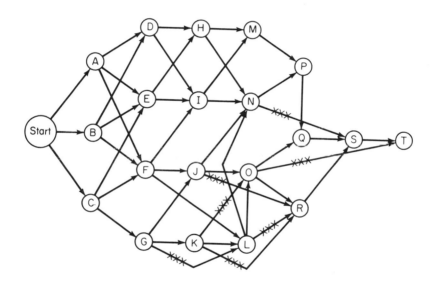

(Redundant arrows are marked with triple X's.)

Chapter 3

1. a. and b.

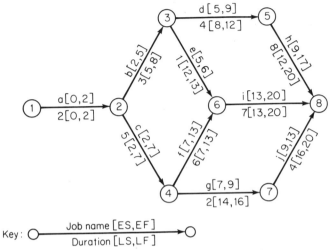

Key: Job name [ES,EF] / Duration [LS,LF]

c. 3 days; 0 days; 7 days.
d. (1, 2), (2, 4), (4, 6), (6, 8).
e. Unaffected. Job (2, 3) would become critical, however.
f. Job (3, 6)—7 days; Job (7, 8)—7 days; Job (5, 8)—3 days.

2. a.

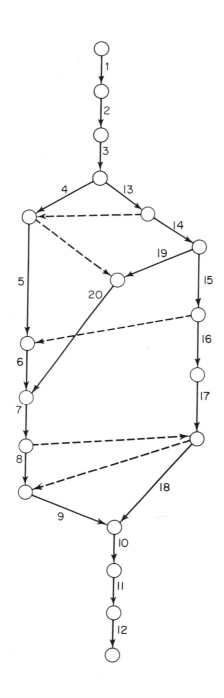

b.

Activity	ES	EF	LS	LF	TS	FS
1	0	0	0	0	0	0
2	0	2	0	2	0	0
3	2	12	2	12	0	0
4	12	34	16	38	4	0
5	34	44	45	55	11	7
6	51	71	55	75	4	2
7	73	76	75	78	2	0
8	76	80	78	82	2	1
9	81	83	82	84	1	1
10	84	85	84	85	0	0
11	85	89	85	89	0	0
12	89	89	89	89	0	0
13	12	28	12	28	0	0
14	28	31	28	31	0	0
15	31	51	31	51	0	0
16	51	71	51	71	0	0
17	71	81	71	81	0	0
18	81	84	81	84	0	0
19	31	36	33	38	2	0
20	36	73	38	75	2	0

c. 1–2–3–13–14–15–16–17–18–10–11–12; 89 minutes.

d. 6:01 A.M.

e. 1. No   4. Yes   7. Yes
   2. No   5. No
   3. Yes   6. No

f. Yes, Mr. Brady has slack in activities 4 through 9. The best time to read the newspaper uninterruptedly would be before or after he gets dressed, when he has 11 minutes slack time. Mrs. Brady must wait until her husband leaves before she can relax with the newspaper.

g.

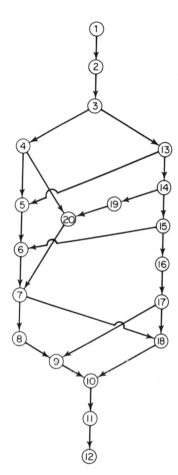

There are 26 arrows in this **AON** diagram, compared to 25 arrows (including dummies) in the arrow diagram of part a.

3. a.

b.

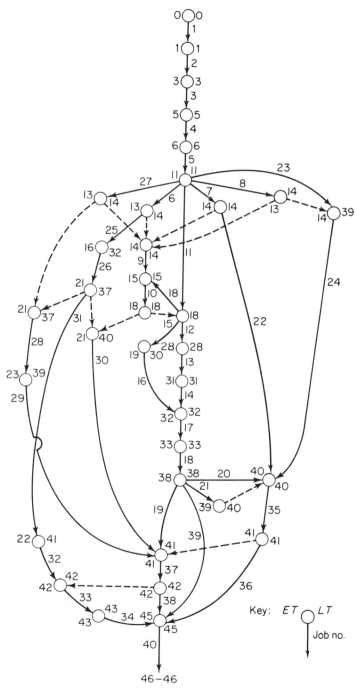

Key: *ET* ◯ *LT*

Job no.

c.

Job	ES	EF	LS	LF	TS	FS
1	0	1	0	1	0	0
2	1	3	1	3	0	0
3	3	5	3	5	0	0
4	5	6	5	6	0	0
5	6	11	6	11	0	0
6	11	13	12	14	1	0
7	11	14	11	14	0	0
8	11	13	12	14	1	1
9	14	15	14	15	0	0
10	15	18	15	18	0	0
11	11	16	13	18	2	2
12	18	28	18	28	0	0
13	28	31	28	31	0	0
14	31	32	31	32	0	0
15	18	19	29	30	11	0
16	19	21	30	32	11	11
17	32	33	32	33	0	0
18	33	38	33	38	0	0
19	38	40	39	41	1	1
20	38	40	38	40	0	0
21	38	39	39	40	1	1
22	14	15	39	40	25	25
23	11	14	36	39	25	0
24	14	15	39	40	25	25
25	13	16	29	32	16	0
26	16	21	32	37	16	0
27	11	13	12	14	1	1
28	21	23	37	39	16	0
29	23	25	39	41	16	16
30	21	22	40	41	19	19
31	21	22	40	41	19	0
32	22	23	41	42	19	19
33	42	43	42	43	0	0
34	43	45	43	45	0	0
35	40	41	40	41	0	0
36	41	42	44	45	3	3
37	41	42	41	42	0	0
38	42	44	43	45	1	1
39	38	39	44	45	6	6
40	45	46	45	46	0	0

d. 1–2–3–4–5–7–9–10–12–13–14–17–18–20–35–37–33–34–40.
 Minimum length = 46 days.

e. See table in part c.

f. There are several alternatives, but the following would probably be among the first to be investigated:
 1. Use more carpenters (shorten job 12).
 2. Use more finishers and painters (shorten jobs 13 and 18).
 3. Use more plasterers (shorten job 10).
 4. Use more framers (shorten job 5).
 Shortening the schedule 10 days might require simultaneous reduction on parallel critical paths or reconsideration of the technological constraints shown (some may not be "firm" constraints).

g. If all jobs were started at their early times, the men engaged in activities 6, 7, 8, 23, and 27 (which all begin on day 11) might well get in each other's way. Other examples may also be found.

Chapter 4

1. a. .50 (that is, a 50 per cent chance)
   b. .31
   c. .84

2. About 65 weeks.

3. a. $20\frac{5}{6}$ minutes
   b. Variance $= +84$ (standard deviation $= 9\frac{1}{6}$ minutes)
   c. $20\frac{5}{6}$ minutes

4. a.

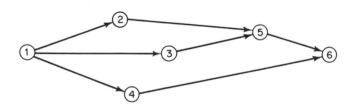

b.

Activity	Expected Duration (weeks)	Variance
(1, 2)	2	1
(1, 3)	4	1
(1, 4)	3	1
(2, 5)	1	0
(3, 5)	6	4
(4, 6)	5	1
(5, 6)	7	4

c.

Node	ET	LT
1	0	0
2	2	9
3	4	4
4	3	12
5	10	10
6	17	17

Expected project length = 17 weeks.

d. Activities (1, 3), (3, 5), (5, 6):   0 weeks slack
   Activities (1, 2), (2, 5)   :   7 weeks slack
   Activities (1, 4), (4, 6)   :   9 weeks slack

5. a. Project variance = 9, standard deviation = 3.
    b. (1) .16
       (2) .84
    c. About .37
    d. About 21 weeks

6. a.

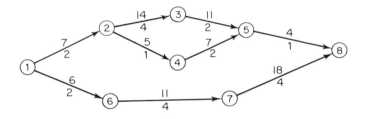

b. Length = 36 days; variance = 25 (path 1–2–3–5–8)
c. .84
d. .84 (path 1–6–7–8)
e. About .71. Since the two paths are independent, the probability of their both being completed within 41 days is equal to the product of their respective probabilities of being completed within that time.

7. a.

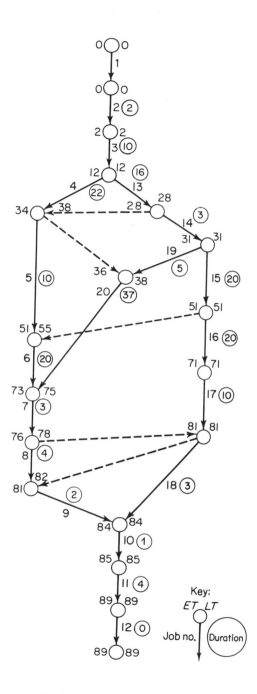

b. See answers to Problem 2 of Chapter 3.

8. See answers to Problem 4 of this chapter. Computer program is essentially event-oriented, but also calculates activity times.

9. a.

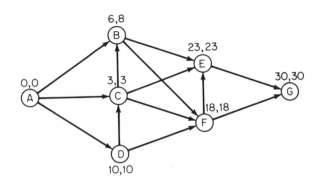

b.

Job	ES	EF	LS	LF	TS	FS
A–B	0	6	2	8	2	0
A–C	0	3	0	3	0	0
A–D	0	9	1	10	1	1
B–E	6	21	8	23	2	2
B–F	6	15	9	18	3	3
C–B	3	5	6	8	3	1
C–E	3	20	6	23	3	3
C–F	3	13	8	18	5	5
C–D	3	10	3	10	0	0
E–G	23	30	23	30	0	0
F–E	18	23	18	23	0	0
F–G	18	28	20	30	2	2

c. .345. Among the critical assumptions are the following: There are no near-critical paths; activities along the critical path are independent of each other; the critical path length T is normally distributed.

Chapter 5

1. a. 30 days; activities 1, 3, 7, 9, 10

b.

Activity Changed	New Length (days)	Cost ($)
3	1	6
7	6	7
9	8	9
		Total 22

2. a. 20 days; 12 days

b.

Length (*days*)	Crashing Cost ($)	Total Cost ($)
20	0	1,200
19	15	1,155
18	30	1,110
17	45	1,065
16	85	1,045
15	130	1,030
14	195	1,035
13	260	1,040
12	335	1,055

c. Optimum length = 15 days (see part b)

Job (1, 2): 9 days
(1, 3): 8 days
(1, 4): 14 days
(2, 4): 5 days
(3, 4): 6 days
(4, 5): 1 day

3.

Project Completion Time (*hours*)	Minimum Total Cost ($)	Jobs Shortened
26	340	
25	*	
24	360	*A*
23	424	*C*
22	*	
21	444	*A* and *C*
20	*	
19	476	*A*, *C*, and *D*
18	*	
17	530	*A, B, C*, and *D*

*Cost is the same as next shorter time, with the same jobs shortened.

4.

Project Completion Time (*hours*)	Total Activity Cost ($)	Total Project Cost ($)
26	340	990
25	352	977
24	364	964
23	376	951
22	396	946
21	416	941
20	436	936

Project Completion Time (hours)	Total Activity Cost ($)	Total Project Cost ($)
19	456	931
18	494	944
17	532	957

5.

Schedule Length	Jobs Crashed	Crash Cost ($)	Cumulative Crash Costs ($)
30	—	—	—
29	A–C	3	3
28	F–E	5	8
27	C–D, E–G	14	22
26	A–B, D–F	14	36

Chapter 7

1.

Job	Crew Size	Start Time
(1, 2)	8	0
(1, 3)	4	0
(2, 3)	5	4
(2, 4)	3	4
(3, 5)	9	12
(4, 5)	3	8

(Schedule is 18 days long; there are no idle man-days.)

2. One possible solution is as follows:

Job	Crew Size	Start Time
a	15	0
b	4	3
c	6	3
d	5	3
e	5	13
f	10	19
g	6	19
h	5	9
i	14	25
j	6	21
k	10	28

Total length = 30 days.

3. The solution in Problem 2 has 42 idle man-days. Can you find a better solution? (Write to the authors if you do!)

Index